Table Matters

Wesleyan Doctrine Series

The Wesleyan Doctrine Series seeks to reintroduce Christians in the Wesleyan tradition to the beauty of doctrine. The volumes in the series draw on the key sources for Wesleyan teaching: Scripture, Liturgy, Hymnody, the General Rules, the Articles of Religion and various Confessions. In this sense, it seeks to be distinctively Wesleyan. But it does this with a profound interest and respect for the unity and catholicity of Christ's body, the church, which is also distinctly Wesleyan. For this reason, the series supplements the Wesleyan tradition with the gifts of the church catholic, ancient, and contemporary. The Wesleyan tradition cannot survive without a genuine "Catholic Spirit." These volumes are intended for laity who have a holy desire to understand the faith they received at their baptism.

EDITORS:
Randy Cooper
Andrew Kinsey
D. Brent Laytham
D. Stephen Long

Table Matters

The Sacraments, Evangelism, and Social Justice

FELICIA HOWELL LABOY

With Questions for Consideration by Andrew Kinsey

CASCADE *Books* · Eugene, Oregon

TABLE MATTERS
The Sacraments, Evangelism, and Social Justice

Wesleyan Doctrine Series 8

Cascade Books
An Imprint of Wipf and Stock Publishers
199 W. 8th Ave., Suite 3
Eugene, OR 97401

www.wipfandstock.com

PAPERBACK ISBN: 978-1-62032-483-7
HARDCOVER ISBN: 978-1-4982-8697-8
EBOOK ISBN: 978-1-5326-4275-3

Cataloguing-in-Publication data:

Names: LaBoy, Felicia Howell.

Title: Table matters : the sacraments, evangelism, and social justice / Felicia Howell LaBoy ; with questions for consideration by Andrew Kinsey.

Description: Eugene, OR: Cascade Books, 2017 | Series: Wesleyan Doctrine Series 8 | Includes bibliographical references and index.

Identifiers: ISBN 978-1-62032-483-7 (paperback) | ISBN 978-1-4982-8697-8 (hardcover) | ISBN 978-1-5326-4275-3 (ebook)

Subjects: Sacraments—Methodist Church. | Wesley, John, 1703–1791—Theology. | Methodist Church—Doctrines. | Methodist Church—United States—Doctrines.

Classification: BX2215.2 .L26 2017 (paperback) | BX2215.2 .L26 (ebook)

Manufactured in the U.S.A.   11/07/17

Biblical quotations from the New Revised Standard Version of the Bible, copyright © 1989 by the Division of Christian Education of the National Council of the Churches of Christ in the USA and used by permission.

For Julia
For Harold
For Adrian

Contents

Acknowledgments

No endeavor is ever done alone and without the gifts of others through the Spirit of God. All the good that is within this research is no doubt present from my family, friends, colleagues, and mentors who have and who continue to influence my life and work.

This work has been primarily forged between the academy and the church, and has been most influenced by my advisor D. Stephen Long and by the seminal work John M. and Vera Mae Perkins. I also wish to acknowledge Drs. Kenneth L. Vaux, Henry Young, L. Edward Phillips, and E. Byron Anderson, who long with Dr. Long helped instill within me the conviction of God's power made available in the sacraments to transform the church such that it could be a transforming agent in the world. As a new doctoral student, I learned in conversations over lunch, suggested (insisted upon) readings, and assignments, the concepts that are contained in this work. I also wish to thank the support of Drs. Ruth Duck and Linda Thomas who insisted that I continue to explore this budding love for the sacraments.

While my professors at Garrett-Evangelical Theological Seminary were instrumental in helping me to conceive much of what is expressed here, I would be remiss if I did not acknowledge the generous support and prodding of my colleagues at United Theological Seminary. Namely, I wish to thank Drs. Richard Eslinger and Kendal McCabe, who expanded my love and understanding of the sacraments; Drs. Lisa Hess and Alicia Myers, who journeyed along with me in the Women Writing for A Change program; and our Vice President of Academic Affairs and Academic Dean, Dr. David Watson, who insisted that I focus on my writing. A special also thanks goes out to my colleague Dr. F. Douglas Powe, who insisted that I answer my call as an evangelism scholar. I also wish to express my extreme gratitude to Dr. Harold A. Hudson, Vice President for Enrollment and Associate Dean for Doctoral Studies for always seeing more in and demanding more of me. Much of what I am doing now is because of your encouragement and faith in me.

I want to offer special thanks to five churches that have helped shaped my perspectives in the necessary connections between the sacraments, evangelism, and social justice. Much thanks and love to the laity and clergy of Revival Center Ministries (Dayton, OH), Greater Allen A.M.E. Church (Dayton, OH), Southlawn United Methodist Church (Chicago, IL), Mandell United Methodist Church (Chicago, IL), and Maple Park United Methodist Church (Chicago, IL). A special thanks to the Maple Park United Methodist Church who allowed me to use them as a living laboratory to see if a commitment to a fuller understanding and practice of the sacraments might reconcile a fractured church such that it could become a reconciling and transformative agent in a fractured community. I would also like to thank Reverend Addison Shields, Jr., Chicago Southern District of the Northern Illinois Conference of the United Methodist Church for your support of my scholarship as I served in pastoral ministry during this time.

I would be remiss if I did not mention the influence of my two "fathers in the ministry," Reverend Russell Knight, Sr. and Reverend Earl G. Harris. Without their prodding and pushing, I would have never accepted my call as scholar and priest. Many thanks to their wonderful spouses as well, Bethany Knight and Jeanette Prear Harris, who taught me so much about the practicality of ministry and scholarship, especially as they pertain to Christian Community and Economic Development and Reconciliation. They have taught me so much about the greatness that lies in small things. I also must mention my "mothers in the ministry" as well—Reverend Dr. Tracy Smith Malone, Reverend Dr. Pamela R. Lightsey, Reverend Margaret Ann Williams, Reverend Lillian I. Gibbs, and Sister Shirley Johnson. They have modeled for me, not only in the church and the academy but also at the many tables they have gathered me around, the importance of hospitality, righteousness and reconciliation, and a love and concern for those who are seemingly not important.

To my family and friends, Ramona Payne, Tony Fitts, Regina and Ron Fisher, Reverend Jacqueline Ford, Dr. Mary S. and Cliff Pellegrini, Kathryn Ling, Jacquie and Tom Johnson, Vivian Matthews, Emma Clay, Dr. Shirley Manigault, Virginia Duffy, Carolyn Head, Brenda and Tony Mills, George and Shirley Johnson, Dorothy Harris, Bettina Riggins, and Reverend Charles Murray, who prayed for and with me, and who provided a listening ear and an encouraging word—thank you. Special thanks to my immediate family: my mother Julia Jewel Howell, who helped me to see that the only limitations in life are those which I place on myself; my father, Harold Howell; and my siblings, Rosalinde, Harold, and Brooke. Special thanks to my sister Rosalinde, who always provided an encouraging ear, a careful eye to my work, and a listening ear.

And special thanksgivings are also in order for the folks at the Orland Park Crossing Panera (Orland Park, IL), who, as I researched and wrote this project, always provided an encouraging word, kind presence, and always a fresh hot cup of coffee. Special thanks to managers Pete Hitterman and Krisann Huff, as well as associates Donna, Shelly, and Clarita, and to Corinne Beyer and Andrew Kinsey for editorial guidance and assistance.

I thank my PhD "Partner-in-Crime," Elizabeth (Liz) Mosbo Ver-Hage and her husband Peter. Your friendship, inquisitiveness, and insistence that we be yoked together (yes, from the first day you were right.), has truly been a gift from God.

I also thank my husband, Adrian LaBoy, who has supported me in every way possible and who has picked up the greater share of our family responsibilities so that I might fulfill my call. Adrian, without your wisdom, love, support, and sacrifice, this journey would have been unachievable and unbearable. I am eternally grateful for your presence in my life and I love you.

Most importantly, I want to thank God because without God's sustaining and abounding grace towards me, none of this would have been possible (John 15:5, 2 Corinthians 9:8).

Finally, as I am growing in my scholarship and ministry, I am constantly learning where my growing edges are. Therefore, any faults in this document are entirely my own.

Preface

I remember how much I disagreed with friend and PhD advisor, D. Stephen Long, when he contended that the sacraments had the power to be transformative. I well understood what our textbooks had maintained. However, during my childhood, and as a pastor of black churches where both Holy Communion and baptism were held in high esteem, I had not seen much of its transformative power in the daily lives of those who participated in these rituals. My issue with Dr. Long's statement about the transforming power of the sacraments was this: while many in the black church routinely participated in Holy Communion, unlike some white congregations at the time who practiced the sacraments somewhat infrequently, I saw no transformation; and in some cases, the people's behavior seemed to have gotten worse. I noticed that although personal piety might have increased (as evidenced in some cases by a growing self-righteousness), in many cases interactions with others—especially those not part of their cliques—had gotten worse. My problem that day in class was that my academic scholarship seemed to have no relevance in the local church I was pastoring, or in many of the churches I had been a part of.

This conversation over the transformative power of the sacraments was also making me wonder if I had heard correctly the call to return to seminary to pursue doctoral studies. I had struggled with leaving the pastorate because I was determined that my academic study would have a direct benefit for the clergy and the laity of local churches, i.e., that it had to be understandable and applicable to the parish setting. As I reflect now, this clash between Dr. Long's academic assertion of the transformative power of the sacraments and my practical experience as the senior pastor of a black church summarized the wrestling in my soul with regard to how I sense my call to both the church and the academy.

Later that day another mentor, theological ethicist Dr. Kenneth L. Vaux sensed my consternation and asked if he could sit with me to discuss how things were going. I explained my dilemma—my experience as a pastor could not reconcile with what I had heard that day in class regarding the transformative power of the sacraments. Simply put, in the vernacular of the black church, Dr. Long's contention that the sacraments were transformative "did not preach." At this point, Vaux invited Dr. L. Edward (Ed) Phillips, the worship and liturgy professor, to join our discussion. I again explained my dilemma to Ed, who affirmed my suspicions regarding the power of the sacraments to be transformative within themselves. Rather, Ed informed me that, unlike early Methodist societies, the contemporary church had failed to help people understand the meaning behind the rituals we practiced, especially with regard to the sacraments. He also made a recommendation that would change my life and ministry—suggesting that I read William T. Cavanaugh's *Torture and Eucharist: Theology, Politics and the Body of Christ*, which told how Chilean Catholic churches used Holy Communion as a social response to the terror and torture being inflicted upon Chilean peasants. Fast forward a few years and this discussion would become the impetus for transformative changes for a black United Methodist congregation on the south side of Chicago, not only in its liturgical practices, but in every aspect of church life—especially our evangelistic and social-justice practices.

After spending a few years in the academy finishing coursework and missing the pastorate, I requested an appointment to serve a local church. Although I expected to be sent back to a church in a poorer community—which was in line with my passion and gifts for faith-based community and economic development—I was appointed to a middle-class black church in the very middle, bordering on upper-middle class community that was on the edge of a very underclass black community. Although the members could be loving one-on-one with me, or their family and friends, it soon became apparent how cliquish the congregation was. More than this, their disdain for the poorer folks who were crossing invisible boundaries, moving into "their" community, and renting Section 8 homes (low income) was also apparent.

Desperate to find a way for our congregation to work together as teams and, more importantly, to evangelize our community and provide ministries of social justice, I sought a theological solution that would bring all of these black folks together, both inside and outside of the church, given that race was not enough to do so. Then I remembered that even in the midst of Dr. Long's assertion of the transforming power of the sacraments, there was this notion that the sacraments were the process by which individuals were brought together across race, ethnicity, class, and gender to be made into the body of Christ. I also remembered Dr. Phillips' suggestion to read *Torture and Eucharist*. So I set out on a quest—to try to understand the sacraments and how they were intended to function, especially with regard to their power to bring people together across class in general, and in a Wesleyan context in particular. I also determined that once I was clear about the power of the sacraments to act as a social discipline to help persons come together across boundaries in a deeply relational and mutually beneficial way, I would experiment on the congregation through our Sunday services of Word and Sacrament. My plan was not to teach a class per say, but rather to begin to alter the regular monthly services of Holy Communion and baptism by preaching about these sacraments and relating the sermons on the sacraments to our how we practiced them in our regular Sunday worship services and how we lived this out in terms of our love of God and neighbor vis-à-vis evangelism and social justice.

Each month as we instituted a change in the practice of either Holy Communion or baptism, I learned what was underlying some of the behavior I saw in our congregation, which provided insight into the next month's preaching on the sacraments. For example, I remember when I changed the wafers to a loaf of bread for the elements. Some persons in the congregation went to my assistant during communion because she was willing to hand them the soft parts of the bread. This provided insight as to some of the pushback I received when challenging my church to serve more. They wanted a "softer" assignment—not to reach our poorer neighbors, some of whom came with a myriad of problems. Rather, they wished I would reach out to more "acceptable" persons about attending our church. The next Communion Sunday, I preached on how you cannot make bread or ministry with only "soft" parts. Then, there was another time when I mentioned that the "passing of the peace" in the ritual was to ensure that partakers were in right relationship with their fellow brothers or sisters in Christ. After affirming the openness of the United Methodist table and having preached from 1 Corinthians 11, I told the congregation that they might want to consider if participation at the table without being in right relationship with sisters and brothers in the room meant that they had failed to "discern the body of Christ" and would cause them to "eat and drink" judgment on themselves (1 Cor 11: 27–29). Several persons, who preferred to stay in conflict with me and with some others in the church, did not take communion that day. I was upset, but colleagues affirmed that I had been heard.

With regard to baptism, before I baptized children I counseled the parents that baptism meant I was taking their child into membership and that they, along with the congregation, were entering a covenant to raise their children in the admonition of the Lord. This meant that in some cases there were children I refused to baptize, and in others their parents went back to their "home" churches for their child's baptism. In some cases, it meant that parents and grandparents got serious with their Christian discipleship and started coming to church. With adult baptism candidates, I explained that I would not baptize them to be in service to the Lord on their own, but rather that baptism was designed to make them a member of our congregation with rights and responsibilities. Imagine the shock on one young man's face when he tried to explain that since he had only been "sprinkled," and had his own church, he just wanted me to baptize him in our pool to be "closer to God," and I refused.

Not only did my preaching and our interrogation of our rituals of baptism and Holy Communion provide a "social discipline" similar to the one of Chilean Catholic churches that I had read about in *Torture and Eucharist*—with the sacraments becoming the heart of the life of our congregation, we then had language to discuss our evangelism practices (or lack thereof). We began to question our motives behind our social justice practices – i.e., were they designed to just make us feel good or did we really want "those" persons to come to Christ and become members of our congregation? When preaching on both Holy Communion and baptism, I had the opportunity to explain the claim laid on us by the words of institution for both evangelism and ministries of social justice. Eventually, our church developed a community development corporation and began to do more things to reach out to the community surrounding them—a community which many had previously ignored. Of course everything was not perfection, but we began to understand how our sacramental practice was related in Bible study, confirmation, reaffirmation of our baptismal vows, etc. As we grew in our understanding and practice of the sacraments, we—the congregation *and* I—grew as Christian disciples.

I finished my dissertation coupling my affirmation of the transformative power of the sacraments on the life of congregants and their theological importance with the practical aspects of evangelism and so-cial justice, but with only a wink at John and Charles Wesley. Because much of the work on sacraments is by Catholic scholars, I used their information modified by my experience at my church without much aca-demic thought to the rich historical and theological legacy of the Wesleys.

After graduation and after serving that black congregation that taught me so much about the transformative power of the sacraments, I was called to serve as the evangelism professor at United Theological Seminary. To my delight, United's worship professor, one of the authors of the liturgy for the United Methodist Services of Holy Communion, and the author of the epiclesis portion of the liturgy, Dr. Richard Eslinger, had just spent a year doing research on the sacraments. It was Dr. Eslinger who introduced me to our wonderful theological heritage with regard to the transformative power of the sacraments coupled with evangelism and social justice in the theology, worship, and practices of John and Charles Wesley. And it was this, my interrogation of my own theological roots— John and Charles Wesley's commitment to the sacraments, in particular, Holy Communion, and their way of helping congregants understand their import for evangelism and social justice which has provided the passion and emphasis for this book.

One could spend a lifetime studying the connection between the sacraments and worship, evangelism, and social justice. In fact, my grow-ing academic study and pastoral practice of the sacraments are at the heart of my current work in trying to understand how to utilize the trans-formative power of the sacraments in discussions of the racial tensions within our church and world. Who would have considered that a simple statement by Dr. Long would be at the heart of my academic and pastoral work? Therefore, I would like to officially thank Dr. Long for challenging me that first day in his class, and affirm with him that the sacraments can be truly transformative—when they are coupled with helping persons understand what is behind the rituals and the claims they make on the life of a Christian disciple.

Felicia Howell LaBoy
August 2017

Note on Discussion Questions

Felicia Howell LaBoy's commentary on understanding holiness with respect to the sacraments, evangelism, and social justice provides a wonderful opportunity for persons and groups to explore the relationship between these key practices of the church's life. Felicia's work builds upon a solid ecumenical foundation while also drawing out the distinctive features of a Wesleyan understanding, especially with respect to the United Methodist Church.

The following questions, then, are meant to assist readers in Felicia's exploration of these connections. They have been created to help the ongoing conversation the Church has been having through the centuries on what it means to bear witness to God's rule. And while the current set of questions may not exhaust all the angles of the sacraments and the work of evangelism and social justice, they will hopefully instigate further discussion, if not action. This present volume is one of several on the Wesleyan theological tradition designed to engage the church in ongoing spiritual formation and instruction.

Introduction

Every family has rituals or practices. While the meaning behind the ritual may be long forgotten, families often continue to follow rituals consciously or subconsciously simply because it is what this particular family does. Said another way, our rituals, especially those that are done often and over generations eventually define and identify us whether we are aware that they do or not. Take for example the old joke in which a newly married husband asks his wife why she cuts the end of the roast off before putting it in the pan only to be informed that this is the way it is done in her family. Curious, the husband contacts his mother-in-law only to find that she cuts the end off because this is the way it is done in her family; and that in particular it is how her mother, who is a wonderful cook, has always done it. Upon further investigation the husband seeks out his wife's grandmother and discovers that the reason she cuts the end off of the roast and uses it for something else is because early on she and her husband could not afford a bigger pan. To her way of reasoning, the delicious, well-cooked roast was more than sufficient for her family and provided a second meal to stretch a meager budget. Thus, her way of making the roast has become not only a ritual that helps to identify her family, the ritual also serves a particular mission (i.e., make delicious food).

While we may chuckle or snicker at this joke, in fact many of the rituals or practices at most churches work the same way—someone who we perceived to be more than competent (i.e., "expert") at something provides a way of doing something, a ritual or a practice so to speak, that seems to handle a particular issue in a particular context and at a particular time. Because the performance of the ritual/practice is consistent, eventually the practice becomes routine. We simply do it this way because it is what we have always done and it seems to work. There's no reason to think about it, this is simply what we do. As long as it seems to be working, then we employ consciously or subconsciously the old adage "if it ain't broke, don't fix it." And it is here, when rituals become devoid of meaning and only done via rote, that we tend to run into some problems, especially in the church.

In fact, many of the things we do in church escape our scrutiny, especially those rituals that we hold sacred. There are many reasons for this. First, we are simply too lazy, too complacent, and in many ways too busy, to investigate why we do things the way we do. We believe that there are matters more pressing. Since someone competent has already figured this out, we should not spend time on this. Second, we are unwilling to investigate whether or not we should continue or change our practices because we do not want to incur the ire of those around us. Third, we have been doing the practice for so long that we assume that everyone knows and cares what is meant by them so we just keep doing them the way we have been doing it. So, to help simplify our already complicated lives, we never take the time to interrogate our practices to determine whether they are meaningful or necessary in our context.

We seldom investigate our rituals to see if our routine, mechanized practice of them has robbed us of either great theological or practical insight that transcends time and space—a deeper understanding and experience of the love and grace of the triune God that transforms us into mature disciples of Jesus Christ, and empowers to be engaged with God as agents of mission and transformation. And, like the newlywed wife in the joke above, we may be depriving ourselves and our families of the fullness of the experience (i.e., the whole roast) because we engage in practices, especially liturgical ones, that we often repeat without any thought as to what it is that we are doing or the meaning behind it.

Many of us either doubt our ability to engage in deep theological reflection about what the church does in terms of liturgy and/or discount the importance of other aspects of worship such as the sacraments as integral to our life together as the body of Christ. For the most part, many of us focus on what we think is the main event of worship—preaching, and perhaps the music. We must understand that the preaching is often strengthened in the midst of liturgy. The sacraments are not supplemental to our worship. They are integral parts of it in that they help make manifest the presence of Christ in our midst. Noted liturgical scholar James White argues,

> At their best, all sacraments include, however briefly, some form of proclamation of God's word as experienced through scripture. Recovering this unity of word and sacrament is high on the list of reforms needed in all churches. Word and sacrament are not distinct realities but part of the same event. It is one and the same Christ who is given to us in both preaching and action. The same Spirit makes Christ manifest in both but by different means. *Thus, word and sacrament are characterized more by similarity than by diversity. They are never in competition, but each is mutually dependent on the other, reflecting our full humanity.*[1]

If White is correct that we need to recover this unity, then it would seem logical to begin our analysis in how we practice the sacraments.

While it can be argued that many of the rituals and practices of the church need this type of investigation, especially in our complex, multicultural, post-Christian American context, this book only examines the two basic sacraments performed by every Christian church—baptism and Eucharist, also known as Holy Communion. Our task is to investigate our theology and practice of the sacraments in the context of our identity and mission. Our goal then is to understand what our theology and practices convey to us and to a watching world about who we are as a family—specifically who we are as United Methodist sisters and brothers gathered together in God's name to give witness to the saving, sanctifying and transforming grace to be found in Jesus Christ. It is also about how are we shaped by our core practices of baptism and Eucharist to grow individually and collectively as disciples of Jesus Christ so that we become agents of change and transformation in our churches, in our communities and ultimately in our world. At the heart of my argument is a conviction, well founded in our Methodist heritage, that it is what we do together as believers—our practices, and specifically with regard to what we can learn and know, and how we are shaped by our sacramental practice of the baptismal and communion liturgies that forms us for work in the world in terms of social justice and evangelism.

What I am after here is whether or not a thorough and robust investigation of our theology and practice of the sacraments can provide us with not only a fuller understanding of the interconnectedness of sacrament, social justice, and evangelism; but also imbue us with the power of the Holy Spirit to engage in acts of social justice and evangelism, not as something we do or are assigned (i.e., we are on the evangelism committee);

---

1. Emphasis mine. White, *Sacraments as God's Self-Giving*, 27.

but rather as understanding social justice and evangelism as constitutive of who we are as Christians in general, and as United Methodist Christians in particular. The critical question at the core of this book is "can/should our practice of the sacraments move us beyond individualized, consumeristic religion?" In turn, our answer may force us to consider whether or not social justice and evangelism are the responsibility of all disciples of Jesus Christ or simply "spiritual gifts" designated to a few. My belief is that the sacraments make claims on disciples that call for to a more holistic faith. What I intend to demonstrate is that the sacraments both affirm our individuality, and mandate a commitment to living into a unified body that exudes holiness, social justice, and evangelism; they also help us reclaim our theological birthright as United Methodists and invite others to become and mature as disciples of Jesus Christ for the transformation of the world.

While volumes could be written on each chapter, it is important to limit our investigative work. To that end, our work will be outlined as follows:

- Chapter 1: What Are the Sacraments and Why Are They Important?

- Chapter 2: Baptism

- Chapter 3: Eucharist

- Chapter 4: Understanding Holiness, Evangelism, and Social Justice in the Midst of Contemporary Challenges

- Chapter 5: Table Matters: Living as Sacramental People

Questions for Consideration

1. What are the two sacraments practiced in the Wesleyan tradition? What Wesleyan ecclesial bodies practice the sacraments of baptism and Holy Communion? What Wesleyan bodies refer to such practices as ordinances? Are such distinctions important? If so, what difference might they make to the church's self-understanding and mission?

2. What dangers are there to practicing the sacraments in a consumeristic-individualized culture?

one

What Are the Sacraments and Why Are They Important?

What Are Sacraments?

The standard Protestant definition of sacrament is "an outward and visible sign of an inward and spiritual grace, given unto us, ordained by Christ himself as a means whereby we receive the same, and a pledge to assure us thereof."[1] But what exactly does this mean? To begin with, our definition and explanation of the overall term "sacrament," let us first begin by understanding how the term "sacrament" came to be used in early Christian communities. As Juan Luis Segundo maintains, although instituted by Christ, the sign-acts that we know refer to as "sacraments" were not "experienced or lived as sacred rites."[2] Rather, Jewish liturgy, ritual, and common practices were interpreted by early followers of Christ in light of the life, death, resurrection, and ascension of Jesus Christ. For example, the Gospels tell of the baptism of repentance that was practiced by John the Baptist in the wilderness (Mark 1:1–5). There was also the

1. Borgen, *John Wesley on the Sacraments*, 49.
2. Segundo, *Sacraments Today*, 42.

traditional Jewish practice of taking bread, blessing it, giving thanks to God, and sharing it. This simple sharing of the Passover meal by Jesus and the disciples in the upper room became known to Christ-followers as the Eucharist/Last Supper (Matt 26:17–30; Mark 14:1–2; Luke 22:7–23).

As time progressed, post-paschal communities used the Greek word for mystery, *mysterion*, to convey the idea that in their practices of baptism and Eucharist, there was a way that Christ was made known in ways beyond human understanding. More than symbols, the sacraments serve as a means of grace by which God disclosed things to human beings that could not be understood by reason alone. The Latin Church began using the word *sacramentum* to describe the word "sacrament" and to connote vow or promise in order to describe the covenant between God and humans. Thus, we understand the sacraments to function not only as signs by which persons may be identified as Christians, but also as indicators of the grace of God towards humankind as manifested in the life, death, resurrection, and ascension of Jesus Christ requiring and received in faith with the express purpose of "awakening and strengthening our faith."[3] This understanding of the sacraments as both indicators of the grace of God and practices that serve as distinguishing marks for Christ-followers, also suggests that there is something active that occurs whenever the church gathers to partake of the sacraments, within individuals and within the corporate body of believers and between the believers and God. Thus, Stamm rightly asserts, "the sacraments are the work of Christ *in and with* the church."[4]

Liturgical scholar James F. White maintains that "God's self-giving is the basis of the Christian sacraments."[5] Rather than considering sacraments as signs that merely point to something abstract (i.e., water pointing to grace), we need to consider the sacraments on a more personal and experiential level. According to White, sacraments are both theological and anthropological.[6] In them, God offers Godself to us in the same manner that humans utilize when giving gifts to one another. Our gifts become a representation of not only who we are, but of the nature of the relationship that we have with the recipient of the gift. Given that God is love, then we can say that in the sacraments the love of God is made

---

3. Borgen, *John Wesley on the Sacraments*, 50.

4. Stamm, *Sacraments & Discipleship*, 17.

5. White, *Sacraments as God's Self-Giving*, 13.

6. Ibid., 15.

known to us in tangible ways (Rom 5:5). The experience of God's love then lays claim to us in that we are now called to extend this same type of love to all that God loves (see Matt 22:38–40 and 1 John 4:19–21).

Critical to understanding the sacraments as God's self-giving is that sacraments are unique sign-acts in which both God and humans act in concert. Of sacraments as sign-acts, White contends,

> People perform them, but through them experience God's self-giving. A human being in not the only actor in these actions. As Luther said: "For (hu)man baptizes, and yet does not baptize. (S) He baptizes in that (s)he performs the work of immersing the person to be baptized; (s)he does not baptize, but in doing so (s) he acts not on (her)his own authority but in God's stead. Hence, we ought to receive baptism at human hands just as if Christ himself, indeed, God him (God)self, were baptizing us with (God's)his own hands." It is God who really baptizes, though we use the water. Human beings perform the outward action, the visible sacrament, but it is God who acts in self-giving to give the inward fruit that makes it a sacrament and not just another sign act.[7]

In sign-acts, words *and* actions are equally important. An overemphasis of either word or action can cause less than a full understanding, can cause less than a full appreciation of the gift being conveyed. Likewise, as sign-acts, when words, signs, or acts are incomprehensible to the recipient, then something is also lost in translation, and what may be a significant gift given may be treated as incidental by the recipient. Thus, sometimes it is necessary that some sort of explanation precedes the gift. This is why White agrees with Calvin and Luther about the unity of the administration of the sacrament and proclamation of the word, in that

> Word and sacrament are not distinct realities but part of the same event. It is one and the same Christ who is given to us in both preaching and action. The same Spirit makes Christ manifest in both but by different means. Thus, word and sacrament are characterized more by similarity than by diversity. They are never in competition, but each is mutually dependent on the other, reflecting our full humanity.[8]

7. Ibid., 23.
8. Ibid., 27.

So, if both words and actions are equally important in conveying God's self-giving in the sacraments, how then should we think about and practice the sacraments theologically and biblically.

First, White contends that rather than focusing on abstract theological constructs when considering the sacraments, we must understand that our theology is derived from sacramental practice rather than trying to impose theological constructs on the sacraments. This means that when we must look at how the Bible displays God's self-giving to humans through the natural order. The Christian God of the Bible is both transcendent and immanent. This is the God that makes Godself known personally in water, wind, and voice. Thus, God does not only make Godself known through the penultimate sacrament Jesus Christ, but God continues to make Godself known to humans in very human ways through sign-acts performed in the natural order.[9]

Second, sacraments are liturgical grammar and theological cliff notes. Sacraments define us theologically by providing us with language that tells us something about who the Triune God is in relation to us and the created order; and who we are as humans in relationship to God, one another, and the created order. As liturgical grammar, sacraments, like all language, form us into being and becoming. Like all liturgy, the sacraments define who and whose we are and provide "both a rehearsal of the narratives and a continual re-embedding of persons in the language of the faith."[10]

As theological cliff notes, sacraments remind us of our theological birthright while re-embedding us into a way of life characterized by Hebrew and Christian Scriptures. Summed up in them, the sacraments provide "shorthand" for us to remember who and whose we are and who we are called to be in Christ. In the same way that practicing a particular language helps us be more adept at it and influences our desires, attitudes, beliefs, and actions, practicing and participating in the sacraments should shape and form us individually and communally in deep and profound ways. To this end, our sacramental practice and our ethical practice are inextricably linked. Renowned liturgical scholar Don Saliers explains this link between liturgical practice and ethics:

> Norms and practices in ethics are never *simply* ethical. The concretization of the moral life requires a vision of a world, and

9. Ibid., 29–30.
10. Saliers, "Liturgy and Ethics," 23.

the continuing exercise of recalling, sustaining, and reentering that picture of the cosmos in which norms and practices have meaning and point. In short, the possibility of religious ethics (or for that matter, of any significant societal understanding and practice of the good) rests upon available *mythoi*—stories and narratives of human existence in, which picture of the moral good and associated ideas are expressed . . . Christian moral intention and action are embedded in a form of life which is portrayed and shaped by the whole biblical story. Such a narrative understanding of the world found in Hebrew and Christian Scripture provides a way of placing human life *in conspectus Dei*, before the face of God. Such narratives are not ethical systems or lists of rules and principles as such; rather they portray qualities of being-before-God which are focused upon features of God such as holiness, righteousness and loving-kindness.[11]

Thus, every time we practice the sacraments, we are remembering and re-membering ourselves and the gathered community of faith in the *mythoi* of our Christian narrative, and into a way of life to which the sacraments point past, present, and future. Simply put, sacraments provide us with "theological shorthand" that reminds and envelops us in the grace of God's salvation history and our place in it both as ones justified and ones being sanctified as our lives more correspond to the story being represented and re-presented in their practice. Therefore, contrary to popular church growth models which relegate sacraments to the margins of contemporary services so as "not to offend," sacraments practiced in unity with the preached word and in rich symbolism that communicate salvation history made known in Jesus Christ has the power to both convert and to renew those gathered. It is no wonder then that many renewal movements start with theological reflection on the church's sacraments to determine if how we practice them is aligned with God's history of salvation as revealed in both the Hebrew and Christian Scriptures. In addition, these movements have also determined what is needed in the practice of them such that participants know and understand what is being communicated in the liturgy. As White maintains, "One cannot disassociate what the church does from what it says it means. Liturgy and theology are intimately connected."[12]

11. Ibid., 17.

12. White, *Sacraments in Protestant Practice and Faith*, 10.

Third, as Christian grammar, sacraments can only be understood in the context of community—past and present. What this means is that the only way that we know that the sacraments are "sacraments" is because of the history and tradition of our faith community both past and present. We only know what baptism and Eucharist mean because we have Scriptures, creeds, history, and ongoing present interpretation and explanation in light of them. It is here in the "ongoing present interpretation and explanation" that we must pay careful attention to sign value and quality versus validity.

To determine validity in sacramental practice we must determine the sign value of our practice. Sign value "indicates the power a particular form or action has to communicate" to real people present. To determine sign value one must ask "does this particular sign-act have any meaning to the people beyond rote practice?" This question about sign value gives us insight to the quality of the sign-act being performed. Thus, high quality sign-acts communicate to persons in powerful and life-giving ways the lavishness of God's self-giving in the sacraments. On the other hand, validity simply seeks to ask "did we do it right?" with no concern about what is being communicated about who God is and our relation to God and one another in profound ways, such that words and actions complement each other. Another way to think about these distinctions is to ask ourselves in the performance of the sacrament is there something awe-inspiring, gracious, and yet mysterious in them? Does our performance of the sacrament focus unduly on us as individuals or do they fully point to the Triune God made known to us in Jesus Christ full of grace and mercy. White clarifies the distinctions between sign value, quality and validity when he writes,

> The sacraments communicate within a community of flesh and blood. Real people have to be able to perceive what the sacraments signify, not just receive sufficient doses of abstract grace. Hence, the sign value of any celebration of the sacraments is of paramount importance. Any celebration that ignores the humanity of the participants may be valid or regular, but a complete failure in ministering to people.[13]

Although, sign value and quality of the sacraments are crucial in communicating the significance of the sacrament, validity, regularity, and efficacy are important as well. Validity determines what a sacrament

---

13. Ibid., 33.

is and what is not, as well as what the conditions are that must be met for the "right administration" of the sacrament. Regularity is concerned with the social laws of the church with regard to the sacraments (i.e., who might administer them and who must be present when they are performed). Efficacy relates to the effectiveness of the sacrament and to the concept of whether the efficacy of the sacraments is dependent upon God or humans—those who perform, as well as those who receive the sacrament.

Sacramental History: Why We Do What We Do

When analyzing our sacramental theology and practice it is important to provide some historical background in that, as in our story of the new-lyweds and the truncated roast above, most often it is tradition rather than theology that shapes practice; and whether we would admit or not, practice shapes theology, no matter how many theological treatises we write. To begin, we must start with how we came to practice the sacra-ments this way. While a separate volume would be needed to trace the history of the sacraments, it is however important to highlight key events that have bearing upon our discussion.

First, an understanding of the history of the Christian sacraments must first begin with an appreciation of Christianity's Jewish heritage, especially an understanding of the significance of Exodus and covenant for Israel. In this context, we must understand the Exodus event as the decisive event that makes Israel "the people of God." By freeing them from their oppressors, passing them through the flood waters of the Red (Reed) Sea, and leading them to the land of promise, God demonstrated that unlike the gods of the Egyptians, Yahweh is an active participant in human history. It is in this context, God, through the delivering of the Ten Commandments to Moses, initiates the divine covenant to which the people are called to respond. Foundational to Jewish faith, practice, and rituals are acts of divine deliverance and covenant as understood by God's act with Israel, as typified by Exodus. Specifically, "Jewish ritual is above all a celebration of covenant community and a historical remem-brance" of Exodus.[14]

This remembrance and celebration is not nostalgia. Because God has been present in the past and promises to be present and active

14. Downey, *Clothed in Christ*, 38–42.

now and in the future, then Jewish remembrance and ritual for those in the present is a re-presentation of historical activities, a process that Downey refers to as the "sanctification of time (history)."[15] For Israel, the celebration of Passover serves as the unequivocal ritual for their annual remembrance of the Exodus event and the consequential covenant for all of Israel—past, present, and future. In the practice of the keeping of the Passover meal and the weekly Sabbath, past and present, Jews signify their belief of the God who made Godself known in the Exodus event, and who daily has the power to intervene in human history and demands their allegiance and obedience to the covenant they received through the Torah.[16]

The reason why we must start with the Judaic history of Exodus, covenant, and Passover, is that the grammar of the Christian faith and its concordant liturgical practices can only be understood in the context of Judaism. As Downey, Rita Nakishima Brock, and others assert, early Christians made central the life, death, resurrection, and ascension of Jesus Christ; and modified Jewish practices within the context of Exodus, covenant, and Passover.[17] Exodus signified liberation from oppression and liberation to live as the people of God in covenant with God and one another. In accordance with God's commands, the first followers of Christ viewed the crucifixion/resurrection/ascension event as that which signified liberation from all that oppressed humanity as typified by the Roman empire, and as that which enabled all to live as the new covenantal people of God as modeled in the life and teachings of Jesus Christ, as typified by mutual love, responsibility, and accountability.

In addition to the recovery of our Jewish roots, also pertinent to our discussion is the influence of sixteenth-century reformers—namely Luther, Calvin, and Zwingli—and the impact of scholasticism on their theology and practice of the sacraments, and their impact on later theologians. The impact of scholasticism on these reformers is critical in that most of the sixteenth-century reformers were priests, and thus deeply

---

15. Ibid., 39.

16. Ibid., 38–42.

17. In their book *Saving Paradise*, Rita Nakashima Brock and Rebecca Ann Parker chronicle their study of the iconicity of the early church throughout Turkey, Palestine and the Mediterranean in which they discovered that prior to the tenth century, most of the iconicity of the Christian Church focused on Christ's resurrection or depicted him as a shepherd and the community's life as living in to paradise. See especially chapters 1–5.

influenced by the late medieval church. As such, these reformers were also mostly influenced by the Western Church tradition, rather than the Eastern Church. Furthermore, as priests, these reformers would have been deeply formed by pastoral ministry which was highly sacramental as White describes:

> By the sixteenth century, the public worship life of the Christian laity in the West was almost monopolized by the sacraments . . .
> One's entire life from cradle to grave was ministered by the sacraments. They formed the basis of pastoral care and provided resources for each stage of life passages as well as for the day-in and day-out journey. By the late Middle Ages, birth was greeted within a very few days of baptism. Marriage was considered a sacrament, and death was preceded by a final anointing and followed by a requiem mass. In between birth and death, one might receive confirmation if a bishop chanced by and through-out life one found a remedy for sin in confession.[18]

Even though the worship life and the theology of the laity were shaped through sacramental practice, there were issues with them. First, White notes that the sacraments were seemingly done minimally based on making the work of the clergy more efficient. In addition, the sacraments, which were most often done in Latin, were shrouded in irreverence, superstition, and avarice.[19] Also, sacraments were highly penitential in nature.

Because of the deficiencies in sacramental practice, a "covert rebellion" began in the fourteenth century, which shifted the focus of Christian worship from outward signs as marks of Christian life to an inner piety. As White reports, this *devotio moderna* was not meant to serve as a renunciation of the sacraments, but rather as a way to liken outward practice to the inner witness of the Holy Spirit.[20] Furthermore, medieval scholastic theologians, in an effort to more accurately define sacraments, narrowed the number of ordinances from seven (baptism, confirmation, Eucharist, penance, extreme unction, marriage, orders) to two (baptism and Eucharist). With this shift two critical theological events occurred. First, sacraments became defined solely by dominical institution. Gone was the freedom and flexibility of earlier church fathers and theologians in identifying a wide range of human activity as sacramental. Second,

18. White, *Sacraments in Protestant Practice and Faith*, 14–15.

19. Ibid., 15.

20. Ibid.

scholastics turned the axiom *lex orandi lex credendi lex vivendi* (the law of praying is the law of believing and life) on its head by emphasizing that abstract theological constructs should shape liturgy (*lex credendi lex orandi lex vivendi*).

Critical to the sixteenth-century Reformation, especially with regard to the church's sacramental practice, was Luther's *Babylonian Captivity of the Church*. A scathing critique of papal sacramental practice, this treatise asserted that with the exception of baptism, the entire sacramental system, in particular, the practice of the Eucharist, was held in captivity to doctrinal and liturgical error. In The *Babylonian Captivity of the Church*, Luther (1) reduces the number of the sacraments from seven to two/three, (2) defends infant baptism, and most importantly, (3) enriches the definition of sacrament so that it links the sign to promise and promise to grace alone.

John Wesley and the Sacraments

For both John and Charles Wesley, the sacraments, in particular the Eucharist, are central to their theology and practice. To understand John Wesley's theology of the sacraments, one must first understand that his theology of the sacraments is derived from primarily several influences. We do this because, as discussed earlier, investigation of our theology and practices must begin with our theological forefathers if we are to be able to claim/reclaim our identity within a particular faith tradition. Because we will discuss baptism and Eucharist more extensively in the upcoming chapters, we will concern ourselves only with laying out a more generalized foundation of Wesley and his theology of the sacraments and the importance of the sacraments in general to Wesleyan theology, doctrine, and practice.

According to Jason Vickers, to best understand Wesley's overall theology one must acknowledge that, whereas many contemporary scholars claim that Wesley inhabited a wide variety of theological traditions—from Roman Catholic to Eastern Orthodox to magisterial Protestantism to Puritanism to German Pietism—he in fact "inhabited and deeply enriched a particular theological tradition, namely, English Arminianism."[21] In fact, Vickers contends, it is because of the English Arminian tradition of the eighteenth century was deeply enmeshed in the scholarly study of Eastern

21. Vickers, "Wesley's Theological Emphases."

Patristic, medieval Catholic, and Magisterial Protestant texts. Thus, it was their study and interpretation of these texts, more than anything else, it led to their disagreement with the Reformed theology of the covenant of grace as related to God's covenant of salvation.[22]

Contrary to the Reformed tradition of placing the covenant of grace under the rubric of divine election, English Arminians maintained that first God's Grace was not only the purview of the few that could discern it, but rather that "God's absolute freedom included the freedom to make God's will known with such clarity that a common plowman could understand it." Second, they asserted that, although God has absolute freedom to enter into covenant with all humans, "grace was not irresistible; it had to be freely received and embraced." Furthermore, although humans had to receive and embrace God's offer of grace, justification by faith as mental assent alone was insufficient proof of salvation. Vickers reports that for English Arminians such as Jeremy Taylor and the so called "holy living divines," holiness (i.e., holy living) is the *telos* of the Christian life and the fruit of salvation. Thus, within the English Arminianism of the eighteenth century, free grace and holiness are brought into dialectical and necessary relationship. It is this theological emphasis and practice of holding grace and holiness in tension within the theology of the covenant of salvation that serves as the foundation for Wesleyan theology, doctrine, and polity.[23]

John Wesley's entire theology of holiness, or what he called the Way of Salvation, centers around his tripart concept of grace. Second, one must consider that although Wesley was influenced by many of the prominent Reformers, namely Calvin, Wesley was also greatly influenced by the theology of the early church fathers, especially those who are most associated with the Eastern Church. Third, we must recognize that Wesley's theology was greatly affected by his practical experience as an Anglican priest, his understanding of the spiritual needs of the congregation, and his development of theological tools to aid his congregation in spiritual growth.

To understand Wesley's theology of salvation, and thus the sacraments, one must begin with Wesley's understanding of sin. Wesley operates within a threefold doctrine of sin. First, there is original sin committed by Adam in the garden, which results in guilt and loss of the

---

22. Vickers, "Wesley's Theological Emphases," 190–91.
23. Ibid., 192.

image of God for all humans. Second, there is the sin of commission or involuntary sin, which are "sins of infirmity, ignorance, and error." Finally, the third category of sin is that of commission in which persons willfully disobey God's commands regarding God and neighbor. According to Borgen, it is this final and third category of sins that humans are "only responsible and condemned" unless these are repented of and thereby forgiven.[24]

For Wesley, the remedy for all sin is the atoning work of Christ. Thus, Christ is both the author and the efficient cause of all of our salvation and the sole meritorious cause of both our justification and sanctification. Contrary to Calvinist theories of the atonement, and following the theology of the English Arminians, Wesley asserts that no one is predestined for eternal damnation because of some pre-determination by God. Rather, Christ's finished work makes possible the prevenient grace of God such that "no person is lost because (s)he has not received grace, but because (s)he has not used the grace (s)he has received."[25] Thus for Wesley, Christ is "the author and efficient cause of our salvation and the sole meritorious cause both of our justification and sanctification."[26] By virtue of the atonement, whosoever accepts Jesus' work as complete is justified, born again, and made a believer. As well, by virtue of the atonement, Christ's work also provides the grace for the believer to grow into holiness and to have all sins of commission and omission forgiven until they feast with Christ in his holy banquet. Thus, it is through the atonement that all grace—prevenient, justifying, and sanctifying—is made available to all humans through the means of grace, including the sacraments.

At the heart of Wesley's theology was an understanding that human salvation was both an instantaneous and a "gradual therapeutic process that grows out of our responsive participation in God's forgiving and empowering grace."[27] To understand how Wesley determined his doctrine of holiness, one must examine Wesley's perspectives and ideas regarding awakening, justification, faith, repentance, sanctification, and New Birth. Wesley described his doctrine as the Way of Salvation, rather than the Order of Salvation, to describe the interconnectedness of these themes

24. Borgen, "John Wesley: Sacramental Theology," 67.

25. Ibid., 76.

26. Ibid., 67.

27. Maddox, *Responsible Grace*, 192.

and the progression of spiritual maturity in the Christian believer. The first key concept in Wesley's doctrine of holiness is *awakening*. By "awakening," Wesley meant the point by which humans recognize their need for God. Wesley believed that although God's salvific work through Jesus Christ had been completed before the foundation of the world, most humans remained ignorant of their need for God's gracious gift of salvation and were thus spiritually "asleep." Thus, God, through God's prevenient grace, provided opportunities though sermons, interactions with other believers, tragedies, and natural disasters, to "awaken" to their need for salvation. Once awakened, people would become aware of their need for repentance.

To counter Reformist claims that he preached "salvation based on human works" and Anglican claims that he had limited repentance to the initial conviction of sin, Wesley developed a dual doctrine of repentance—one that discussed repentance prior to justification and one that discussed repentance in the life of Christian believers. Wesley defines repentance prior to justification as "a thorough conviction of sin, an entire change of heart and life," and as such a gift of God. As Maddox describes, "The key point is that it was only this aspect of repentance that he [Wesley] placed prior to justification. In this way he hoped to make clear that repentance prior to justification was not a human initiative but a response to God's gracious prevenience in awakening."[28]

Wesley's second doctrine of repentance addressed the need for repentance in the life of Christian believers. To fully understand Wesley's doctrine, one must understand that Wesley believed that it was entirely possible for Christians to reach "perfection" such that they would never sin. Wesley was so committed to his concept of perfection, he often emphasized that Christians undertake regularly the spiritual disciplines that led to personal and social holiness as a way to grow in this perfection.[29] Because Wesley understood salvation as a process, he understood that repentance in the life of the believer was key to their growth. As Wesley matured, he became more convinced of the importance of the dialectical and dynamic relationship between faith and repentance for the sanctification of the believer. As Maddox contends,

> The mature Wesley became increasingly convinced of the importance of repentance within the Christian life. In this context,

28. Ibid., 162.
29. Ibid., 163.

he also came to a much more dynamic understanding of the relationship of repentance and faith. He now saw them as "answering one another" throughout our Christian journey: in repentance we repeatedly acknowledge our failure and inherent helplessness, while in faith we progressively receive God's gracious forgiveness and empowerment. Repentance forces us to confess that apart from God's Grace we can do nothing, while faith assures us that, "I can do all things through Christ strengthening me."[30]

Once persons acknowledge their need for God, they are justified, which Wesley defined by one word: forgiven.[31] Wesley concurred with the assertion of the Reformers that justification of believers happened by faith alone—that through Christ, God's salvific work was sufficient for humans to receive full pardon of their sins and to begin anew empowered by the Holy Spirit. Wesley called this type of justification *initial*, and believed that it not only delivered believers from the power, but also the guilt of sin. However, Wesley believed in the idea of final justification. For Wesley, sanctification was necessary because it signified the believer's full assent to God's justification. Different from the Reformers, Wesley emphasized that this faith was not simply a mental assent to Christ's salvific work, but rather justification implied that one was "pardoned to participate," and this participation in the triune life of God is exactly what Wesley hoped to convey in his doctrines of New Birth and sanctification.[32] Maddox explains the interrelatedness of sanctification and final justification by contending that

> while initial justification constitutes the crucial base line of our entry into pardoning Divine acceptance, God desires and smiles upon our subsequent recovery of the Likeness of God. Indeed, if we *purposefully* neglect such transformation of our sinful lives following our initial justification, Wesley was convinced that we would eventually forfeit a pardoning relationship with God. Unless we later returned to responsive relationship, we would not enjoy God's eschatological pardoning acceptance (i.e., final justification). In this sense, while initial justification is not contingent upon prior sanctification, final justification is![33]

30. Ibid., 174.
31. Ibid., 166.
32. Ibid., 168.
33. Ibid., 171.

For Wesley, the New Birth, or regeneration, is the beginning step in sanctification and occurs simultaneously with justification. Cobb describes the relationship between justification, New Birth, and sanctification thus: "Justification is a changed relation to God; the new birth is the beginning of that process in which grace, now sanctifying grace, strengthens love for God and for neighbor."[34]

As this love for God and neighbor is strengthened, Wesley believed that it would be manifested in inner and outer holiness, which arises "from a conviction wrought in us by the Holy Ghost of the pardoning love of God."[35] Thus for Wesley, faith was not simply the mental assent to doctrinal creeds or formulations, but rather the belief in the pardoning love of God. In particular, Wesley described "faith as the handmaid" of love and built on Roman Catholic and Protestant understandings of the biblical text "faith working by love." According to Maddox,

> Roman Catholic theology continued the majority practice of the Early Church in translating (*Greek word for "work"*) as a passive participle, with the implication that our faith is generated (worked) through our repeated acts of love or virtue. Protestant exegetes argued instead that the participle was active in voice, insisting that Paul's point was that faith is the energizing source of any acts of real love. While Wesley endorsed the Protestant exegesis of this specific text, his broader perspective on the relation of faith and love integrated aspects of both interpretive traditions. On the one hand, he affirmed that Christian faith (understood subjectively) is evoked in us as an act of love. On the other hand, he was equally convinced that faith (understood "objectively" as the Witness of the Spirit) is the energizing source of our dispositions and acts of love for God and others.

Related very closely to Wesley's theology of grace and holiness is his understanding of the theological and practical importance of means of grace, including the sacraments, in assisting believers grow in holiness (i.e., love of God and neighbor). For Wesley, the sacraments function in the *via salutis* in four primary ways: "1) as effective signs, 2) effective means of grace, 3) effective pledges of glory to come, conjoined with the added aspect 4) sacrifice."[36] Key to Wesley's understanding of the function and efficacy of the sacraments was his distinction between "outward sign"

34. Cobb, *Grace & Responsibility*, 97.

35. Maddox, *Responsible Grace*, 174.

36. Borgen, "No End Without the Means," 67.

(*signum*) and "thing signified" (*res*). As outward sign, Wesley understood the relation between the material elements utilized in the sacraments in conveying to participants God's action within the sacrament (i.e., bread as nourishment; water as cleansing agent). While outward signs conveyed inward grace, they could never be thought of as a substitute for them. This is because it is the Holy Spirit that effects grace within the hearts of human beings. Thus, "whatever is, or becomes, or happens in, with or through any means whatever, or any action or words connected therewith is done by God through (His) Holy Spirit."[37]

As effective signs, the sacraments serve as a memorial in which the real presence of Christ is made known in the power of the Holy Spirit such that time and space are collapsed. Simply put, as an effective sign, the liturgy of the sacraments are to enact within participants the experience of being present not only within the contemporary practice of the sacrament, but in the work of Christ as it unfolds. Borgen describes Wesley's theology of the sacrament as effective sign when he writes,

> Thus there is a two-way suspension of time and place: Christ is crucified now and here; *my* sins drive the nails through his hands on Calvary, then and there. But as the believer repents, almost crushed under the burden of acknowledged guilt, [s]he also realizes the full importance for him [her] now: Christ invites him [her] to his sacrifice "not as done and gone many Years since, but a to Grace and Mercy, still lasting and *new*, still the same as when it was first offer'd for us." Christ himself is present here and now to save and uphold. And his presence is as real as God is real, and, as a means the sacrament actually conveys what it shows.[38]

In addition, the sacraments are effective means of grace for Wesley in that through them the grace worked in the atonement is applied. In his sermon "The Means of Grace," Wesley contends that first and foremost the sacraments are not optional because they are the "outward signs, words, or actions, ordained of God, and appointed for this end, to be the ordinary channels whereby he might convey to men, preventing, justifying, or sanctifying grace."[39] Thus for Wesley, there can be no ends (i.e., grace applied and appropriated) without the means. In this both Wesley and his brother Charles withdrew from the Fetter Lane society because they

37. Ibid., 68.
38. Ibid., 72.
39. John Wesley, Sermon 16, "The Means of Grace."

could not defend the doctrine of enthusiasm which maintained that the practice of spiritual disciplines were unnecessary for spiritual growth and experience.[40] In addition, Wesley maintained that while necessary, the means of grace—or in the context of our discussion, the sacraments—are not the ends. They are simply tools—means that God uses to convey the grace wrought at Calvary, which are rendered ineffective without God's Grace at work in them. Making the means the ends involves engaging in rote practice of them is to misuse them. For Wesley, the solution against making the ends the means is not to discard the means as ineffective but to investigate them so as to discern their proper use.

As means of grace, the sacraments are also effective pledges of heaven in that they signify God's commitment to the covenant God has made with humans that is made effective through the atonement. No more sacrifice need to be made, Christ's work is enough. God has committed Godself and God's Grace in remaining faithful to the covenant, and it is something more. Through the remembrance of Christ's sacrifice for us, we are to sacrifice our entire beings for the cause of Christ in the power of the Holy Spirit. As Borgen explains, "For Wesley, the sacramental sacrifice is neither propitiatory nor expiatory. The Lord's Supper is a means of conveying Christ's sacrifice *both* ways. First, Christ's sacrifice is received and feasted upon. Secondly, it is this sacrifice, already received, which 'set forth' before the Father as a pleading sacrifice together with the offering up of 'self.'"[41]

More importantly, while Wesley affirmed the efficacy of the sacraments because of God's divine power, he also reminded his followers that rote performance of the sacraments without an appropriate response to the divine enablement provided to participants in the sacraments rendered the sacraments ineffective to aid one in the Way to Holiness. Maddox explains it this way:

> Wesley did indeed develop a creative alternative to the common Western antimony between (1) the dependence of human responsiveness upon the Divine gracious empowerment conveyed in the sacraments, and (2) the prerequisite of the human responsiveness to the effectiveness of sacraments. This alternative exemplifies the co-operant tension of *responsible grace*. On the one hand, Wesley rejected as strongly as anyone the (supposed) implication of *ex opere operato* that sacramental rites

40. Ferrel, "John Wesley and the Enthusiasts," 182.
41. Borgen, "No End Without the Means," 81–82.

are effective intrinsically, apart from the responsiveness of the recipient. He constantly reminded folk that rote performance of such actions as regular worship and prayer are not salvific unless one recognizes and responds to God's gracious provenience expressed through them. On the other hand, while God's grace offered in the sacraments must be responsively received, Wesley was equally convinced that our response-ability is progressively nurtured by this very grace. Thus, he repeatedly denounced the folly of those who desire "the end without the means"—i.e., those who expect growth in faith and holiness without regular participation in the means through which God has chosen to convey grace.[42]

As mentioned earlier, key to this theological understanding of the "co-operant" nature of the sacraments, in particular, the Eucharist, was Wesley's familiarity with the early church fathers and his experience as an Anglican priest. During Wesley's day, within Anglicanism, there was much debate on the importance of the *anamnesis* (the words of institution) versus the *epiclesis* (the invocation of the Holy Spirit on the elements and on the gathered community). The Western Church, most notable the Catholic Church, as did the major Reformers such as Luther, Calvin and Zwingli, focused on the *anamnesis*. With a focus on *anamnesis*, the Eucharist focused more on Christ's sacrifice and its efficacy for the remission of sins. The net result of this is that grace becomes solely the responsibility of Christ's work and receiving of the elements becomes the way one maintains one's status as justified by God. As Maddox notes, the effect on the clergy is that their focus is now on helping to determine who is worthy of "recertification."[43] Simply put, in a system that focuses more on the *anamnesis* and omits *epiclesis*, baptism becomes cosmic life insurance to keep one's soul from hell and the Eucharist become the monthly payments to keep that policy current. The social ramifications are that if one only has to worry about one's soul and one's allegiance, then there can be a distinction between the sacred and the secular.

On the other hand, a focus on the *epiclesis*, which some Anglicans and Puritans—as well as the Eastern Church—advocated, emphasizes the presence of the Holy Spirit to transform both the elements and the gathered congregation. The result of more emphasis on the *epiclesis* moves the participants from mere recipients and empowers them to grow in love of

42. Maddox, *Responsible Grace*, 196.
43. Ibid., 198.

God and neighbor. This focus on the *epiclesis* by Wesley clearly fits with his belief that grace is not only present to pardon, but is also present to empower, to help Christians grow in holiness.

What has been called the genius of Wesley is this theology which affirms God's Grace while affirming that this grace not only pardons but empowers the believer to live Christlike.[44] Because Wesley's theology of the sacraments is based on his theology of holiness, they of necessity link personal and social holiness. For Wesley, the sacraments provided only one aspect of the works of piety, which were too balanced with works of mercy. For Wesley, holiness "was the aim of his life, the organizing center of his thought, the spring of all action, his one abiding project."[45]

> [T]he account of how the saving power made possible and ac-
> tual through Christ becomes effective in the lives of individual
> people. What is the experience of those who are justified and
> sanctified by this power? How should we preach and live so that
> more people can be saved? In short, what is our role, and what is
> God's, in the process of salvation?[46]

Wesley's doctrine of holiness, which he called "the Way of Salvation," was distinct from many of his Protestant and Catholic contemporaries in that Wesley so closely linked the concept of personal holiness with the concept of social holiness, that he declared that there was "no personal holiness without social holiness." By personal holiness, Wesley meant that holiness which comes from salvation in Jesus Christ. For Wesley, personal holiness signifies that, as those who receive the grace and love of Christ, they grow in love of God and humans, and strive to live according to God's will. For John and his brother Charles, works of piety such as prayer, Bible study, and sharing in the Eucharist served as the principal means of grace, as regular ways by which the spiritual lives of Methodists might be built up through God's Spirit. The Wesleys also stressed the necessity of meeting in small groups, called classes, so that mutual care and accountability would help their members grow spiritually.

In addition to the works of piety that would help believers grow spiritually inwardly, the concept of social holiness was crucial to Wesley's quest to have members of his societies grow spiritually. John Wesley said that the goal of Methodists was to "reform the nation, and particularly the

---

44. Ibid., 201.

45. Jennings, *Good News to the Poor,* 140.

46. Cobb, *Grace & Responsibility,* 22.

church; and to spread scriptural holiness over the land."[47] Thus there is no holiness but social holiness, which is worked out in community rather than by individual pursuits for Christian perfection. Wesley's model of Christian lifestyle is life marked by mutual accountability, which does not allow for one to do anything that caused harm to another, but involves respecting and caring for our own material and spiritual well-being.[48]

Bishop Walter Klaiber of the United Methodist Church in Germany and Manfred Marquardt contend in their book *Living Grace: An Outline of United Methodist Theology* that Wesley believed love is the outward and visible evidence of our salvation in Jesus Christ.[49] They claim the basic principle of Methodism is love of neighbor, social holiness, born out of personal holiness, that is, the experience of God's love. Social and personal holiness are indivisible parts of the wholeness of salvation. Thus, "personal holiness and the struggle for social justice are inextricably linked in the Wesleyan tradition."[50] Therefore, striving for a "perfect fellowship with God is inseparable from a right relationship to one's fellow human beings."[51]

Sacraments as Spiritual Resource for Evangelism and Social Justice

In his book *Biblical Perspectives on Evangelism: Living in a Three-Tiered Universe,* Walter Brueggemann contends that if the church is to remain vital, it must remember that in addition to those outside of the church, current members, especially children and youth, must be continually reminded of the faith in which they have been incorporated. Specifically, he argues that to do this, the faith communities must understand that the narrative into which they have been incorporated is more than a handbook on morality or doctrine, but rather the "articulation of imaginative models of reality in which 'text users' are invited to participate."[52] To this end, Brueggemann maintains that "when the community of faith 'uses' a text in its own life and practice, it re-enacts not only the substantive

---

47. Klaiber and Marquardt, *Living Grace*, 286.
48. Wesley and Methodist Studies Centre at Oxford Brookes University.
49. Klaiber and Marquardt, *Living Grace*, 292.
50. Wesley and Methodist Studies Centre at Oxford Brookes University.
51. Klaiber and Marquardt, *Living Grace*, 292–94.
52. Brueggemann, *Biblical Perspectives on Evangelism*, 8.

(moral, doctrinal) claims of the text, but also the dramatic, transformational potential of the text . . . Evangelism, I propose, is 'doing the text' again as *our* text and as 'news' addressed to us and waiting to be received, appropriated and enacted in our time and place [emphasis mine]."[53]

As we have seen from our discussion of the sacraments, the sacraments, especially as theological shorthand and effective sign as the means of grace, invite us to not only to live into the biblical drama as spectators through our imagination, but empower us to experience of being present not only within the contemporary practice of the sacrament, but beyond time and space as well. In the work of Christ as it unfolds in which the real presence of Christ is made known in the power of the Holy Spirit such that time and space are collapsed. We are invited and empowered (i.e., made "response-able") to not only understand the Bible as an "imaginative model of reality," but to live into that reality in our participation of the sacraments and to continue the ongoing work of evangelism and mission that the sacraments, through the *epiclesis* invite us to participate.

In the sacraments, "wherein God hath bound Godself" to us, we are actually incorporated into not only the life of Christ, but into the Triune God, that is ongoing and beyond the limits of time and space. To this end, it can be said that through Christ we are incorporated into the mission of God which is ongoing and redemptive of all creation which is by definition evangelistic. Building on the work of Christopher Wright in *The Mission of God: Unlocking the Bible's Grand Narrative*:

> Missions, therefore, arises not simply as a response to a command given to the church (although it is never less than that), but as a joyful invitation to *participate* with God in His [God's] redemptive work in the world. God the Father is unfolding a grand narrative of which His [God's] Son Jesus Christ is the central figure and we, as the church, are being called and empowered through God the Holy Spirit to participate in the unfolding of this grand narrative . . . *Therefore, missions is about simultaneously entering into the inner life of God as a missionary God, as well as entering into the world where the triune God is actively at work.*[54]

As individuals are incorporated into the physical and mystical body of Christ—and thus into the life of the triune God through baptism—disciples are then continually remembering and re-membering the church

---

53. Ibid., 8.

54. Tennent, *Invitation to World Missions*, 61. Emphasis mine.

through the Eucharist. Through both baptism and Eucharist, they are continually reminded that the gospel does not stop at the Cross and the Resurrection, but continues to unfold in God's ongoing initiatives at Pentecost and in the life of the church.[55] This aspect of participation in the body and life of the triune God renders moot the idea of the sacraments as ends unto themselves (i.e., spiritual vitamins or "fire insurance") and emphasizes God's action in the sacraments and the response of those that receive them to engage in God's work in the world. Thus, in addition to the preached word, faithful sacramental practice with the appropriate and accompanying catechesis helps followers of Jesus to be mindful that the sacraments are about what God has done through Jesus; and what God, through the Holy Spirit in God's holy church, invites and intends to do through us until the culmination of all things when we feast at the final heavenly banquet. While it is true that the sacraments are pledges of heaven, they also invite participants to pledge themselves to the work of God in the world beyond individualistic morality and pietism.

It is these aspects of being incorporated into the divine drama of the Triune God, who is engaged in mission through the sacraments, that also help the church to evaluate its current theology and practices to determine if they are in accord with this divine drama. This idea of self-examination, which includes denunciation, confession, and repentance is critical when one understands the modern church's tendency to make theological reflection the purview of ecclesial experts (i.e., clergy and scholars) and the church's tendency to privilege the functional aspects of ministry over theology. When the church abandons these aspects of her liturgy and life, she not only mimics, but privileges the larger society's paradigms for leading organizations. In his book, *Practicing Gospel: Unconventional Thoughts on the Church's Ministry*, Ed Farley contends when churches and their leaders allow such cultural paradigms to determine church leaders' (and also members') self-understanding and set the agenda for the church's work, then church leaders, both clergy and lay, deny themselves and their congregations of the alertness and openness (or to use Wesley's terminology, "the awakeness") to the gospel's power for transformation and renewal. In fact, Farley argues that church leaders need to be particularly aware of three cultural trends: bureaucracy, moralism and individualism that have attained paradigmatic standing within modern churches and thus make it difficult for the church to respond to

55. Ibid., 63.

world issues any differently than other worldly organizations. Farley explains this danger of the church's privileging of these three cultural trends over Gospel when he writes,

> These three paradigms of ministry or leadership share a common trait: they mirror and foster the prevailing trends of current secular society. A subtle secularism colors the congregation that focuses totally on the welfare of its individual members, offers to them moralizing or therapeutic bromides, and directs most of its energies to its own growth or success. *When Gospel is the congregation's paramount referent and symbolic word, bureaucracy, moralism and individualism may not disappear, but they lose paradigmatic status.* When church leaders are oriented to the prophetic summons of authentic faith, they resist defining themselves by their institutional functions. Their task is not simply to maintain the social institution but to assist the community of redemption to transcend its own self-orientation. When Gospel is paramount, church leaders are hesitant to be simply moralizing scolds or therapeutic consolers.
>   . . . Church leaders become suspicious of these secularizing paradigms when they *interpret* their tasks under Gospel. . .(that) is impelled by ongoing theological struggle with the meaning of Gospel, faith and church [emphasis mine].[56]

Thomas B. Dozeman also insists that sacraments are spiritual resource in that the liturgy of the sacraments are not only about invoking our memory of God's salvific acts, but that God is also reminded about the new covenant mediated through Jesus Christ. Although it is the priests (clergy) who perform the rituals of the sacraments, the emphasis is on the empowerment of the laity to be "ethical agents for God in the profane (sinful) world."[57]

While Farley is not explicit in making an argument for the sacraments what else are they than the *symbolic word* referenced above to define *Gospel*. Proper practice of the sacraments that are in line with the totality of Gospel have the power in powerful ways to provide a prophetic lens to the worldliness of the church and the world; and thus serve as spiritual resource not only for ethics but also for mission and ministry. When sacraments are practiced only by rote with no catechesis that has meaning for contemporary participants and that is only comprehended

---

56. Farley, *Practicing Gospel*, 10.
57. Dozeman, "Priestly Vocation," 98–99.

through the Gospel, then they are in danger of becoming "therapeutic and moralizing bromides," that is, simply ends unto themselves.[58] This is why it is important that communities of faith do not truncate the liturgy of the sacrament or not practice them in concert with the preached word that culminates in the sacrament. As Wesley maintained, the proper practice of the sacrament places each of us at the foot of the cross, makes us aware of Christ's sacrifice for sin, and my sin specifically. It also reminds us that the Cross and Resurrection is not the end of the story, but that with Pentecost and through baptism, each of us are called to participate in the life of the triune God which is about mission and ministry. Continual practice of the Eucharist keeps the message of the Gospel ever before congregants as referent such that we may be provided with an interpretive lens by which to determine the secularization and self-occupation of ourselves as individuals, churches and ecclesial institutions.

Given that we have provided a foundation for the sacraments as spiritual resource for evangelism and missions in general, now we will now turn our attention to a more comprehensive understanding of how baptism and Eucharist each serve as spiritual resources for evangelism and mission.

---

58. I maintain this is what happens when ministries offer single-serve communion cups as "spiritual vitamins" or offer baptism as "fire insurance" to keep persons from the fires of hell and earth.

Questions for Consideration

1. What are sacraments?

2. What importance does *remembering* have in practicing the sacraments of baptism and Holy Communion? What are the consequences of forgetting?

3. How might popular church growth models, which seek not to offend those who have gathered to worship, play into a consumeristic, therapeutic, understanding of faith? How might the deep "sign-acts" of God's salvation lose their purpose and meaning?

4. What is the relationship between the validity, regularity, and efficacy of the sacraments? Why are these concepts important?

5. What are the consequences of separating the outward practice of the sacraments from the inner witness of the Holy Spirit? What shifts in church history made such separation possible?

6. How did John Wesley and the early Methodists understand the sacraments?

7. How did John Wesley bring to bear his understanding of God's Grace and salvation (i.e., the holiness of heart and life) on the sacraments?

8. What role does Christ's atoning work on the cross have in Wesley's understanding of the life of faith and in the practice of the sacraments?

9. What role do the means of grace have in assisting believers in growing in holiness toward God and neighbor? Why did Wesley insist on the constant usage of these means in the spiritual life?

10. What is the relationship between the sacraments and the church's evangelistic and social justice ministries in the world?

11. What cultural obstacles are there to the church's practice of baptism and Holy Communion and to what Wesley calls the Scripture way of salvation? How does hyper-individualism distort what Wesley was teaching?

two

Baptism

Introduction

In my experience as both a pastor and a professor of evangelization, many times I have found that when I ask someone what does it mean to be saved, they will inevitably begin to discuss baptism as a "mark of salvation." In addition, at many funerals, many obituaries include the fact that many persons were "baptized at an early age" as justification for both a Christian funeral and as a guarantee that regardless of how they lived their lives, their baptism has clearly reserved for them a place in heaven. Not only have lay persons made these assertions, many clergy, when making appeals for persons to "get saved," often add to this appeal the need for persons to be baptized. This has occurred so frequently in the communities in which I have served as clergy that persons, when coming forward in response to the altar call, have requested that they be "rebaptized" as a sign that they are committing their lives to Christ. In fact, this practice of equating baptism with salvation has led me to label this behavior as equating baptism with "eternal fire insurance."

Not only are there these clear links between baptism and salvation (i.e., baptism = salvation), I have also found that there is also concern amongst many with regard to validity of one's baptism as being necessary for salvation based on one's age, and the mode by which one was baptized. Many parents in the United Methodist churches and the communities in which I served were not clear about the difference between baby dedications, christenings, and infant/child baptisms, or their relationship to adult or "believers" baptisms. Parents and grandparents simply saw the baptism/dedication/christening as something they and I were "supposed to do;" and were frequently more than a bit perturbed with me when I refused baptism because they did not practice their faith within a Christian community of faith and/or were unwilling to commit to rearing their child in a Christian lifestyle.

In my experience I have also found that because many people within and outside of the church equate baptism with salvation that, once baptized, many persons seem to believe that they are now part of a cosmic communion with no need of a relationship to a local church. This occurred many times even though this has been clearly explained to them prior to and was a part of their baptism in which they made vows to be a vital and active member of both the local church and church universal. Rather than making the connection between baptism as incorporation into the Christ body universally over time and space, and as incorporating them into a local community of faith, many of these persons have simply seen themselves as in a "contractual agreement" with God in which they have appropriated the work of Jesus Christ in his crucifixion, death, and resurrection as atonement for their sins and the necessary appeasement for them to enter heaven. Since, they believe, at least for right now, that baptisms only happen at church, they know they must come to the church to be baptized. However, while they understand the necessity of the church for baptism, many of these same folks believe that it is their "right" to determine their own formation and growth as Christians, thus nullifying the need for the church once baptism has occurred, except perhaps for the occasional visit. Simply put, for these believers, baptism can happen at any church, by any cleric, those that have submitted themselves to a more formal process of ordination/licensure or their friends who simply obtained a license to practice ministry on line for a nominal fee. For them, formation is not the responsibility of a gathered group of believers, but is determined by each individual alone and can happen through the faithful "shopping" of beliefs, teachings, or worship experiences across a wide variety of venues (i.e., a multiplicity of Christian churches, television/internet, nature, non-Christian religious entities, etc.). In addition, they simply see no need to be tied to a particular body of believers when all the church currently offers in terms of formation can be easily obtained, especially across the internet and that they can enter/exit Christian communities of faith at will without fear of church discipline.[1] Even more disturbing has been the practice of some to be[7] baptized by smaller congregations because they want a "more personal, intimate setting" so as to celebrate their or their child's baptism; but not to become a member of these congregations because they would rather attend a larger church so that they "will not have to do any work" or craft their own way of serving, giving and participating online.

Given this wide range of understandings and misunderstandings regarding baptism and to continue our discussions on developing faithful practice of the sacraments so that they are experienced as more than a rote performance, or worse a commodified experience, and on the importance of the sacraments for evangelism and social justice, we must consider these questions: what is baptism and what is it meant to do in the life of the Christian? Also, because the subject of baptism is sufficient within itself to fill several volumes, we must impose some limitations on our analysis. Therefore, the remainder of this chapter will review the theology and practice of baptism from a Wesleyan, and a decidedly United Methodist perspective. Thus, while we acknowledge that other denominations will have a decidedly different theology and practice of baptism which is hinted at in the anecdotal information above, this treatise is written so as to recover our theological heritage as United Methodists and to help us better understand and live faithfully into the practice of baptism as found in the Baptismal Covenants of the *1989 United Methodist Hymnal* as best outlined in *By Water and the Spirit: Making Connections for Identity and Ministry*, the study commissioned by the General Conference of the United Methodist Church to help United Methodists recover their theology and practice of baptism in a faithful way.

To this end, this chapter will discuss the following:

- *The Meaning and Significance of Baptism*

    In this section we will not only discuss the meaning of baptism and its theological history with regard to the people of God, but we will also discuss the various modes of baptizing and their signification.

---

1. For more on how persons are seeing the church as obsolete, see John Edmiston's "The Ubiquitous Gospel," presented at the Biola Digital Ministry Conference in 2013.

- *Baptism, Salvation, and New Birth*

  As was suggested in the anecdotal suggestion baptism and salvation are clearly linked, not only in the minds of laity and clergy, but also in the teaching of the early church and from our theological forefather John Wesley. Because of the links between baptism and salvation and the implication of this, we will also discuss infant and adult baptism in this section. Finally, this section of the chapter will define salvation and describe the links between salvation and baptism from a Wesleyan, decidedly United Methodist, perspective.

- *Baptism as the Sacrament of Initiation, Incorporation, and Integration, and Commissioning*

  As we proceed through our definition of baptism and how baptism is linked to salvation, it will become apparent that we can discuss baptism's implications on the life of the Christian in terms of initiation; incorporation and integration; and commissioning.

The Meaning and Significance of Baptism

As James F. White states in *The Sacraments in Protestant Practice and Faith*, baptisms are recorded more often in the New Testament than observations of the Eucharist, which is understandable if one considers the missionary and eschatological aspect of the Early Church.[2] While a quick review of the book of Acts affirms White's assertion, we must ask ourselves why was this so? What was so significant about baptism, in particular Christian baptism that there is this emphasis on it not only in the book of Acts, in the commissioning of the disciples in the Great Commission (Matt 28:19–20)? In addition, as Scripture and the current United Methodist baptismal liturgy remind us, there is something in the process of baptism that incorporates us into the narrative of the people of God as told through key narratives in both the Old and New Testaments:

> Eternal Father:
> When nothing existed but chaos,
> you swept across the dark waters
> and brought forth light.
> In the days of Noah
> you saved those on the ark through water.

2. White, *Sacraments in Protestant Practice and Faith*, 52.

After the flood you set in the clouds a rainbow.
When you saw your people as slaves in Egypt,
you led them to freedom through the sea.
Their children you brought through the Jordan
to the land which you promised.

Sing to the Lord, all the earth.
Tell of God's mercy each day.

In the fullness of time you sent Jesus,
nurtured in the water of a womb.
He was baptized by John and anointed by your Spirit.
He called his disciples
to share in the baptism of his death and resurrection
and to make disciples of all nations.[3]

In addition, if Sarah Coakley is correct that "religious beliefs and doctrines are not to be demonstrated by 'evidences,'" but rather are learned through embodied practice, then clearly there is something in the baptismal liturgy that is meant to teach and remind us of our theological heritage and to help us embody our faith.[4] Furthermore, if baptisms were already a part of Jewish liturgical life, we must also ask how and why the early church utilized this practice when incorporating and initiating new converts to the faith. To begin, let's investigate the early origins of baptism and their implications for the meaning, theology and practice of baptism.

Baptism's Early Origins

As discussed earlier, baptism and Eucharist must be understood in the context of Jewish faith and practice. Foundational to Jewish faith and practice is the recognition that these rituals are sign-acts of divine deliverance and covenant as understood by God's act with Israel, as typified by Exodus. Specifically, "Jewish ritual is above all a celebration of covenant community and a historical remembrance" of Exodus.[5] As early Christians made central the life, death, ascension, and resurrection of Jesus Christ, they modified Jewish liturgical practices within the context

---

3. Felton, *By Water and the Spirit*, 54.
4. Coakley, "Resurrection and the 'Spiritual Senses,'" 143.
5. Downey, *Clothed in Christ*, 38–42.

of Exodus, covenant, and Passover.[6] Exodus signified liberation from oppression and liberation to live as the people of God in covenant with God and one another. In accordance with God's commands, the first followers of Christ viewed the crucifixion/resurrection/ascension event as that which signified liberation from all that oppressed humanity—as typified by the Roman empire—and as that which enabled all to live as the new covenantal people of God as modeled in the life and teachings of Jesus Christ—as typified by mutual love, responsibility, and accountability. Thus, it can be argued that early Christians correlated baptism with the Exodus event of liberation and the creation of "the people of God." Furthermore, this correlation can easily be determined by reviewing Jewish water rites.

As noted by Pat E. Harrell, water rites were in use by Jewish and Hellenist communities prior to the baptism of John the Baptist.[7] For Jews, these water rites were used in three primary ways, all having to do with one's covenantal relationship to God and to the community. First, water was used as a means of cleansing and consecrating humans and animals before their encounter with God (see Exod 19:10–14; 29:3–5; 30:19–21; 40:11–12). Second, water was used as a means of purification for those who had becoming ceremonially unclean and who were temporarily removed from the community (i.e., Lev 15:8). Third, water was used not only as a means of physical purification but as a means of repentance—a means of heart purification from idolatry and from breaking covenant especially with the oppressed, especially widows and orphans (i.e., Isa 1:16; 4:4; Jer 2:4:14). In addition to these meanings behind Jewish water rites was also the use of water to make Gentiles Jewish proselytes in a three-fold ceremony that included circumcision, baptism, and sacrifice. According to Harrell, these Gentile proselytes were immersed in water (i.e., baptized) after they vowed in the presence of at least three witnesses their willingness to live according to the mandates of Judaism, specifically the Torah.[8] In fact, it is this practice of baptizing Gentiles that can be

---

6. In their book *Saving Paradise*, Rita Nakashima Brock and Rebecca Ann Parker chronicle their study of the iconicity of the early church throughout Turkey, Palestine and the Mediterranean in which they discovered that prior to the tenth century, most of the iconicity of the Christian church focused on Christ's resurrection or depicted him as a shepherd and the community's life as living in to paradise. See especially chapters 1–5.

7. Harrell, "Jewish Proselyte Baptism," 159–65.

8. Ibid., 161. See also Hultgren, "Baptism in the New Testament," 7.

seen to most correlate with the Christian practice of baptism. As Harrell describes the practice,

> Proselyte baptism should be interpreted as having both a negative and a positive aspect. Negatively, it removed the noahide[9] sins of the candidate. R. Judah affirmed that a convert was not held accountable for his pre-baptismal sins. Positively, it was a "new birth" by which the old life was left behind and a new life inaugurated. When the candidate emerged from the water he was "an Israelite in all respects." This latter statement suggests what was perhaps the motif of the baptism. As the Jews were saved through their baptism in the Red Sea, so proselytes were made to share this experience by a water baptism that placed them on an equal footing.[10]

In fact, the practice of baptizing Jewish proselytes also is similar to certain forms of Christian baptism in that when Gentiles were baptized so was their entire household including children and servants. It is important to note, however, that any children born to the household after the conversion of their parents were thought to be "Jews by generation" and would not be deemed apostate if they decided upon the age of accountability to denounce Judaism.[11] In addition, to Judaic water rites, it is also probable that the water rituals from Hellenistic mystery cults were also influential on early Christian practice. In particular, Arland Hultgren, citing the work of both William Bousset and A. D. Nock which maintain that as early as the second-century Gentile Hellenistic mystery cults utilized baptism as a means of initiation into the cult and as a sign of death and rebirth.[12]

Not only is the baptism of Gentile proselytes significant for our understanding of the meaning of baptism as established by the early church. As Hultgren and others assert, it is the baptismal practice of John the Baptist which focused on repentance and forgiveness of sins, the passivity of those baptized and on regeneration that would have had the most influence on early Christian practice and thus provide us with critical

---

9. Harrell defines "noahide laws" as "those moral requirements of the whole human race against idolatry, adultery and incest, bloodshed, blasphemy, robbery, social injustice and eating flesh from a living animal" ("Jewish Proselyte Baptism," 162). Thus, noahide sins would be those acts that are not in line with these requirements.

10. Ibid., 162–63.

11. Ibid., 163.

12. Hultgren, "Baptism in the New Testament," 6–7.

theological insight as to the significance and meaning of baptism in the early church.[13] More than the conversion of Gentiles to Judaism, Hultgren asserts that John's baptism is significant for both Jew and Gentile in that

> What is fascinating, even distinctive, about John is that he called upon the people of Israel—not just gentile would-be proselytes—to undergo baptism. By so doing he was saying, in effect, that even the people of Israel are not prepared for God's kingdom; they are as gentiles, in need of repentance and rebirth. It can be concluded, then, that Christian baptism is immediately related to John's baptism, but then John's is a prophetic adaptation of proselyte baptism. All of this belongs to the background of Christian baptism.[14]

In addition to its Jewish roots, liturgical scholars also assert that to understand the theology of baptism we must turn to the practices to discern what distinguished Christian baptism from both the baptism of Gentile proselytes and those who were of John's baptism. In particular, these scholars contend that we must analyze the early church "formulas" of baptism to determine what were the other theological meanings implied in the baptismal ritual for early Christians.

According to Hultgren and others, the two major differences between the baptismal rites for Gentile proselytes and those baptized by John the Baptist are the admonition to baptize "in the name of . . ." and the move from baptism as solely christological to Trinitarian. Referencing the work of Lars Hartman and others, Hultgren maintains that the use of "in the name of" was designed to distinguish Christian baptism from other baptismal rituals. The use of the christological formulation signified that Jesus through his life, death, resurrection, and ascension proved that he was the messianic fulfillment of the Law and the Prophets and thereby authorized by God to usher in a new kingdom. Thus, those baptized into the name of Jesus Christ signified that they were entering into this new covenantal community initiated and culminated in Jesus. The move from the christological to the Trinitarian formula was utilized as "eschatological shorthand" to extend the early church's understanding and adoption of the baptismal rites of John the Baptist which included repentance, forgiveness, and conversion to include the ongoing work and

13. Ibid., 8.
14. Ibid.

necessary empowerment of the Holy Spirit in the lives of believers individually and corporately.[15]

From this discussion of the origins of the baptismal practice of the early church, it can be argued that the following metaphors/meanings are critical in developing a theology of baptism:

- Baptism as the rite of repentance and forgiveness of sin;

- Baptism as union with Christ's death and resurrection;

- Baptism as the rite of initiation and incorporation into the people of God;

- Baptism as reception of the Holy Spirit; and

- Baptism as New Birth or regeneration.

We will discuss these metaphors under two categories. First, we will look at baptism as the rite of repentance and forgiveness of sin under the category of baptism, salvation, and New Birth. We will then look at the remaining metaphors under the category of baptism as the sacrament of initiation, identity, incorporation, integration, and commissioning.

Baptism, Salvation, and New Birth: Baptism as the Rite of Repentance and Forgiveness of Sin

As discussed in the introduction, many persons both within and outside of the church understand that there is a significant connection with baptism and salvation. What is critical for us as Wesleyan Christians is to understand the connection between salvation and baptism so that we might live fully into our theological birthright. To do this, we must first define what the term *salvation* means for Wesleyan Christians. Then we can determine the relationship between a Wesleyan, and decidedly United Methodist understanding, of baptism and salvation.

If we are to keep in mind the Jewish heritage undergirding baptism, we must acknowledge the correlation between baptism and the Exodus. In the Exodus, people are liberated from (i.e., "saved" from) oppression and liberation ("saved" for) to live as the people of God in covenant with God and one another. If baptism is to be correlated with Exodus in this way, then for modern Christians we must ask what is it that we must be "saved" or liberated from, which in turn leads to a discussion of sin.

15. Ibid., 9.

Although out of vogue, it is the discussion of sin that causes us to recognize our need for salvation. As explained in the early chapters of Genesis, humans were originally created to be in loving relationship with God and with one another, and to accomplish God's will and purpose for all of creation and humanity by recognizing that even though humans are in fellowship with God, humans are not God. Unfortunately, in Genesis 3 we are told that because of human rebellion sin enters the world and distorts not only our relationship with God and one another, but also with the created order which is now subjugated to futility (Rom 8:19–21). Thus sin corrupts more than individuals. Sin has a corporate nature to it in that it corrupts institutions and practices created by corrupt individuals no matter how good their intentions. More importantly, we are now "slaves to sin" in that we have an innate inclination to sin (Rom 6:14–23). Like Adam and Eve, we are incapable of liberating ourselves from sin; and although we can practice good works, we can never escape the effects of sin, namely guilt and fear. All humans need someone who is beyond sin's grasp to liberate us.

The Judeo-Christian story let us know that while humans may have abandoned God, God has not abandoned us. Instead, God is working throughout history to restore us to our true selves and to loving relationship with God, with others, and with all creation. Furthermore, because God's restoration of humans and creation is initiated by God alone, we can understand the process of our salvation as pure gift or grace, not only in making us "right with God and with one another," but in bringing to our awareness the need for salvation and enabling us to say "yes" to the divine invitation. Felton describes this grace when she writes, "Since God is the only initiator and source of all grace, all grace is prevenient in that it precedes and enables any movement that we can make toward God. Grace brings us to an awareness of our sinful predicament and our inability to save ourselves; grace motivates us to repentance and gives us the capacity to respond to divine love. In the words of the baptismal ritual: 'All this is God's gift, offered to us without price' (*The United Methodist Hymnal*, 33)."[16]

Under Wesley's theology of atonement, not only are we liberated individually from the effect of sin, but because of the grace of God, Christ's atoning work is universal. While God's Grace for salvation is universal, under Wesley it is not irresistible. One must choose faith, not simply as

16. Felton, *By Water and the Spirit*, 10–11.

intellectual assent, but rather as personal trust. Thus, according to Wesley salvation through faith for the believer entails

> even in the present world: a salvation from sin, and the conse-
> quences of sin, both often expressed in the word justification;
> which, taken in the largest sense, implies a deliverance from
> guilt and punishment, by the atonement of Christ actually
> applied to the soul of the sinner now believing on him, and a
> deliverance from the power of sin, through Christ formed in
> his heart. So that he who is thus justified, or saved by faith, is
> indeed born again. He is born again of the Spirit unto a new life,
> which "is hid with Christ in God." And as a new-born babe he
> gladly receives the adolon, "sincere milk of the word, and grows
> thereby;" going on in the might of the Lord his God, from faith
> to faith, from grace to grace, until at length, he come unto "a
> perfect man, unto the measure of the stature of the fullness of
> Christ."[17]

Thus, for Wesley, salvation from sin through faith not only entailed assurance of being freed from sin and its consequences, but also signified a new beginning, in his words, of being born again with an expectation of spiritual growth (i.e., obedience and works) as evidence of being born again. Although Wesley puts in dialectical tension the application of water through baptism and the inner grace that signifies New Birth, Wesley was not convinced that these two had to occur simultaneously. For Wesley, baptism serves the same function as the instituted means of grace in that he believed it, "in an ordinary way, is necessary to salvation, but not in the *absolute* sense."[18] Thus, baptism serves as the means to the New Birth (i.e., conversion), not as its equal. For conversion, like the atoning work of Christ, is the ministry of God. Wesley makes this point abundantly clear in his sermon "The Marks of the New Birth":

> Who then are ye that are *thus* born of God? Ye 'know the things
> which are given to you of God'. Ye well know that ye are the
> children of God, and 'can assure your hearts before him'. And
> every one of you who has observed these words cannot but feel
> and know of a truth whether at this hour (answer to God and
> not to man!) you are thus a child of God or no! The question is
> not what you was made in baptism (do not evade!) but what you
> are now. Is the Spirit of adoption now in your heart? To your

---

17. John Wesley, Sermon 1, "Salvation by Faith."
18. Borgen, "No End Without the Means," 75.

own heart let the appeal be made. I ask not whether you *was* born of water and the Spirit. But are you *now* the temple of the Holy Ghost which dwelleth in you? . . .

Say not then in your heart, I was *once* baptized; therefore, I *am* now a child of God. Alas, that consequence will by no means hold. How many are the baptized gluttons and drunkards, the baptized liars and common swearers, the baptized railers and evil-speakers, the baptized whoremongers, thieves, extortioners! What think you? Are these now the children of God?[19]

Thus, while Wesley believes that infants are born again through baptism, he also believes that the grace they receive in their baptism may be lost, and if lost, it might be renewed without the concomitant rebaptism. Thus, it is "extremely important that children be taught in order to counteract the natural corruption and make it possible for them to grow in grace."[20] In fact, according to Henry H. Knight, it is this concern for the loss of baptismal grace, the causes Wesley to not only develop the Methodist class system for adults, but to extend it to baptized children and to create spiritual formation materials for families to use with children to encourage their spiritual growth, especially as it pertains to prayer.[21]

The Baptism of Infants and Adults

Given that we have discussed the correlation of baptism to salvation (i.e., conversion and the New Birth) and that we have introduced infant baptism as intrinsic to Wesley's theology and practice of baptism, we will now turn to a more detailed discussion of infant and adult baptism. We do this because of the inconsistencies even in United Methodist practice, as hinted at in the introduction and in numerous United Methodist books on the theology and practice of baptism as exercised by local pastors and congregations. To aid us in our discussion, we will first look to Laurence Hull Stookey's analysis of the inclusivist versus exclusivist views regarding who is eligible for baptism, then apply this analysis to our Wesleyan, albeit United Methodist, understanding of infant and adult baptisms, and the concept/practice of re-baptism.

19. John Wesley, Sermon 18, "The Marks of the New Birth," 181.
20. Borgen, "No End without the Means," 77.
21. Knight, "Significance of Baptism," 139.

Inclusivist vs. Exclusivist View of Baptism[22]

With regard to who may be baptized, clergy and congregations generally tend to fall into one of two camps—the inclusivist or the exclusivist view. The inclusivist view maintains that all who request baptism for either themselves or their children should be admitted to the baptismal font. The exclusionist view is that baptism is for those who make a conscientious profession of faith for themselves. As we shall demonstrate, each view has its strengths and weaknesses.

According to Stookey, the inclusivist view is most commonly associated with state churches, especially those of the pre-reformation era. Stookey cites that it was this view—that everyone should be baptized—that allowed military officials to baptize conquered peoples at will, thus bringing them and their possessions both into the empire and into the church. While this practice obviously highlights a misuse of baptism, Stookey asserts that the strength of the inclusivist position is that it emphasizes that all of salvation is initiated and facilitated by the grace of God. Further, it highlights the "whosoever will come" nature of the gospel in that all are eligible for the salvific grace of God made known in Jesus through the power of the Holy Spirit. As we noted, the weaknesses of the inclusivist position can lead to utilizing the church's practices for oppression rather than liberation. In addition to this, Stookey maintains that an overemphasis on divine activity can "lead to misunderstanding so that the rite comes to be viewed mechanically, or even magically. In its worst distortions, baptism can is considered a kind of escape hatch from perdition or a guarantee of salvation."[23]

Under an inclusivist view—especially operating in a postmodern, hyper individualistic, consumeristic culture in which the church is seen only as a vendor or religious goods and services—baptism simply becomes a commodity that one "purchases" by submitting oneself to the ritual of baptism without any need to further one's spiritual growth, especially within the confines of a faith community. In addition to the commodification of the baptism, under the inclusivist model, baptism can also be seen as a "right," especially when the lines between Christian discipleship and national citizenship become blurred such that everyone believes that they have a "right" to not have withheld from them what

22. For a more detailed discussion of this, see "The Who's Who of Baptism," in Stookey, *Baptism*, 41–74.

23. Ibid., 42.

seems available to everyone else. Simply put, the danger of the inclusivist position is that the signs of the sacrament are separated from the *res* such that the means (i.e., the water and the ritual) are equated to be the end (i.e., the inward grace of conversion/New Birth).

At the opposite end of the spectrum is the exclusivist view which highlights the need for human response and commitment to divine activity. Thus, churches that maintain exclusivist doctrines of baptism often seek to ensure that persons are committed to the vows they make in baptism. The weakness of the exclusivist view is that while those holding the view believe that baptism is not possible without God's initiative and Christ's atoning work, "baptism is more likely regarded as a reward for faith."[24] Further, as Stookey argues this view of baptism can be highly personalized in that it relies solely on the experience of one coming for baptism and as such it is susceptible to being "a voluntary association" of like-minded persons who profess faith rather than the creation of Christ. Therefore, instead of "whosoever will" with regard to Christ's atoning work as universal, the emphasis in exclusivist is on the individual and their experience of faith, rather than the communal aspects of baptism.[25] In this way, the local faith community has the danger of becoming a collective individuals rather than a body of diverse believers gathered by Christ across race, ethnicity, gender, sexual orientation, or physical/mental competency. Furthermore, as Stookey notes, under an exclusivist position it is quite possible to keep those who are not physically or mentally competent from the sacrament, which is to disavow God's graceful action within the sacraments.[26]

Stookey contends that by holding both of these views in creative tension, the church overcomes the weaknesses of each and stays in line with Scripture and church tradition. Thus, he maintains that with regard to defining eligibility for baptism while keeping this dialectical tension, that the appropriate answer is: "baptism is to be granted to those who are committed to the Christian faith and to their children, provided they have not been baptized before."[27]

---

24. Ibid., 43.
25. Ibid.
26. Ibid., 59–60.
27. Ibid., 44.

Wesley's Theology and Practice of Infant Baptism and Its Correlation to United Methodist Theology and Practice

For United Methodists, this dialectical tension between inclusivist and exclusivist views was well developed by John Wesley centuries ago and was at the heart of the class system of his Christian formation. Following his Anglican heritage and in accord with early church practice that most likely began in the New Testament era, Wesley affirmed infant baptism for children of committed Christian believers who were brought up in Christian homes and faith communities.[28] As Borgen notes, Wesley argues for infant baptism based on "Scripture, reason, and primitive (i.e., early church) practice." First, Wesley maintains that infants, like all humans, are inheritors of original sin and as such in need of salvation, which must be received through the means that God has ordained—baptism. Once baptized, infants are justified and born again.

Second, Wesley states that infants ought to be baptized because they ought to come to Christ, because Christ has commanded them to come (Matt 19:13–14; Luke 18:15) and once coming to Christ, they are members of the Body of Christ and admitted to the local church.[29] Further, once infants are admitted to the church, Wesley advocates that in their baptism there ought to be a component that entails the parents' intention of consecrating their child to Christ. Wesley understands that this consecration of infants entails an understanding that upon their baptism, infants are also consecrated because they receive the Holy Spirit. Thus, upon baptism, infants are able, as are adults, to begin the process of sanctification, which is why the commitment by parents to work toward their own and their children's spiritual growth is a crucial component of Wesley's, and of our United Methodist, baptismal service for infants and children unable to speak for themselves.[30] To this end, Wesley developed many spiritual formation tools for families to assist their children in their spiritual growth—as do United Methodists.

In his *Thoughts Upon Infant Baptism*, Wesley contends that infants and children are to be baptized also because of Scripture and the apostolic tradition of the church. For Wesley, baptism can be likened to circumcision as a mark of entering into covenantal relationship with God

28. Brewer, "Evangelical Anglicanism," 111–12.

29. Felton, *By Water and the Spirit*, 29. See also Borgen, *John Wesley on the Sacraments*, 142.

30. Borgen, *John Wesley on the Sacraments*, 143.

in which Abraham was to circumcise his entire household including children. By equating baptism in the New Testament with circumcision in the Hebrew Bible, Wesley also argues that given that it is highly unlikely that when Scripture mentions entire households being saved and baptized that children where omitted. Finally, citing such church fathers as Irenaeus, Clement of Alexandria, Origen, Cyprian, Ambrose, and Augustine, Wesley asserts that recent baptismal practices that only allow for baptizing adults and those that can attest to their faith is no reason to jettison over 1,700 years of Christian thought and teaching, especially as it comes from the apostolic tradition.[31]

As is clearly demonstrated in both *By Water and the Spirit*, as well as the Baptismal Covenants in the United Methodist Hymnal and Book of Worship, United Methodists advocate for infant baptism based on the same reasons that Wesley provided. In addition, they affirm that baptism is the act of God through the church. While human response is important, as demonstrated by the inclusion of both parental and congregational vows in the baptismal covenant services, baptism is not primarily the work of humans. Given that baptism is primarily an act of God in the church, then in accordance with the inclusivist view, it is only to be received once. The assertion of unrepeatable baptism is based on the idea of baptism as covenant. While humans may, and often do, break our covenantal commitments to God, God is ever faithful and does not do so with us, even when we are unfaithful. As Scripture tells us, nothing can separate us from the love of God in Christ (Rom 8:38–39). When, as adults, we repent and return to God, our covenant with God does not have to be remade—God has kept his end of it. Like the covenant made with Abraham, God has already allowed for our failures and makes covenant with us, by putting the reliance of keeping the covenant on Godself (Gen 15:9–21, in particular vv. 17–18).[32]

The question, then, if we are to keep the inclusivist and exclusivist themes in Wesleyan dialectical tension, must be what ought to be our practice regarding adults—both those who have never been baptized and those who, though baptized at a younger age, have fallen away from the faith and thus are not living as children of God? Furthermore, what are we to do with those who have been baptized, but are not living fully into their baptisms, especially if our theology and practice is to not rebaptize?

31. Ibid., 145–47.

32. For more on this, see Felton, *By Water and The Spirit*, 30–31.

To answer this, we must investigate Wesley's theology and practice to discern how we might assist adults into living within in their baptism.

Wesley's Theology and Practice of Adult Baptism and Its Correlation to United Methodist Theology and Practice

When one considers Wesley's ministry, we must be mindful that for the most part Wesley's followers would have been those who had been baptized through state churches a as infants and children. Thus, while Wesley has a fully developed theology of baptism which includes both infants and children, as well as adults, Henry H. Knight contends that it is precisely Wesley's concern for those who were not living fully into their identity as children of God that drove much of Wesley's development church formation and spiritual growth as evidenced by the Methodist classes and societies.[33] This is also easily understood when one considers Wesley's sotierology and how it relates to baptism. In particular, as cited above, Wesley is clear that baptismal ritual is not the end, but rather the means for persons to be born again. In fact, in his sermon *The Marks of the New Birth*, Wesley contends that there is a difference between those who have experienced the New Birth (i.e., are born again) and those who are not, even though most may be baptized.[34] His concern with the difference between nominal Christians, whom he often referred to as "practical atheists," can easily be seen in this extended citation from his sermon "The Almost Christian":

> A second thing implied in the being "almost a Christian" is the having a form of godliness, of that godliness which is prescribed in the gospel of Christ—the having the outside of a real Christian. Accordingly, the "almost Christian" does nothing which the gospel forbids . . .
>
> He that hath the form of godliness uses also the means of grace, yea, all of them, and at all opportunities . . . he who uniformly practices this outward religion has the form of godliness
> . . .
>
> Are not many of you conscious that you never came thus far? That you have not been even "almost a Christian"? That you have not come up to the standard of heathen honesty? At least, not to the form of Christian godliness?

33. Knight, "Significance of Baptism," 133–42.
34. John Wesley, Sermon 18, "The Marks of the New Birth," 173–82.

. . . The great question of all, then, still remains. Is the love of God shed abroad in your heart? Can you cry out, "My God and my all"? Do you desire nothing but him? Are you happy in God? Is he your glory, your delight, your crown of rejoicing? And is this commandment written in your heart, "that he who loveth God love his brother also"? Do you then love your neighbor as yourself? Do you love every man, even your enemies, even the enemies of God, as your own soul? As Christ loved you? Yea, dost thou believe that Christ loved *thee* and gave himself for thee? Hast thou faith in his blood? Believest thou the Lamb of God hath taken away thy sins, and cast them as a stone into the depth of the sea? That he hath blotted out the handwriting that was against *thee*, taking it out of the way, nailing it to his cross? Hast *thou* indeed redemption through his blood, even the remission of *thy* sins? *And doth his Spirit bear witness with thy spirit, that thou art a child of God* [emphasis mine].[35]

Thus, for adults, while Wesley affirmed that through baptism God was faithful to forgive persons of their sin and begin the process of re-generation. While Wesley agreed that baptism was the primary means of regeneration, he did not believe that it was the only means. Following his Anglican heritage, Wesley maintained that if baptism was the only means of being born again, then there was no "second chance" for back-sliders. For Wesley, baptism is what God does for us and in us, in that in baptism "something new is *born*, comes into being, a 'principle of grace is infused,' the Holy Spirit is given, and the baptized is 'mystically united to Christ. . . . From which *spiritual*, vital union with *him*, proceeds the *influence* of his grace on those that are baptized.'"[36]

Although Wesley believes that baptism occurs in the same manner for both infants and adults, he does believe that baptism functions differ-ently in the lives of adults. For Wesley, those who had been "born again" prior to their receiving baptism, "he should also be born of the Spirit." Borgen concludes that the reason why Wesley insisted on the rite of bap-tism for those who were already converted as to insure that the other im-portant functions of baptism, namely incorporation into the church and that they be "born of water and the Spirit," were enacted in their lives.[37]

For those who had not been baptized as infants, Wesley insisted on their baptism for the same reasons as for infants. While scholars report

---

35. John Wesley, Sermon 2, "The Almost Christian," 62–67, selected.

36. Borgen, *John Wesley on the Sacraments*, 158–59.

37. Ibid., 159–60. See also Knight, "Significance of Baptism," 137.

that Wesley baptized many adults, Borgen and Knight also report that Wesley, who was most concern for how adults lived into the grace of their baptisms, allowed for the possibility of the sacrament not being "duly received," as well as for the falling way from the grace received in one's baptism, thus making baptismal grace inefficacious. To this end, Borgen writes,

> Thus, as late as 1760 Wesley could affirm . . . "I baptized a gentlewoman at the Foundery, and the peace she immediately found was fresh proof that the outward sign, *duly received, is always accompanied with the inward grace.* Nevertheless, faithful to his doctrine, he also allows that not everyone experiences the fullness of grace. First, God in his wisdom grants his grace to each person according to his state and need, and in some he even withholds his grace for some time. And, when the sacrament is not "duly received," God's grace does not become operative; *lack of repentance and some degree of faith will effectively block God's grace. A man may prevent Baptism from being efficacious for him, but the contrary is not true: a man's faith and repentance is not constitutive of the efficacy of the sacrament* [emphasis mine].[38]

Given that it was possible for adults to prevent God's Grace made available to them in their baptism, Knight contends that Wesley developed a system of spiritual formation designed specifically for those persons new to the faith or those who had practiced nominal Christianity or had fallen away completely. According to Knight, following the model of the early church, Wesley developed the pattern of "proclamation, enrollment in a class, accountability to discipline, and new birth."[39] In addition, Wesley's model hinged on his belief that persons who responded to his message were simply reawakened, having received convincing (or convicting) grace. Therefore, "seeing themselves now as God saw them, they responded with the faith of a servant, dutifully trying to obey God yet remaining under the power of sin. They yearned for God to give them New Birth, an experience of God's forgiving and transforming love which enable them to have the faith of a child and to begin to grow in love of God and neighbor."[40]

For these persons practicing all of the means of grace—prayer, fasting, fellowship, Eucharist, Bible reading was meant to nurture them in

---

38. Borgen, *John Wesley on the Sacraments*, 162–63.

39. Knight, "Significance of Baptism," 135.

40. Ibid., 134. See also Vickers, "Wesley's Theological Emphases," 198–201.

their growth of the love of God and neighbor. Through this process of spiritual formation, rebaptism is not needed in that nominal or backslidden adults are now provided within a process whereby they can respond to the God who has never broken covenant with them. Furthermore, Wesley's process ensured that adults did not have to rely solely on an intellectualized or overly emotional faith based on themselves alone. Rather, his process help person progress until they were assured of the inner witness of the Holy Spirit that they are the children of God. Through his insistence on the participation of adults within the sacraments, especially his practice of baptism within community Wesley provided for his followers a path toward sanctification, which has at its foundation a clear understanding of the grace of God enacted and present to us, and also human responsibility in cooperating with the Holy Spirit in covenantal community to move forward in spiritual growth.

Baptism as the Sacrament of Initiation, Identity, Incorporation and Integration, and Commissioning

Baptism as the Sacrament of Initiation

For early Christians the act of baptism was more than a washing away of sin and a rising to new life for catechumenates. The act of baptism brought into the present God's covenantal acts of creation and redemption as depicted in the early chapters of Genesis; as well as God's act of saving nascent Israel from Pharoah's army and making covenant to be their God, while making them God's people through the passage of the Red (Reed) Sea. Thus, baptism, as understood and practiced by early Christians, incorporated them into the community of God's people across time and space through baptism as a rite similar to Passover in which they were incorporated into God's original covenant with Israel and fully realized in Jesus Christ. Simply put, for post-paschal communities, baptism was the seminal event for theologizing about and practicing the Christian faith. As Stookey explains, "In contrast to later understanding, baptism was a process that extended over a period of time and possessed a unity within itself and in relation to the whole of the Christian life; baptism was connected to everything in the Christian life."[41]

41. Stookey, *Baptism*, 117.

From our discussion above with regard to Wesley's theology and practice of baptizing, it is easily discerned that he views baptism as the initiation of people into life in Jesus Christ and into the body of Christ, the church. For Wesley, there is no baptism without the church. Simply put, the church is God's primary chosen vehicle through which to birth those into the kingdom of God. Baptism does not mark the end of one's spiritual journey or simply attest to the work of the Holy Spirit within them. Rather, baptism signifies that new life in Christ has begun. As evidenced in the previous section, Wesley's linking of baptism with salvation and primarily the New Birth, as well as his development of an extensive system of catechesis makes clear that, for him, baptism is the starting point for the work of sanctification in a believer. According to Wesley, the regeneration wrought in our baptism brings about justification and New Birth, which, while closely related, has a differing effect within the life of the believer. Justification implies the change of the relationship that we have with God (God does something *for* us); whereas the in the New Birth there is a change in our spiritual condition in that God does something *in* us—makes it possible for us to grow in holiness through the power of the Holy Spirit so that we can grow in love of God and love of neighbor.[42] Wesley makes this distinction clear with regard to baptism as initiation in these words from his sermon "The Great Privilege of Those That Are Born of God": "When we undergo this great change we may with such propriety be said 'to be born again,' because there is so near a resemblance between the circumstances of the natural and the spiritual birth; so that to consider the circumstances of the natural birth is the most easy way to understand the spiritual."[43]

Vickers maintains that Wesley was so convinced that baptism marked initiation into the life in Christ through the Holy Spirit that he develops doctrines of awakening and spiritual regeneration. With awakening that occurs in the New Birth the Holy Spirit not only restores the spiritual senses so to be able to "see 'the light of the glory of God . . . in the face of Jesus Christ' and to 'hear the inward voice of God, saying 'Be of good cheer, thy sins are forgiven thee: Go and sin no more.'"[44] Once awakened, Wesley's doctrine of spiritual generation contends that the Holy Spirit is ever present in the life of the awakened believer until "by

42. John Wesley, Sermon 19, "The Great Privilege of those that are Born of God," 184.

43. Ibid., 185.

44. Vickers, "Wesley's Theological Emphases," 200.

this intercourse between God and man, this fellowship with the Father and the Son, as by a kind of spiritual respiration, the life of God in the soul is sustained: and the child grows up till he comes to the 'full measure of the stature of Christ.'"[45]

This process of initiation is easily seen in the United Methodist Baptismal Covenant service which states quite clearly in the introduction of the service that baptism is initiation into "Christ's holy church" which is eschatological and which spans time and space.[46] Even in the United Methodist's *Baptismal Covenant IV: Congregational Reaffirmation of the Baptismal Covenant*, participants are reminded of the fact that through baptism they have already been initiated into Christ's church at our baptism. Once we enter into the covenant of grace made available by God through Christ's atoning work, there is no need to re-enter that covenant again for the covenant, like all of our covenants with God is based on God and God's Grace alone. We may deny that covenant through our sinning or prevent our receipt of the full measure of the covenant of God's Grace toward us, but God is ever faithful in keeping God's end of the bargain.

With our initiation also comes a change in our identity as noted above in the passages from Wesley. We will now turn our attention to how our identities are transformed in baptism.

Baptism as the Sacrament of Identity

As Christian theology asserts, sin distorts us from who we are to be in relation to God, ourselves, and others. Felton describes beautifully the effects of original sin in terms of our understanding of who and whose we are and what that means for the created world when she writes,

> Tragically, as Genesis 3 recounts, we are unfaithful to that relationship. *The result is a thorough distortion of the image of God in us and the degrading of the whole creation.* Through prideful overreach or denial of our God-given responsibilities, we exalt our own will, invent our own values, and rebel against God. Our very being is dominated toward an inherent inclination toward evil which has traditionally be called original sin. It is a universal condition and affects all aspects of life. Because of our condition of sin, we are separated from God, alienated from one

---

45. John Wesley, SS II.4, *Works*, 2:192–93, 200.
46. The United Methodist Church, *The Book of Worship*, 87, 95, 103, 106.

another, hostile to the natural world and even at odds with our own best selves.[47]

Through God's prevenient grace, God quickens in us the ability to know that while we are still yet in sin, we are like the prodigal son in the pigpen, this is not who we are and we were meant for more than this, for in our Father's house (kingdom) even servants are treated better. Like the prodigal son, we have to acknowledge that it was us that abandoned our Father's house to live according to the world's standards. We have to be willing to make the journey to our Father's house, where there is provision for servants and sons, and be willing to confess the error of our ways, even the error of our ways embodied in us through original sin, and ask for forgiveness. Once there, we must receive the Father's lavish gift of forgiveness and restoration of who we are—children of God. Then, we have a choice to make—will we only accept the identity that we have claimed for ourselves because of our sin-consciousness (i.e., remain a servant) or will we claim the identity our Father gives us in spite of our sin as a son and join joyfully in the abundance of joy that God lavishly provides solely as gift.

Wesley makes this point of the distinction of the restoration of identity as children of God in terms of God's justifying grace (what God does for us) and New Birth (what God does in us) in many of his writings. In addition, his process of spiritual formation by placing persons who were awakened to his message of God's justifying grace (i.e., who made a decision for Christ), in class meetings and societies so that they could begin to divest themselves of their sin-consciousness of living as servants and move to living as children of God with all of the rights and the responsibilities. Wesley describes this living as servant versus sin in his sermon "The New Birth" and maintains that it is through the New Birth that one is able to claim one's full identity in Christ. He makes this point well when he asserts that the only way that one grows into the full stature of sonship in God is when in New Birth

> the change wrought in the whole soul by the almighty Spirit of God when it is "created anew in Christ Jesus," when it is "renewed after the image of God," "in righteousness and true holiness," when the love of the world is changed into the love of God, pride into humility, passion into meekness; hatred, envy malice, into sincere, tender, disinterested love for mankind. In a word,

---

47. Felton, *By Water and the Spirit*, 9.

it is that change whereby the "earthly, sensual, devilish" mind is turned into "the mind which was in Christ." This is the nature of the new birth. "So is everyone that is born of the Spirit."[48]

Just as justification and New Birth can occur in the infant/child baptism, baptism does not guarantee that one has fully accepted his/her privileges and responsibilities as a son. In the sermon "The New Birth," Wesley describes those who are baptized and evidence no inward or outward holiness in that they "continue to be the servants of sin." He also describes those who have fallen away or live nominal Christian lives as forfeiting the privileges of the covenant that God made in their baptism.

In the United Baptismal Covenants we see that in our rites, whether for infants/children unable to answer for themselves, adults, confirmands—or even in the reaffirmation of our faith—we are invited to make a change in or acknowledge the change in our identity begun at our baptism. Through the Renunciation of Sin and the Profession of Faith and in the Apostle's Creed, we are reminded of who we are and whose we are. Thus, we are reminded that "be you [we] baptized or unbaptized, you [we] must be born again. Otherwise it is not possible you [we] should be inwardly holy; and without inward holiness as well as outward holiness you [we] cannot be happy even in this world; much less in the world to come."[49]

And while we acknowledge that our identities are changed personally (i.e., we are now, as individuals, children of God), our baptismal covenant suggests that the only way we can fully know who we are is as we are incorporated into Christ's body across time and space—the church, and in the local congregation that is called to nurture us in mutual fellowship and accountability. In this way, we can begin to claim the truth behind the African proverb that insists "I am because we are." Just the limbs of our natural body cannot survive without being connected to the overall body, we must be a part of the body of Christ. Furthermore, our being a part of the body of Christ cannot be subsumed such that the diversity of who God has created and gifted us to be—through the power of the Holy Spirit through a process of assimilation or dismissal of how these gifts manifest themselves through our gender, race, ethnicity, ableness, sexual orientation or socioeconomic status (1 Cor 12)—is diminished. Not only are we incorporated into the body of Christ as the church, but

48. Wesley, Sermon 45, "The New Birth," II.5, 340.
49. Ibid., IV.4, 344.

also through our dying and being raised with Christ we are incorporated into the life of the Triune God, a process that Wesley described as spiritual respiration. Corporately then, the entire body of Christ is empowered to function as the present body of Christ in unity, while maintaining the diversity of each unique part. Further, as 1 Corinthians 12 delineates, the individual aspects of the body of Christ do not function as a collective, but maintain care, balance, and concern for one another. This is demonstrated in the *Reconciliation* aspect of the eucharistic liturgy. As persons who have been reconciled to God through repentance and forgiveness, disciples are now required to be reconciled to one another as evidenced through the "passing of the peace." These two moves within the liturgy thus symbolize, through word-act, the Great Commandment to love God and to love neighbor as oneself.

Questions for Consideration

1. What is baptism? What is the meaning and significance of baptism?

2. What are some of the cultural challenges of consumerism on understanding what baptism means and how it relates to the life of holiness in and through the life of the church?

3. What do the early rites and symbols of baptism tell us about the importance of baptism in the church and its communal nature?

4. How does John Wesley's understanding of sin and salvation influence the way he views and practice of baptism as a means of grace, for instance, regarding the New Birth or the life of sanctification or holiness?

5. What are the strengths and weaknesses of "exclusivist and inclusivist" views of baptism? Do they help or hinder conversations about infant and adult baptism?

6. What was John Wesley's practice and theology of baptism? Of infant baptism? Of adult baptism? How are these practices and theologies carried out, or not carried out, in various Wesleyan bodies, specifically in the United Methodist Church? What are the strengths and weaknesses of these practices?

7. How is baptism as initiation linked to the Holy Spirit's work of sanctification and regeneration in the life of the believer and to Christian discipleship? How is such an understanding of baptism central to knowing our true identity as children of God?

8. What kinds of responsibilities does the church have when we become incorporated into God's mighty acts of salvation, especially when the church pledges to love those who cannot answer for themselves? What is the role of the Holy Spirit in awakening us unto salvation as we confess our sin and love God and neighbor?

9. What are the dangers of a contractual view of baptism or church membership? How might such a view fail to appreciate the depths of the church's baptismal covenant?

10. What are the social and evangelistic implications of baptism in the life of the church? In terms of reconciliation? In terms of welcoming the stranger? In terms of reaching out to the marginalized?

three

Eucharist

Introduction

> In baptism we receive our identity and mission as Christians.
> Holy Communion is the sacrament that sustains and nourishes
> us in our journey of salvation.[1]

Regardless of what one calls it—Eucharist, Holy Communion, the
Lord's Supper—this sacrament is the one that helps us to fully appropriate our identity as Christians and to understand the claims this identity
has on us with regard to the world around us. From those first Christians,
the Eucharist was understood as not only something instituted by Christ,
but also as a ritual that provided a divine-human representation and representation of the reign of God that is both present and not yet. This
meal was a mark of the new covenant initiated by Christ and referenced
the covenant that God had made with early Israel as symbolized by the
Passover meal.

The Passover meal signified for early Israel, not only in the form of
a memorial, but also *anamnesis*—a way of making past events present,

---

1. Felton, *This Holy Mystery*, 16.

that their God was gracious. Because of God's Grace, their God rescued them from the oppression of Pharaoh, saved them from death, promised to be their sovereign God, provided for them from heaven and led them to the Promised Land. Although the covenant demanded the faithfulness of both sides, Israel's God proved Godself faithful even when Israel was unfaithful. However, this was no cheap grace, the Passover also reminded early Israelites that there were consequences to disobedience. Their disobedience required sacrifice, repentance, and the intention to live under the lordship of Christ in the power of the Holy Spirit such that they grow in holiness and Christlikeness.

These themes are also prevalent in the Eucharist and can be found in most liturgies of the sacrament, as demonstrated in the order of worship for *The Great Thanksgiving* found in the United Methodist Hymnal. There is the first part of the service, the *anamnesis* that reminds us of what God in Christ has done for us—atoned for our sin, because we could not do this for ourselves. In the latter half, the *epiclesis*, we are reminded that Christ's work is not over. There is more for us to do in union with Christ to bring about God's kingdom that is both present and not-yet. But to do the work, the God will have to pour out the Holy Spirit on us such that we become one with Christ, not as individuals, but as members of his mystical body so that we might carry out his ministry to all the world.

A hallmark of the movement started by our theological ancestors, John and Charles Wesley, was the fact that it was highly Eucharistic. At the core of the renewal ideals for the church was a renewal of how the Eucharist was traditionally practiced. Because they were primarily concerned with the evangelization of nominal Christians, specifically by helping them grow in holiness and Christian discipleship, the Wesleys utilized sermons and songs, and modified text as well as the traditional Sunday service such that those who attended the services went through a process of Christian formation that utilized a variety of media targeted at inculcating them into the Wesleys' theology, especially their theology of salvation, holiness, and the Eucharist. In this chapter we will first review the different names of the sacrament.

Different Names of the Sacrament

The New Testament highlights at least six major ideas regarding the Eucharist: thanksgiving, fellowship, remembrance, sacrifice, action of the

Holy Spirit, and eschatology. In the varying names these themes are high-lighted so as to emphasize these major aspects. First and foremost, we can refer to the sacrament as the Eucharist, because as such it is an act of joy-ful thanksgiving for all that God has given in terms of creation, covenant, redemption and sanctification. In fact, the United Methodist liturgy for this sacrament is called "The Great Thanksgiving" (i.e. Eucharist) so as to remind us of the many reasons that we have to give God thanksgiv-ing and praise for all that God has done and is doing for us through the power of the Holy Spirit by God's Grace to express his love toward us.

The sacrament may also be referred to as the Lord's Supper. This is to remind us not only of the fact that Christ instituted it when he served as both host and servant of the supper, but that he continues to serve as host, servant, sacrifice, and priest in it with us now. As the Lord's Supper, the sacrament reminds us that we observe the sacrament in "remembrance of Me" (Christ). More than nostalgia, the sacrament is both representation and re-presentation of what God has done through Jesus Christ such that these acts are present now. Christ is risen and alive now—not just 2,000 years ago—and is present to us in the sacrament.

The sacrament is also referred to as Holy Communion to remind us that the sacrament is the communion of the church—gathered and universal, across all time and space. Those gathered are not a collective of individuals but comprise the mystical body of which Christ is the head. The communion of the church is not only with human beings across time and space, but also represents our communion with the triune God. As a type of sacrifice, Holy Communion is a re-presentation of Christ's sacri-fice which we present in union with Christ before the Father to be made available in the God's work of redemption, reconciliation, and justice in the world.

The sacrament is also eschatological in that it reminds us that in Christ, God has acted decisively to determine the outcome of the end of history. As the United Methodist liturgy for "The Great Thanksgiv-ing" declares, "Christ has died, Christ has risen, Christ will come again." While we feast physically at the communion table, this is meant to be a foretaste of the heavenly banquet when we feast with Christ and the church triumphant. Our partaking of the communion elements signifies that we are feasting at the banquet of God's kingdom that is both present and not yet.

For our purposes, we will utilize the terminology of the Eucharist since it is the one utilized within our liturgical documents. We will also use the terms communion and Lord's Supper because these are the terms that both John and Charles Wesley, as well as their theological mentors, used in developing their theology and practice of the Eucharist.

Understanding Wesley's Eucharistic Theology and Practice: "The Duty of Constant Communion" and the Hymns on the Lord's Supper

Two critical documents for understanding John Wesley's theology of the Eucharist are his sermon "The Duty of Constant Communion" and the *Hymns on the Lord's Supper*, John Wesley's collaboration with his brother Charles. In these two documents John Wesley carefully crafts for the hearers of his day and ours a rich sacramental theology that is grounded in the worship of God and is consistent with his mission of helping Christians become mature disciples, a process he referred to as sanctification. Although, Wesley originally wrote *The Duty of Constant Communion* in 1733 while at Oxford, he boldly states in his update of 1788 that he had "not yet seen cause to alter [his] sentiments in any point" in it. In fact, many have argued that Wesley's entire theology was sacramental in general, and specifically eucharistic.[2] To gain a better grasp of Wesley's eucharistic theology, we will now look at the specific contributions of each of these on Wesley's theology and practice of the Eucharist.

"The Duty of Constant Communion"

It can be said that Wesley wrote "The Duty of Constant Communion" to address two concerns. First, building on the theology of Richard Hooker, Joseph Hall, William Law, and other Caroline Divines, Wesley understands that as the instituted means of grace, both baptism and Eucharist—but specifically the Eucharist—are those means by which God strengthens the spiritual senses and that assists partakers in growing in sanctification. Second, Wesley was committed to utilizing reprinted early Christian documents as well as secondary historical surveys as a means of renewal for the Church of England as a whole, and for the nominal Christianity that plagued his society. As Karen Westerfield Tucker explains, Wesley continued resourcing of early patristic documents and

---

2. See both Martin, "Toward a Wesleyan Sacramental Ecclesiology," 19–38, and Hunter, "Toward a Methodist Communion Ecclesiology," 9–18.

historical overviews, a process defined as *ressourcement*, because he believed that the "doctrine and practice of the church of the first 100 years
to exemplify true, uncorrupted, and scriptural Christianity."[3] Third, and
more importantly, Wesley pens this sermon to address the infrequency
of Holy Communion/Eucharist in the Church of England, as well as misunderstandings of the Eucharist as practiced in the Catholic church in his
day. Based on his own experience of communing at least four to five times
weekly, and during certain seasons even more, Wesley was convinced that
a sure way to address the nominal Christianity of his times was to address
specifically the concerns persons had with the necessity and frequency, as
well as their own worthiness to partake of the sacrament,

According to Stamm, communion was infrequent during Wesley's
time due primarily to four reasons: (1) apathy, (2) misunderstanding of
1 Corinthians 11 on personal unworthiness to receive the sacrament,
(3) the doctrines of both con- and transubstantiation, (4) the belief that
in the sufficiency of the Protestant Reformers increase in the frequency
of communion to at least four times per year, and (5) the length of the
Sunday Service of Word and Holy Communion.[4] In *The Duty of Constant
Communion*, Wesley begins his apologetic for constant communion by
insisting that the primary reason for constant communion is simply because "the Lord commands it" without stipulation by all who name themselves as Christians until the end of the world. Second, Wesley, in line
with his understanding of the benefits of the means of grace, asserts that
the reason for constant communion is because of the benefits of doing
so, specifically, the forgiveness of past sin and "the present strengthening
and refreshing of our souls." In this manner, Wesley reminded his hearers and readers that no one is above constant temptation, or without sin.
Therefore, the surest way to have these blotted out and to be strengthened
in the battle for our souls by being able to withstand temptation, was
to partake in communion, constantly.[5] Thus, in the first two paragraphs
of this sermon, Wesley lays the foundation for constant communion by
reminding listeners of the grace of God in the atoning sacrifice of Jesus
Christ, their need for this grace, and their right response to God's Grace
made available in Holy Communion in order for them to appropriate
all of the benefits of Christ's atoning work. He then reminds them that

3. Westerfield Tucker, "Wesley's Emphasis on Worship," 223.

4. Stamm, *Sacraments & Discipleship*, 80–81.

5. John Wesley, "The Duty of Constant Communion," 65.

this pattern of constant communion is also foundational in the lives of early Christians. To this end Wesley writes, "Let everyone therefore, who has either any desire to please God, or any love of his own soul, obey God and consult the good of his own soul, by communicating every time he can; like the first Christians with whom the Christian Sacrifice was a constant part of the Lord's day service. And for several centuries they received it almost every day: Four times a week always, and every Saint's day beside."[6] He then reminds them that with regard to the early church, those who attended the worship services without communicating where "excommunicated, as bringing confusion into the Church of God."[7]

Next, Wesley advocates for constant communion over the objections that the new Protestant reforms of quarterly communion are sufficient by maintaining that "the phrase 'frequent communion' is absurd to the last degree." He does this by asserting that every claim for frequent communion is reasoning for constant communion. In this, he appeals to the Lord's command to "do this as often" as we can, contending that Christians are obliged to obey God's commands constantly, emphasizing that whatever believers can do, they should. Thus, while affirming the Church of England's teaching with regard to the need for repentance and for reconciliation, Wesley removes the efficacy of the sacrament from human responsibility by simply noting that while penance is important, more important is God's bid to come, even if one cannot prepare adequately. In so doing, Wesley reminds us that Holy Communion is also a converting ordinance in that in it, God in the power of the Holy Spirit transforms us and makes us response-able to do that which we cannot do in our own power. This insistence that we come whether we believe ourselves "ready, adequate or not," is congruent with Wesley's sotierology grounded in the grace of God that reminded his hearers and us that we are (unable) at any point to save ourselves or make ourselves acceptable to God. We simply invited to the Lord's Table and in the words of Isaiah 55:1–3a:

> Ho, everyone who thirsts,
> come to the waters;
> and you that have no money,
> come, buy and eat!
> Come, buy wine and milk
> without money and without price.

6. Ibid., 66.
7. Ibid.

Why do you spend your money for that which is not bread,
and your labor for that which does not satisfy?
Listen carefully to me, and eat what is good,
and delight yourselves in rich food.
Incline your ear, and come to me;
listen, so that you may live.
I will make with you an everlasting covenant.

Wesley then refutes the argument against constant communion with regard to the unworthiness of the recipient by explaining the misconception of 1 Corinthians 11's admonition to not eat and drink unworthily and by appealing to humans' need for the grace and mercy of God present in Holy Communion. Beginning by appealing to human need, Wesley explains that in terms of unworthiness, of course, no one is "worthy" to partake of Holy Communion. Rather, in grace and mercy, God offers each of us the opportunity to receive mercy, pardon for sin and strength for our souls. If we refuse this gift of God's Grace and mercy, then Wesley declares "what can God himself do for us farther?"[8]

Next Wesley provides a proper exegesis of the understanding of "unworthiness" in 1 Corinthians 11 by clarifying that to eat and drink unworthily is to take "the holy Sacrament in such a rude and disorderly way." This Wesley presumes to be impossible, especially given the orderliness of the worship services. Wesley contends that since no one should come to the table without self-examination and repentance, then even those who have committed sins for which they believe themselves unworthy are in position to receive the sacraments. He utilizes this same argument for those who maintain that they are unable to live the holy life they vow within the sacrament. Again, Wesley contends that our inability and propensity for sin is exactly the reason for constant communion. He also uses this defense for those who claim they have no time for self-examination if communion is to be held on every Lord's day (i.e., weekly) maintaining that it is precisely by engaging in constant communion that one matures spiritually. Thus, Wesley maintains, "Make not reverence to God's command a pretence for breaking it. Do not rebel against him for fear of offending him. Whatever you do or leave undone besides, be sure to do what God bids you to do. Examining yourself, and using private prayer, especially before the Lord's supper is good; but behold 'to obey

8. Ibid., 67.

is better than' self-examination; and 'to hearken,' than the prayer of an angel."[9]

For those who state that they have yet to "experience" the benefits that are made available in Holy Communion and for those who have grown apathetic, Wesley simply states that our feeling/experience is not sufficient grounds in the face of the Lord's command. In addition, he asks those who base their contentions against constant communion, have they prepared themselves with regard to self-examination and expectancy (i.e., are they willing to obey the commands and receive all the benefits). Finally, Wesley states that the church's inability or unwillingness to offer Holy Communion more than three times per year is no excuse for not receiving. This is a direct refutation of those who do not participate in Holy Communion either because of the length of the service or its un-availability. As Stamm reports, the norm of the Church of England was to offer Holy Communion weekly.[10] Therefore, although some argued that the church taught that partaking Holy Communion at a minimum of three times per year, the believers of his day, had the opportunity to take communion constantly. This they were to do because of the command of the Lord, not the minimum requirements of church polity.

At this point it is also critical to note that while Wesley advocates for constant communion, he does not advocate for solitary communion. Thus, communion is to be taken within the context of Christian community. Although Wesley understood the importance of family and private prayer, Wesley insisted that Methodists participate in public worship weekly. In fact, Westerfield Tucker purports that Wesley's design of Methodist worship services, in particular his hymnody and the reinstitution of the ancient love feasts was due to Wesley's commitment to public worship in which believers were not recipients of the worship services, but rather active participants. She surmises that this is because of Wesley's commitment to historical writings and reviews of early church practice that emphasized congregational participation across social classes.[11] Moreover, Rattenbury in his *Eucharistic Hymns of John and Charles Wesley* highlights that in these hymns there is a profound sense of the church as the priesthood of all believers. Thus, the priestly function is shared by the church, not as a collective of individuals, but as the corporate body of Christ, in participation with Christ's offering for us.

9. Ibid., 69.

10. Stamm, *Sacraments & Discipleship*, 81.

11. Westerfield Tucker, "Wesley's Emphasis on Worship," 230–33.

Key Eucharistic Themes in the Wesleys' Hymns on the Lord's Supper

As important as is Wesley's sermon "The Duty of Constant Communion," probably no other work of his provides as much insight into Wesley's Eucharistic theology as the 1745 *Hymns on the Lord's Supper*, which he copublished with his brother Charles. In the introduction, as well as the compilation and arrangement of these hymns, the Wesley's provide a theological and deeply devotional document that could have been comprehended by all, which expressed the Wesleys' core teaching and doctrine, especially as it pertained to sotierology, ecclesiology, and the Eucharist. In addition, it can be argued that in these Eucharistic hymns, the Wesley's informed Methodist faith through music and song. They enhanced their learning ability of key theological concepts through multisensory level learning by congregational hymn singing and participation in the Eucharist.[12]

Although the Church of England in Wesley's day was "slow to adopt hymn singing," especially the expressive hymns of the Wesleys, Stevick argues that the key purpose of the *Hymns on the Lord's Supper* was for preparation of the Eucharist and to maintain the fervor of the celebration "during the administration of communion when the members of the Methodist societies, crowding the churches on sacrament Sunday, protracted the time for serving the elements."[13] In particular, Rattenbury writes that a key aspect of the hymns was the devotional verses which facilitated their use in large communion services.[14] Thus, in the creation of the hymnal, Rattenbury contends that John and Charles Wesley were able to balance in creative tension the institutional Christianity of their day with the emotionalism of revival. To this end, Rattenbury writes,

> The Eucharistic hymns and the emphasis on the Lord's Supper were a particularly valuable product of the times: they expressed deep evangelical emotion, but repressed some of the by-products of a Revival which endangered not only decency and order, but even morality. The hymn book was a product of two outstanding facts of the Revival: its experimental religions, the orderliness of the Wesleyan-Anglican tradition. And both were

12. For more on how music influences learning and helps with retention, see Brewer, "Music and Learning." See also Hawn, "Hymnody and Christian Education."

13. Stevick, *Altar's Fire*, 5.

14. Rattenbury, *Eucharistic Hymns*, 15.

necessary for that permanent work of God which the Wesleys were instruments. It should never be forgotten that these hymns were Revival hymns, and that Sacramental worship was not only not contrary to Evangelical, but in the eighteenth century, in its intensified form, one of its chief results. While these hymns were corrective of extravagance, they were the fruit of the Revival.[15]

Even though the Wesleys are credited with enhancing Eucharistic worship by providing these hymns, we must understand that the hymns were not written in a vacuum. As noted earlier in this document, the Wesleys (in particular John) were greatly influenced by historical texts and reviews of the early church, as well as theological writings that were products of Protestant Reformers, such as Calvin and Luther, and English Arminians.[16] In addition, Stevick also writes that the Wesleys were influenced by the sacramental hymns of Isaac Watts.[17] Although the Wesleys drew on these sources in their hymnbook, they also hold them in creative tension so that the distinctive theology, doctrine, and practice of Methodism was maintained.

Specifically, Stevick illustrates that the Wesleys glean from both Calvin and Luther the doctrine of the real presence of Christ in the Eucharist as not in the actual elements (i.e., transubstantiation) nor as only in the individual heart of communicants. Rather, the Wesleys believed, along with Calvin and Luther, that Christ was made known in the breaking of bread. Therefore, the Eucharist is not an act of commemoration based in nostalgia, but rather the present act of the living Christ. Thus, Eucharist in Luther's theology, and in Wesleyan thought, God's gift of atonement for sin, which Christians receive gratefully, thereby entering into Christ's sacrifice. In this way, we as Christians "lay ourselves on Christ by a firm faith in his testament and do not otherwise appear before God with our prayer, praise, and sacrifice except through Christ and his mediation."[18] In this way, Christ becomes our eternal high priest, a concept that, as we will see later, the Wesleys develop more fully in their hymns. Although Wesley agreed Luther with regard to Christ's presence and priestly nature in the sacrament, they disagreed with his doctrine of consubstantiation.

With regard to Calvin, Stevick contends that the Wesleys have stronger ties to Calvinism and Puritan Nonconformist thought mostly

---

15. Ibid., 16.

16. For more on this, see Vickers, "Wesley's Theological Emphases," 190–206.

17. Stevick, *The Altar's Fire*, 13–14.

18. Ibid., 9.

through their parents Samuel and Susanna. In this way, the Wesleys followed Puritanism in terms of their insistence on monitoring one's "own interior life for signs, more or less evident, of [one's] election or of [one's] immediate relation to God."[19] In addition, Stevick demonstrates that the Wesleys are congenial with the Calvinist doctrine of "virtualism," which taught that in the sacrament Christ's presence is known by the Holy Spirit. Thus, the "virtue of the Holy Spirit is joined to the sacraments when they are duly received."[20] Although indebted to Calvinism, the Wesleys do disagree with Calvin on several critical issues. they disagree with his doctrine of predestination, which they believed could lead to antinomianism.

From the Moravians, the Wesleys understand Christianity to be a religion of both heart and head. They are also influenced by the Moravians' evangelistic impulse, as well as their simplicity, faith, and sense of community. More importantly, motifs emphasized in their hymns such as the communicants presence at the crucifixion of Christ within the sacrament, the wounds of Christ, and Christ as the Victorious Lamb, are motifs that are easily seen in the Eucharistic hymns.[21] Although the Moravian influence is seen in the Wesleys' theology and practice of the Eucharist, Sunday service and hymnody, Wesley does fall out with them over their doctrine of stillness which was in direct contrast with John Wesley's understanding of the means of grace, as vehicles that convey God's Grace to believers. For the Moravians, in particular Philip Molther, by attaching grace to particular means was to trust in the means more than in God's Grace. Therefore, the Moravians upheld the view that rather than engaging in the means of grace, "instituted" (i.e., baptism or Eucharist) or otherwise, one should "be still, ceasing from outward works" for to engage in the sacraments was "folly."[22]

For his design of the hymns, Charles Wesley had two models from which to draw. First, Charles had the twenty-five sacramental hymns of Isaac Watts in Book III of his *Hymns and Spiritual Songs*, first published in 1707 and part of the "singing diet" of the Holy Club at Oxford to which both Wesleys belonged. In these hymns, Stevick asserts, "Watts pioneered for English-speaking Christians what hymns on the Holy Communion

19. Ibid.
20. Ibid., 10.
21. Ibid., 12.
22. Ibid., 13.

should talk about, what tone they should adopt, [and] what vocabulary they should employ."[23] From these hymns, Wesley adopts the motifs of the focus on the cross of Christ, the triumphal feast of Christ and his church, the divine reversal in the gospel in that Christ's suffering has raised us to his throne, and the sacrament as the pledge of heaven. Stevick writes that the only difference in motifs between the Wesleys and Watts was the Wesleyan emphasis on the high priesthood of Christ in the Eucharist.

More than any other, the Wesleys' theology and practice of the Eucharist, including their hymnody, was influenced by the "churchly" Anglican tradition that they inherited from their parents and that was practiced in their homes.[24] It is from this Anglican tradition, that the Wesleys would receive their doctrine of Eucharistic Presence and Eucharistic Sacrifice. Against both the doctrines of transubstantiation and consubstantiation, but somewhere in between, these Anglican theologians were agreed that Christ was made known in the "breaking of bread," even if *how* he is known is a mystery. Further, mystery or no, the Anglicans were agreed that communicants could be sure of Christ's presence and receive his benefits in the sacrament. This was possible because the Eucharist is made efficacious by the Holy Spirit.[25] Thus, the Anglican doctrine of Eucharistic Presence can be easily summarized in the following words by the eighteenth-century Anglican theologian William Law: "To eat the *Body* and *Blood* of Christ, is neither more nor less that to *put on* Christ, to receive Birth and Life and Nourishment and Growth from him . . . Neither Christ, nor his Benefits and Blessings have the Nature of things *done*, or *gone* and past, but are always present, always in being, always doing and never done . . . To remember God as absent, is but a very little way to *Atheism*."[26]

As important as understanding the Eucharist as a Sacrament, was also to understand it as a sacrifice. This doctrine of Eucharistic Sacrifice, builds on the description of Jesus as the etern al high priest in the book of Hebrews, and maintained that Christ was both high priest and sacrifice in the Eucharist. We as the church offer nothing in the Eucharist because of the sole saving efficacy of Christ's sacrifice upon the cross. Thus, in the Eucharist, the church in acknowledgement of Christ's sacrifice and in

23 Ibid.

24. Ibid., 15.

25. Ibid., 16–17.

26. Law, *Demonstration of the Gross and Fundamental Errors of a late Book*, 17–18.

conjunction with it, offers a sacrifice of praise and thanksgiving for what Christ has done, and is continually presenting every time the Eucharist occurs.

Although many of these Anglican theologians and priests had significant influence on the Wesleys' theology and practice of the Eucharist, no other Anglican was more important to their work than Daniel Brevint. As both Rattenbury and Stevick acknowledge, the Wesleys introduce their *Hymns on the Lord's Supper* with an abridgement of Brevint's book *The Christian Sacrifice and Sacrament*. Both theological and devotional, Brevint's book is organized into the following two parts, further delineated into eight sections:

Part I: Eucharist as a Sacrament
Section I: The Importance of well understanding the Nature of this Sacrament.
Section II: Concerning the Sacrament, as it is a Memorial of the Sufferings and Death of Christ.
Section III: Concerning the Sacrament, as it is a Sign of Present Grace.
Section IV: Concerning the Sacrament, as it is a Means of Grace.
Section V: Concerning the Sacrament, as it is a Pledge of Future Glory.

Part II: Eucharist as a Sacrifice
Section VI: Concerning the Sacrament, as it is a Sacrifice.
Section VII: Concerning the Sacrifice of Ourselves.
Section VIII: Concerning the Sacrifice of our Goods.

In Sections II–V, Brevint makes clear that in the Eucharist, Christ's atoning work has past, present, and future implications for communicants and as such makes demands on us when he writes, "As it is a Sacrament, this great mystery shews three faces, looking directly toward three times, and offering to all worthy receivers three sorts of incomparable blessings—that of *representing* the true *efficacy of Christ's sufferings, which are past, whereof it is a* memorial; that of *exhibiting* the first fruits of these sufferings in real and *present graces*, whereof it is a moral *conveyance* and *communication*; and that of *assuring* me of all other graces and glories to *come*, whereof it is an infallible *pledge*."[27]

Not only do the Wesleys extensively utilize Brevint's schema and work extensively in the wording of the hymns in the *Hymns on the*

27. Brevint, *Christian Sacrament and Sacrifice*, II.1.

Lord's Supper, specifically, John develops an abridged version of Brevint's schema for the organization of the eucharistic hymns, reducing Brevint's original eight sections to the following five parts with a short supplement:

Part I: "As it is a Memorial of the Sufferings and Death of Christ" (27 hymns).

Part II: "As it is a Sign and Means of Grace" (65 hymns).

Part III: "The Sacrament as a Pledge of Heaven" (23 hymns).

Part IV: "The Holy Eucharist as it Implies a Sacrifice" (12 hymns).

Part V: "Concerning the Sacrifice of Our Persons" (30 hymns).

"After the Sacrament" (9 hymns).

Overall, we shall see that for the Wesleys, following Brevint, their primary theology, doctrine and practice of the Eucharist is that it is a place of mutual exchange between God and humans—a place where "people appear to worship God and where God is present to meet and bless the people."[28] By presenting the Eucharist as both Sacrament and Sacrifice, the Wesleys and Brevint, make clear that both humans and God perform as priests (i.e., the church as the priesthood of believers) which participate in union through the sacrifice of Christ, and as both making sacrifice (i.e., the communicants by offering their entire being and their possessions; see also Phil 2:5–13). Brevint describes this exchange when he writes, "The Christian Communicants are in special manner invited to offer up to God their souls, their bodies, their goods, their vows, their praises, and whatsoever they *give*; and God, on the other side, offers to us the body and blood of his Son, and all those other blessings withal, that will surely follow this sacred gift."[29] To better understand the theological themes in each part of the hymnal, which in turn help us to better understand the Wesley's overall theology of the Eucharist, we will now analyze each section independently, highlighting the various theological themes present within the work.

28. Stevick, *The Altar's Fire*, 55.

29. Brevint, *Christian Sacrament and Sacrifice*, I.i, 55.

Part I: "As It Is a Memorial of the Sufferings and Death of Christ" (27 Hymns)

In this section, the Wesleys are expounding on the theme of memorialism in the Eucharist. Specifically, they are wrestling with the question of what the words "in memory of Me" (*eis anamnesis*) mean for communicants. Acknowledging that *anamnesis* means "calling to mind," they are focused on whether or not something more than "memorial" (i.e., the calling of a past event) is what is being conveyed. Although they agree that the Eucharist calls to mind the previous event of Calvary, Rattenbury notes that within Brevint's and the Wesleys' theology of the Eucharist, *anamnesis* does not refer Calvary, but rather to Christ.[30] To limit the *anamnesis* in the Eucharist to Calvary would be to deny that Christ is risen and risen indeed. For Christians, Good Friday (i.e., Calvary) is not the last word—Resurrection (the empty tomb) is. Thus, to limit the *anamnesis* to Calvary is not congruent with their doctrine of Eucharistic Presence, or the Real Presence of Christ made known in the breaking of bread; but rather Real Absence. And in so doing, it limits the divine-human exchange in the sacrament, and reduces it to a memorial service to celebrate a dead and beloved hero, without acknowledging the benefits of the hero's death ready and available to those who participate now. This practice also eliminates the collapsing of time and space in which believers are present to the crucifixion as though it were happening now right before their eyes.

Further, as Rattenbury surmises and with which I agree, when the Eucharist is reduced to a simple memorial, then why should persons continually pay homage by participating in the service? In addition, when the sacrament is reduced to a memorial, then there is the danger of both antinomianism and spiritual voyeurism which negates the mutuality of the divine-human exchange as it relates to worship, especially in terms of humans offering their entire lives and possessions as a sacrifice in union with Christ's work.[31] Also, when Eucharist is seen as a memorial of the

30. Rattenbury, *Eucharistic Hymns*, 19.

31. This statement can be likened to the fact that the U.S. observes Memorial Day to remember the fallen heroes and heroines who have given their lives in service to the country. While persons may watch the Memorial Service and laying of the wreath at the tomb of the Unknown Soldier, Memorial Day for the U.S. has simply become the unofficial start day of summer, a "free" vacation day with which to offer worship services and sacrifices at the altar of the grill, held at the church of the barbecue; and a huge sales day.

past—rather than a sacrament which collapses time and space and places communicants at the foot of the cross—it can allow for the communion between God and humans to be interpreted as contractual. This is easily seen when certain prosperity gospel preachers interpret the partaking of the sacrament as humans fulfilling a contractual agreement in which God is now obligated to bless them, without emphasizing the horrors of Calvary, that our sin placed Christ on the cross, all of which should evoke our worship and praise. In this system, neither recognition of the salvific work of Christ nor the worship that this work should evoke is necessary. Communicants only need to partake of the sacrament so that they may be blessed; which in turn makes God not only the agent and sacrifice, but the sole servant in the sacrament.[32] Without emphasizing that *anamnesis* refers to Christ not Calvary, Brevint and the Wesleys would have reintroduced the same misuse and misunderstanding of the Eucharist by the Catholic Church that the Reformists had sought to correct.

Thus, in this section, the hymns are designed to teach communicants while they are participating in the sacrament that the Eucharist is more than mere memorial of a historical event. We are to remember Christ and his story—all of it, not just Calvary. When we gather at the Lord's Table first we are to remember the historical event of Calvary and why our Lord died on the cross and in doing so to remember God's Grace

---

32. From a transcript between televangelists Paula White and Perry Stone on the Paula White show, October 9, 2004, in which both Stone and White insinuate in the following conversation that by buying Stone's book and taking communion, one would receive a magnificent financial blessing:

Paula White: "I believe that as you take communion that there is protection through that blood. Then the Bible declares that the blood not only saves us, not only protects us, but it also provides for us. You said there's a couple that we know very dear that had a financial need."

Perry Stone: "Yes!"

Paula White: "And their father, a great pastor, pastor Scott told them God gave him a revelation."

Perry Stone: "Yes."

Paula White: "To take communion once a day."

Perry Stone: "He said, 'Take it everyday and as you're praying thank God for blessing you financially. Thank Him that that's part of the provision. They needed $50,000 and they got an amazing, remarkable $50,000 miracle, this couple did!"

Paula White: "Call that toll free number! We want you to get the 'Meal That Heals!'"

Televangelist and Pastor Gregory Dickow offers a thirty-day prepackaged self-contained communion kit for individuals and emphasizes that through daily communion, one is "to take communion today over a situation where you don't feel God has turned to your favor." (See Brian Thorton, "Can You Say, 'Uh-Baugh-Mih-Nay-Shun?'")

by offering Christ for our sin. But not only are we to remember what led to Christ's crucifixion, we are to elicit the Holy Spirit's power to realize Christ's passion and death and what through them he has done for us. Thus, Rattenbury contends that the theological emphasis of the hymns in Part I are designed to bring about theological reflection and devotion— divine contemplation that leads communicants to gratitude and praise.[33] This emphasis is easily seen in Hymn 21, verses 1 and 2, of the Wesleys' *Hymns on the Lord's Supper*:

> 1. God of unexemplified grace,
> Redeemer of mankind,
> Matter of eternal praise,
> We in thy passion find:
> Still our choicest strains we bring;
> Still the joyful theme pursue;
> Thee the Friend of sinners sing,
> Whose love is ever new.
>
> 2. Endless scenes of wonder rise,
> With that mysterious tree;
> Crucified before our eyes,
> Where we our Maker see;
> Jesus, Lord, what hast Thou done?
> Publish we the death divine;
> Stop now and gaze, and fall, and own
> Was never love like thine![34]

In this section, the Wesleys also acknowledge that while we are in remembrance of Christ, Christ is remembrance of us. These hymns are do not speak of one sided devotion, but also ask the communicants to remember that in the Eucharist, Christ is also remembering and bringing as great high priest the continual offering of himself which brings us peace.[35]

Part II: "As it is a Sign and Means of Grace" (65 Hymns)

This section of the Wesleys' *Hymns on the Lord's Supper* comprises the longest grouping of hymns in the collection. The significance of these

---

33. Rattenbury, *Eucharistic Hymns*, 25–27.

34. John Wesley and Charles Wesley, *Hymns on the Lord's Supper*.

35. Rattenbury, *Eucharistic Hymns*, 27.

hymns is to remind persons that Eucharist is not an "ends" unto itself, but rather a means, albeit, according to the Wesleys' the chief, means of grace. Thus, while the sacrament is a memorial of the passion of Christ, it also provides grace anew for communicants. Therefore, the Eucharist is both representation and re-presentation in that it "represents at once both what Our Lord suffered and what He still doth for us."[36] Thus, the Wesleys' primary aim of this chapter is to assist communicants' understanding of the definition of sacrament and how the sacrament functions within their lives collectively and personally. Furthermore, in this section it can be ascertained that the Wesleys are also helping Methodist communicants understand the difference in Methodist theology and practice of the Eucharist from other Reformists of the day, namely, Luther, Zwingli, and eventually the Moravians.[37]

As Rattenbury reports, the hymns can be loosely classified into two sections, symbolic (nos. 29–52) and instrumental (nos. 53–92). Sandwiched in between both sections is a small section of Sacred Poems which include devotional poems on the symbolic nature of the Eucharist, as well as a group of short hymns for personal devotions.[38] In the section of symbolic hymns, Wesley utilizes various biblical metaphors to relay to communicants not only how the sacrament is efficacious for them, but also how there is mystery within it. One of the key symbols that the Wesleys employ is that of the "mixed chalice." Rattenbury surmises that the Wesleys utilize the mixed chalice (i.e., the mixture of water and wine in the cup at the Eucharist) to emphasize the justifying and sanctifying nature of what Christ has done in the atonement, and how the grace from that is being made afresh to communicants to cleanse them from present sin. In this theology of sacrament and congruent with Wesley's teaching on the sacrament and the duty of constant communion, the Eucharist functions as both a means of justifying and sanctifying grace, while relating the Eucharist to our baptism. Rattenbury explains this concept when he writes,

> The essential teaching of the Hymns of the Mixed Chalice is expressed by Toplady's words: "Cleanse me from its guilt and power." The argument seems to be that the blood of Jesus saves from guilt but does not cleanse. Water is a necessity as well as

36. John Wesley, *The Letters of John Wesley*, as quoted in Rattenbury, *Eucharistic Hymns*, 31.

37. Rattenbury, *Eucharistic Hymns*, 30.

38. Ibid., 34, 36.

blood . . . Some allusion to baptism is probably to be found in the use of the word "water" . . . What seems plain here is that the blood and water were means of both justifying and sanctifying grace, as John Wesley claimed this sacrament to be—not only a symbol, but a means of grace.[39]

The emphasis on the instrumental section is to explain how the sacrament is a channel (i.e., instrument) for God's Grace which can only be received by faith alone. Thus, the channel/instrument (i.e., the communion elements) are not grace, but simply the vehicles that God uses to relay grace to the one who believes. Key phrases in the hymns of this section invite communicants to "draw near," "receive," "feed." Emphasizing that in the Eucharist God is pleased to provide spiritual nourishment, but the communicants must receive it in faith. This reemphasizes the Reformation understanding that one is justified by faith alone. Thus, like the atonement, the benefits of the sacrament are acquired by faith alone. The channels/instruments are not the means and the efficacy of the sacrament rests in God's self-giving grace alone.

Also key to this section is the emphasis on the presence of Christ made known in the breaking of bread. Thus, the Wesleys highlight the mystery in Eucharist on what cannot be understood by rational thought but only by faith and at God's own self-disclosing. It is the Holy Spirit that makes Christ present and known to those who partake of the sacrament. Here we can see the practical application of Wesley's sermon *The Duty of Constant Communion*, in that one partakes of the Eucharist simply out of faith and obedience, there is no rationality to it. The one who partakes must come with an expectation of meeting Christ in it, and meeting Christ in it by the grace of God who makes Godself known unto humans. In this way Stevick suggests that in the Eucharist, "the *doctrine* of the sacrament is validated (or else it is not validated) in the *experience* of the sacrament."[40] In this way, theology and worship coexist and communicants are spiritually formed in the experience of the Eucharist which ministers to both heart and head, personally and collectively within corporate worship. In the Eucharist, those gathered are the Body of Christ, engaged with their Lord and one another and walking on the path of holiness. Thus, Eucharist should be constant because it assists believers in "communing" with Christ and others. Feasting on Christ and

39. Ibid., 37.
40. Stevick, *The Altar's Fire*, 93.

contemplating his presence increases the believers faith in and love of God

Another key theme present in these hymns is the concept of the forgiveness of sins. When one comes to the communion table one is reminded that Christ's atoning work is sufficient for all past, present, and future sin in that the Eucharist continually "gives anew what the cross gave."[41] Utilizing the healing stories in the Bible as references for hymns in this section, Wesley correlates physical healing with internal transformation available within the sacrament as communicants experience the forgiveness of God and are bid to "go and sin no more" (John 8:11). In this way, forgiveness and holiness are seen to work in tandem with one another to assist communicants on the path of sanctification. Thus, "Forgiveness enables holiness; holiness completes what forgiveness begins. Unless forgiveness leads to a life of sanctity, it is as though Christ had died to no purpose."[42] Again, this interplay between forgiveness and holiness is the grace, albeit sanctifying grace, which enables humans to do that which they cannot do in their own strength but what is made available to them in the Eucharist by the power of the Holy Spirit and as they continue to grasp the presence of Christ in their midst. Holiness is not and cannot be achieved by one's own efforts, it is all the gift of God made present and available in the Eucharist to everyone who will partake of the elements in faith. Therefore, communicants are encouraged in these hymns to petition the Holy Spirit to enable them to perceive Christ and to assist them in drawing near to him and receive the gift of transformation and sanctification.

In all of these and in contrast to the "stillness" doctrine of the Moravians, communicants are invited to enter into the joy that his to be found in Christ's presence knowing that they have been forgiven and cleansed. The Eucharist prefigures and is a foretaste of the heavenly banquet in which there is joy unspeakable and full of glory. This is no somber occasion to remember solely the cross—this is the invitation to joyfully remember Christ who is not dead, but who is alive and who has promised to sustain his own until his return. It is he who has promised to sup with them and in the midst of doing is sanctifying them and transforming them into the persons that he already says they are. Like the Father in the prodigal Son biblical stories, their participation in the Eucharist is a time of great joy and celebration. And while recognizing the joyfulness in the

41. Ibid., 96.
42. Ibid., 101.

Eucharist, Wesley is particularly aware that sometimes the presence of God is not felt, that the God who makes Godself known in the breaking of bread and sharing of the cup is also above all knowing. It is in these times, the hymns encourages believers to participate in the Eucharist regardless of whether they have the "experience" or not. Rather, they are to come in faith, understanding that whether they experience the triune God or not, God is present and will make Godself known and relay all of the internal benefits of the sacrament to those who continue to come and receive the Eucharist in faith.[43]

Part III: "The Sacrament the Pledge of Heaven" (23 hymns)

The hymns of this section, which are also the last section under the concept of the Eucharist as "Christian sacrament," serve to remind communicants that the Eucharist does not only pertain to the past and present, but to future events as well. They serve as a reminder to communicants that the Eucharist is a foretaste of the heavenly feast that will occur when Christ returns at the end of history as we know it. In this section the Wesleys utilize Brevint's terminology of "earnest," "pledge," and "title" to explain how the Eucharist encourages all of that great day when we with the church triumphant shall feast at that great heavenly banquet of our Lord. Simply put, in these hymns the Eucharist looks back to Calvary seeing Christ's salvific work as completed, but waiting to be fulfilled. They are designed to help believers be encouraged and move toward perfection while they are in-between the now and the not yet.

In this way the terms "earnest," "pledge," and "title" are meant to convey different aspects of God's promised future for communicants made possible in the atoning work of Christ. Brevint defines "earnest" as "something given on account, in anticipation of the future; for instance, the graces of zeal, love and holiness, which remain our possession always and will not pass away."[44] "Pledge" signifies that which is something given in anticipation of a greater future thing that will be taken back when the future thing is received in full by the one holding the pledge. For example, the Eucharist serves as pledge because once Christ comes and we feast with him and the church triumphant, we will no longer need to partake of the earthly elements of bread and wine because our salvation will be fully realized and there will be no need for the early elements.

43. Ibid., 114–18.

44. Rattenbury, *Eucharistic Hymns*, 63.

Brevint uses the term "title" to refer to the legal document which suggests that through the Eucharist, communicants are gaining title deed to the mansions/dwelling places in heaven that Jesus promises to his disciples (John 14:1–3).[45] Although Wesley utilizes all three terms in the hymns of this section, he privileges the concept of the sacrament as a pledge and as earnest.[46] Furthermore, Wesley demonstrates a two-way movement between God and communicants in that the Eucharist brings communicants up before the throne of God and God sends down the benefits of love, grace, and peace.

Similar to the theological themes present in other sections, this section focuses on the theme that the Eucharist provides sustenance for communicants, and specifically for communicants as they are making their way in this world and moving toward their heavenly home. Not only does the Eucharist provide sustenance, it, like natural food, provides communicants with nutrients for becoming mature disciples. In this way, heaven is a continuation of what one begins as life in God on earth.[47] Other key themes in this section are that heaven is a place of abundance, especially in term of eating and feasting; eternal rest and joy unspeakable. Thus, in heaven, and at the heavenly banquet, life will be quite different from the struggles of this world. Because of the abundance, rest, peace, joy, and love of heaven, it will also be a place of unending praise. In the Eucharist, we are to experience some of this in that the celebrant reminds those communicating that they are celebrating not only with the body of Christ present in their midst but also with the church in heaven who are joined with them in unending praise for what Christ has done.

While the emphasis of this section is that heaven, with all of its benefits, is to be anticipated in the future, Stevick also asserts that the Wesleys have an emphasis on the fact that some of the benefits of heaven are to be enjoyed in the present, especially in the present experience of the Eucharist. Just as the Eucharist is to collapse past and present time and space in its memorial aspect, it also collapses present and future time and space such that the present communicants recognize that they "see the sights and hear the sounds of heaven itself."[48]

In addition to benefits, Christ's return also signifies the final judgment of all things. In this section, there are some hymns that refer to the

45. Ibid.

46. Stevick, *The Altar's Fire*, 130–31.

47. Ibid., 133.

48. Ibid., 138.

apocalypse. Stevick describes how the Wesleys include this apocalyptism in several hymns of this section when he writes,

> In a remarkable emphasis, when Wesley says that faith "ante-dates the final doom" (98:4,3) he means that at the sacrament the communicant is present beforehand at the final judgment. The sacrament makes present to faith the redemptive crisis of Jesus' death, but also the vindicating and judging crisis of Jesus' return. By this eschatological symbolism Wesley unites, at least implicitly, redemption and the eucharist with universal history and its consummation—the "dreadful joyful day" towards which time moves and which waiting believers have already encountered.[49]

In this section of the sacrament as the pledge of heaven, there is no cheap grace. There will be those who reject the saving grace of God in Jesus Christ. Communicants present themselves at the sacrament so that through it in the power of the Holy Spirit, they might be sustained, sanctified and ready to meet their Lord. In this way, the Wesleys are tying the concept of the Eucharist as the means of grace with the sacrament as the pledge of heaven. There is no fear for those who recognize that the Eucharist imparts the spiritual means for believers to grow in holiness. For those who are faithful, watching and waiting, engaging in the means of grace and growing in love of God and neighbor, Christ is waiting for them as well. In one of the most beautiful sections of one of the hymns, Wesley explains how the day of Christ's return will be both dreadful and joyful when he writes,

> 3. Then let us still in Hope rejoice,
> And listen for th' Archangel's Voice,
> Loud echoing to the Trump of God,
> Haste to the dreadful joyful Day,
> When Heaven and Earth shall flee away
> By all-devouring Flames destroy'd:
> While we from out the Burnings fly,
> With Eagles Wings mount up on high,
> Where Jesus is on Sion seen;
> 'Tis there He for our coming waits,
> And lo the Everlasting Gates,
> Lift up their Heads to take us in![50]

49. Ibid., 141.

50. John Wesley and Charles Wesley, *Hymns on the Lord's Supper*, Hymn 93, as quoted in Stevick, *Altar's Fire*, 145.

Part IV: "The Holy Eucharist as it Implies a Sacrifice" (12 hymns)

Up until now, the primary emphasis of the Wesley's hymnbook has been on understanding the Eucharist as a sacrament, and primarily as the chief means of grace. As sacrament the emphasis has been on what communicants see and receive from God by faith when they commune with God. As has been demonstrated thus far, although there is somewhat an emphasis on the sacrament as memorial, the primary emphasis has been on assisting communicants in understanding that the memorial is not so much of Calvary as it is of Christ. In the previous three parts, communicants are invited not only to remember the horrors of Calvary, but to remember the benefits of communing with Christ. Thus, they are urged to engage in constant communion by faith because God has promised to meet them there and will provide through the power of the Holy Spirit the ability to perceive and receive the benefits (i.e., the justifying and sanctifying grace) contained therein.

If the first three parts of the Wesleys' *Hymns on the Lord's Supper* were designed to provide catechesis and spiritual formation in communicants regarding the Eucharist as sacrament, Part IV: "The Holy Eucharist as It implies a Sacrifice" begins the second primary section following Brevint on comprehending the Eucharist as Sacrifice, specifically not only the sacrifice of Christ, but also the sacrifice of his body, the church, collectively and upon individual members. In a sense this last section which is comprised of Parts IV and V, are the "so what" of the first section (i.e., if God has provided both justifying and sanctifying grace through the Eucharist in addition to a slew of benefits, the least not of which concern our eternal future, then what is, required of those who partake of the sacrament?). These two parts help us understand that grace, while freely given, is never cheap and that those of us who have experienced the justifying and sanctifying grace of God in Jesus Christ ought to, not out of duty but gratitude, render unto God a precious offering—our very selves. As Stevick summarizes both the Wesleys and Brevint on this point, "The sacrament is more than something recalled; it is something done, and the doing has the character of sacrifice . . . Sacrifice, as the church's Godward action, follows sacrament. Life is offered on the basis of prior grace received. Christian sacrifice is response sacrifice."[51]

---

51. Stevick, *Altar's Fire*, 148.

There are only twelve hymns in this section of the hymnbook, with six of them directed toward God the Father. Although this section is the smallest within the Wesleys' *Hymns on the Lord's Supper*, some scholars believe it to be their greatest contribution to Eucharistic thought, in particular Hymn 116.[52] Furthermore, since while this section of hymns highlight the sacrament as sacrifice, the theme of sacrifice is also prevalent in other parts of the collection as well. Stevick records that the word sacrifice appears more than fifty times in all parts of the hymnbook and other referents to the word, such as "oblation," "offer/offering," "victim," and "atone/atonement" further demonstrate the theme of sacrifice throughout the whole work. In addition, the depiction of Christ as "Lamb" to correlate him to the Levitical lamb that is slain on the Day of Atonement for the sins of the people.

In addition, while the Wesleys emphasize the Eucharist as a sacrifice that believers make, their priority in this section is to underscore the unique, sole-sufficient, atoning sacrifice that Christ makes for believers. Therefore, all sacrifices of the people of God, whether those made by ancient Israel or by Christians only have their reality and are only comprehended through the salvific work of Christ. While affirming Christ's sacrifice of himself on the cross, the Wesleys are quick to point out that that Christ's sacrifice, while a concrete historical event, is also ongoing in that the Eucharist makes Calvary present to the communicant, while at the same time making the communicant present to Calvary. In this way, the Eucharist is more than memorial, in the sense of recalling what Christ has done; but in the Eucharist, the church joins Christ in making the sacrifice.[53]

To understand this concept that in the Eucharist, the church unites in Christ's sacrifice, both the Wesleys and Brevint rely heavily on the theology of the high priesthood of Christ as found in the New Testament book of Hebrews which proposes that Christ's redemptive work is ongoing in heaven. In Hebrews, Christ's work continues beyond his death at Calvary in that he is the high priest as outlined in the Levitical rites. But Christ is no ordinary high priest, at Calvary is also the sacrificial lamb. Because Christ is both priest and lamb-sacrifice, Christ opens through his wounds the throne room of God for believers. Furthermore, the Levitical high priest entered into the holy of holies only on the Day of Atonement

52. Ibid., 165.
53. Ibid., 150.

and then returned to the people to continue this process annual. Because Christ's sacrifice is the only sufficient sacrifice and only needs to be made once, Christ does not have to repeat the sacrifice. Rather, according to the Wesleys and Brevint, Christ as the eternal high priest "offers at the heavenly altar his sacrifice which belongs to an eternal order."[54] As such, Brevint writes,

> The Sacrifice of Jesus Christ being appointed by God the Father for a propitiation that should continue through all ages, to the worlds' end; and withal being everlasting by the privilege of its own order—which is *an unchangeable priesthood* (Heb 7.24), and by his worth who offered it—that is the blessed Son of God, and by the power of the Spirit by whom it was offered—which is the *Eternal Spirit* (Heb 9.14) . . . it must in all respects stand everlasting and eternal.[55]

The Wesleys explain how Christ continues as the eternal high priest by maintaining that while Calvary is a past, unrepeatable act, Christ's death, is continually presented or shown in heaven and as such makes intercession for sinners. In addition, while Christ is continually presenting his sacrifice to the Father in heaven, the church in union with Christ is presenting his sacrifice in the Eucharist to the Father and to the world. To explain this and building on their Anglican heritage, the Wesleys utilize 1 Corinthians 11:26: "For as often as ye eat this bread, and drink this cup, ye do shew the Lord's death till he come" to undergird their claim for the church's participation in Christ's priestly sacrifice as a royal priesthood. Therefore, "Christ, as the obedient Son on earth, addressed his work to God; and now as the eternal priest in heaven he still addresses his work to God. When the eucharistic church offers its life to God, it does so dependently and in union with the self-offering of the obedient divine Son depicted in the book of Hebrews."[56] In his work expounding the Wesleys' eucharistic theology, Stevick also cites that there are critics of the concept of Christ's ongoing priestly offering in heaven. Critics mostly cite that the Wesleys and Brevint, relying on Anglican theology of their day, are taking exegetical license with regard to the use of Hebrews to describe Christ's ongoing presenting of his sacrifice to the altar.

---

54. Ibid..

55. Brevint, *Christian Sacrament and Sacrifice*, II.8, as quoted in Stevick, *Altar's Fire*, 151.

56. Stevick, *Altar's Fire*, 152–53.

Christ's work is not only as high priest in heaven, his work also extends to that of mediator, the one who continually makes intercession for those on earth though his sacrificial deed. Wesley describes this work of mediation through Christ's priestly work to present the sacrifice of himself to the Father. As the Father looks upon Christ, who is united with his body, the church, God the Father sees the church through Christ. In that way, our sins are covered by Jesus' blood and our justification and righteousness are not ours, but rather are those of Christ which have accrued to us.

Again, this understanding of the priestly and mediating work of Christ makes our justification and sanctification an act of grace. Not only because Christ does for humans what we could not do for ourselves, but also because in the Eucharist and in the power of the Holy Spirit, the church is united with Christ's sacrifice and presentation of that sacrifice to God the Father. Just as the church cannot constitute itself, it also cannot redeem and/or sanctify itself. Christ, as priest-mediator, not only offers intercessory prayers on our behalf, but he also presents us before the great throne of God. As the church receives the Eucharist, it "presents itself in Christ and Christ in itself to God, (and) [it] offers what it has first received. The church has been gathered into the God-ward movement of the Incarnate Lord, crucified and living."[57]

To describe our union with and in Christ, Wesley describes Christians as being "wrapped in the smoke of his sacrifice and covered with his blood . . . so bound into him that when he presents himself before God, he presents his people with him."[58] In this way, Wesley argues that the church is "dead in Christ's death"; incorporated as individual, and mutually dependent members of Christ's very body; "raised and made holy by his sacrifice; named on his high priest's garment and on his hands and heart, and spoken for by the heavenly intercessor."[59] Believers are not only his in terms of possession, but by his justifying grace and in the power of the Holy Spirit, we are in him and discover that in him we move and have our being. Each time we commune with God we are given sustenance to grow more fully on earth into Christ already is (Eph 4).

An important theological theme in this section are what Stevick refers to as the "three centers of sacrifice": (1) Christ's sacrifice at Calvary,

---

57. Ibid., 157.

58. Ibid.

59. Ibid., 158.

(2) Christ's eternal sacrifice made in heaven, and (3) the Eucharist that the church makes continually on earth. For Wesley, these are not three different sacrifices; rather, they interpenetrate one another in perichoresis such that they form a vital unity.[60]

> Line a: As the hymns of Part I had said, the Eucharist makes communicants present at the cross, and the cross is, in a sense, present at the Church's table.
>
> Line b: At the same time, the heavenly altar is the eternal counterpart of the once-for-all act of the cross, and the cross is the historical act in which the eternal Son was wounded.
>
> Line c: The often-repeated Eucharistic act presents Christ to the Father, while the living Christ is the reality of the Church's sacrament of the Table.[61]

Neither the Wesleys nor Brevint thinks that the required sacrifice ends with what happens during the Eucharist. All are clear that what happens at the Eucharist has some claim on communicants' lives, individually and collectively, once they leave the church. We will now turn to their considerations which are outlined in Part V.

Part V: "Concerning the Sacrifice of Our Persons" (30 hymns)

Although this section of hymns in not the longest, it does correspond to two of the longest sections in both Brevint *The Christian Sacrament and Sacrifice* and John Wesley's abridged version of it: Section VII, "Concerning the Sacrifice of our Persons" and Section VIII, "Concerning the Oblation of Our Goods and Alms."[62] In these two sections of *The Christian Sacrament and Sacrifice* and in Part V of the Wesleys' *Hymns on the Lord's Supper* the key theme is to remind communicants that while Christ's sacrifice is the sole-sufficient atonement for our sins, those who are beneficiaries of it, must also respond by placing their entire beings— mind, body, soul, spirit and possessions at God's disposal for God to do with them and with their belongings whatever God chooses. Their response is not to be done out of duty or out of fear, rather their self-giving is in grateful response to the grace they have received. The offering of

60. Ibid., 168.

61. Ibid., 168–69.

62. Ibid., 200

themselves and all that they have and are serve as offerings of praise and thanksgiving for what God has done for them and is doing through them in Jesus Christ in the power of the Holy Spirit. Brevint describes this self-giving of Christians when he writes, "We, beneath, in the Church, present to God his [Christ's] body and blood in a *memorial*; that under the shadow of his cross, and image of his Sacrifice [that is, in the sacrament], we may present ourselves before him in very deed and reality."[63]

Thus, this section continues the concept of sacrifice by explaining that Christians are not only joined mystically to Christ in the Eucharist in the past (i.e., *anamnesis*) and in heaven, they are joined to him in the present. They are to be his body continually dedicating themselves to the work which he began when he walked among humans. Both the Wesleys and Brevint explain that the sacrifice of our persons is united with Christ's sole-sufficient sacrifice, being both supplemental and dependent upon it. To assist communicants and us, Wesley follows Brevint in utilizing the Jewish daily sacrifice of both the lamb and the meal and drink offering. Christ, as the Lamb of God which takes away the sin of the world, is nevertheless joined by the offering of the meal (fine flour mingled with oil) and drink (wine) (see Exod 29:38–42 and Num 28:3–10).

As Rattenbury notes, the hymns of this section emphasize consecration—the dedicated offering of one's entire self to God for God's purposes. In this way, Wesley says that Christians are not only to enter into Christ's death and resurrection, they are to allow Christ to live in them in the power of the Holy Spirit which means they will identify with him and suffer with him because they follow him into the way that leads to life. Thus, Christians who allow Christ to live in them by sacrificing themselves (i.e., giving themselves over to the will of God) will suffer as Christ suffered. They key is that they will remember that at no point is Christ not with them. He is as He as promised to be with them until the end of the age. This union, or communion with God is not the work of the people, but rather it is the work of the Holy Spirit within them, conforming them to Christ-likeness and maturing them in holiness (i.e., love of God and neighbor). Wesley describes this process well when he writes in Hymn 139,

> 1. God of all redeeming grace,
> By thy pardoning love compell'd,
> Up to Thee our souls we raise,
> Up to Thee our bodies yield.

63. Brevint, *The Christian Sacrament and Sacrifice*, 183.

2. Thou our sacrifice receive,
Acceptable through Thy Son;
While to Thee alone we live,
While we die to Thee alone.

3. Just it is, and good, and right,
That we should be wholly thine;
In thy only will delight,
In thy blessed service join.

4. O that every thought and word,
Might proclaim how good thou art;
Holiness unto the Lord
Still be written on our heart.[64]

Key to this section of hymns and to the Wesleys' thought is that of mutuality. Communicants can only give what they have received. As God gives Godself to communicants in the Sacrament, they receive him and in receiving him they offer, with Christ, themselves back to God. This continually giving and receiving takes place within the sacrament and is lived out amongst believers as they allow Christ's life to be lived through them in the power of the Holy Spirit beyond the ritual of the Eucharist offered in the community of faith. They follow Christ into the world, and by placing themselves at God's disposal renouncing sin and any claim to worldly possessions and to self-will, and willingly offer to others what they have received from God. They do so knowing that like Christ, any suffering they encounter in doing the Father's will, will bring joy and fulfillment in that if they share in Christ's sufferings, they will share in his glory (Rom 8:17–18).

Part VI: "After the Sacrament" (9 hymns)

This section, the smallest of all, is meant to serve as devotional material for those after the sacrament. This section follows the service of Holy Communion from the 1662 *Book of Common Prayer* in which, after the Eucharist has been received, communicants offer prayers of thanksgiving or self-dedication and then end with *Gloria in Excelsis*.[65] The focus of these hymns are praise, joy, thanksgiving for what Christ has done for and in communicants and reminds them of many of the key themes

---

64. John Wesley and Charles Wesley, *Hymns on the Lord's Supper*, Hymn 139.
65. Stevick, *The Altar's Fire*, 214.

in the previous sections. These hymns also remind communicants that not only are they in union with Christ in terms of his continual offering before God the Father in heaven, and in union with Christ on earth; but that in their praises they unite with angels and archangels, with fellow communicants and with the saints in heaven, to give glory to God what has been accomplished by God's Grace through Christ's sacrifice. It also reminds them to be aware of decay and decline with regard to the church's devotion so that the church can be renewed once through the sacrament. Finally, this section reminds communicants of Christ's immanent return and that the faithful ones will join in his glory and joy.

Relating Modern Wesleyan Eucharistic Practice and Theology to Wesley's Work: *This Holy Mystery* and *The Great Thanksgiving*

When we look at the two foundational documents that have been adopted by the United Methodist Church in their practice of the Eucharist, *This Holy Mystery: A United Methodist Understanding of Holy Communion* and the order of worship for celebrating the Eucharist, *The Great Thanksgiving*, we can see the rich legacy of Wesley's sermon "The Duty of Constant Communion" and of the themes present in the *Hymns on the Lord's Supper*. Thus, it is important that we highlight key portions of these texts as we analyze the theology and practice of the sacraments in current context, both from an institutionalized/doctrinal standpoint and from how it is practiced in actuality within United Methodist Churches. It is also important that we do this in light of the fact that we must remember that while United Methodism is a strain of Methodism, in addition to the Methodism as practiced by John and Charles Wesley and their English followers in the midst of the eighteenth century, it is also Methodism that has been influenced by the American context, specifically by nineteenth-century revivalism, especially the influence of Baptist theology and practice on American Methodism; liberalism; and American rugged individualism. Furthermore, we must also keep in mind that when the Wesleys began they did not have in mind an institutionalized church; but rather saw themselves as a renewal movement within the context of the Church of England. Accordingly, the Wesleys understood Methodism as a "reforming movement that called established institutions and their hierarchies to scriptural account."[66]

To determine the institutionalized/doctrinal United Methodist theology and practice of the Eucharist, we will review each of these and highlight the legacy of primary Wesleyan sources for Eucharistic theology and practice, namely the sermon "The Duty of Constant Communion" and the *Hymns on the Lord's Supper*. Next, I will suggest how and why the institutional theology and practice of the Eucharist may be recreating the same problems that it sought to correct in that institutionally the denomination has not considered how the influence of church growth strategies, especially those in the last fourteen years, in light of declining and aging membership have affected what is actually taught and practiced in local congregations. In addition, I believe we must also consider the influence of American culture in the technology age in terms of how members are catechized and discipled. We will now turn our attention to these matters.

This Holy Mystery and The Great Thanksgiving

In response to a survey conducted by the General Board of Discipleship prior to the 2000 General Conference, there was a general consensus of the importance of Holy Communion in the lives of individuals and for the church overall. Also, the survey reported an equally strong consensus that there was something missing in terms of United Methodist Eucharistic theology and practice. According to researchers, "United Methodist recognize[d] that grace and spiritual power are available to them in the sacrament, but too often they do not feel enabled to receive these gifts and apply them in their lives. Many laypeople complain of sloppy practice, questionable theology, and lack of teaching and guidance."[67]

To remedy this, and building on the success of similar work done on United Methodist theology and practice of baptism which culminated in the resource *By Water and The Spirit: A United Methodist Understanding of Baptism*, a study committee comprised of bishops, scholars, pastors, deacons, church leaders, and laypersons was commissioned at the 2000 General Conference to develop a comprehensive document on Holy Communion/Eucharist. In addition to the study committee, there were also listening sessions held in each of the five jurisdictions, as well as in

---

66. Martin, "Toward a Wesleyan Sacramental Ecclesiology," 22.

67. Felton, *This Holy Mystery*, 7.

the central conferences, to provide input to the theology and practice. *This Holy Mystery* was approved by the 2004 General Conference with a concomitant call for widespread dissemination of the document and implementation of the practice as determined by the denomination. In addition, seminaries, theological schools and boards of ordained ministry ensured that new clergy were well acquainted with both *By Water and The Spirit* and *This Holy Mystery* by including these books as required reading in their syllabi and in the responses to doctrinal questions for those pursing commissioning and ordination. Furthermore, the documents on sacramental practice were written such that clergy and lay leaders could utilize them for small group study.

A quick overview of *The Holy Mystery* reveals that it is a comprehensive and thoughtful document that provides denominational and local church leaders, both clergy and laity, with theology, principle, and practice information for each step of the liturgy for the Eucharist, also known as the Great Thanksgiving. In addition to providing these important and useful steps with concomitant background material, Dr. Felton provides a helpful introductory section which outlines the reasons behind the creation of the document and provides a very Wesleyan, albeit United Methodist understanding of the sacrament, including the various names for Eucharist and what each implies, as well as a section that defines the term "sacrament." In this section, which describes the "why" of what we believe and do concerning the Eucharist, Felton includes a helpful section on how the theology and practice of the Eucharist evolved from Early Methodism to present day American Methodism, including the contributions made to the United Methodist practice due to the 1968 merger between the Methodist Episcopal Church and the Evangelical United Brethren. With this helpful background, Felton then does a brief section on the theology of the sacraments and the specific meaning of Holy Communion/Eucharist in the context of both sacrament and sacrifice as outline by the Wesleys in the both the abridged version of Brevint's *The Christian Sacrament and Sacrifice* and their *Hymns on the Lord's Supper*. Key to this first section of the first part of the document is to understand that Felton is "building a case" as to why United Methodist need to move toward a deeper sacramental spirituality—because of the spiritual benefits we receive in it which go much beyond divine love and grace and "involve forgiveness, nourishment, healing, transformation, ministry, mission and eternal life."[68]

The second part of this first section then moves onto our union with Christ and how Christ is present at the table in ways we do not and cannot fathom with our rational minds, but rather have to believe by faith. At the end of the section that speaks of the mystery of the presence of Christ at the communion table, Felton, now that she has clearly laid the theological foundation for the Eucharist, then begins to unpack what does it mean that this is the "Lord's Supper," by discussing the invitation to the Lord's table, specifically the concepts of open communion and unworthiness. From here, she then goes through the liturgy step by step, informing each step with principle, background and practice. Not only does Felton explain the order that the liturgy follows in this fashion, she also provides key theological and doctrinal information as to who may preside at communion, what is the role of the gathered community present at the sacrament and how the table is set and what may be as communion elements. Finally, Felton discusses how the communion table is extended into the world in terms of evangelism and mission.

In addition to the theology, principle, background and practice of the Eucharist, Felton provides those who teach and those we may study *This Holy Mystery* with an outline for small group questions, extended personal study that is accessible for laity, clergy, denominational leaders and seminary professors. The beginning of the book includes helpful hints for those who will lead these sections, as well as a list of supporting documents, including standard denominational texts such as the *United Methodist Church's (UMC) Book of Worship* and *Book of Resolutions*, as well as helpful articles and essays. In addition, the sidebars for each chapter, provide material for deeper reflection and life application with a series of questions for group response. At the end of the book, she includes both Wesley's sermon on *The Duty of Constant Communion* and the order of A Service of Word and Table I and V (for homebound persons). Simply put, a quick review of *This Holy Mystery: A United Methodist Understanding of Holy Communion* reveals that it is a comprehensive theological and practical resource that is faithful to our theological, doctrinal and historical heritage. This same assessment can be offered for the *Service of Word and Table I and V* that are included within *This Holy Mystery* and in both the UMC *Book of Worship* and *Hymnal*.

68. Ibid., 19.

With such comprehensive resources at our disposal written and accessible for every level of the United Methodist denomination (i.e., clergy, laity, denominational leaders and seminary professors), we must ask ourselves, in our investigation of the practice of the sacraments what may at work to hinder the theology and practice of them that hinders communicants from experiencing the fullness of what is promised in the sacraments in spite of all of our good intentions. In the next section, I offer the following observations to point to what I suggest may be hindering our practice of the sacraments, in particularly the Eucharist, in the United Methodist denomination.

Current Implementation of the Theology and Practice of the Eucharist in *This Holy Mystery* and the Service of Word and Table/Great Thanksgiving

To qualify my observations, first let me disclose that at the time *This Holy Mystery* was being implemented, I was in my second year of seminary, a second-career licensed local pastor, appointed to my first church, and also working through the candidacy process for ordination as an elder. Thus, in terms of understanding the document I did so from the perspective of a seminarian and the strange mix of being somewhere in-between clergy and laity, even though I was a licensed local pastor. Second, when I assumed these responsibilities I had only been a member of the United Methodist church since I began seminary at a United Methodist related school. Prior to this, I had been unchurched until I was thirteen and had spent the majority of my church life with the African Methodist Episcopal Zion (A.M.E.Z.) Church; an Assemblies of God church modeled after Willow Creek Community Church, a megachurch located in the suburbs of Chicago; and several years with church plants that were growing to be large membership churches whose theology was mostly based on the Church of God in Christ denomination. In fact, prior to attending seminary, much of my Christian formation happened via Christian television and megachurch conferences. Realizing this was not enough, I eventually enrolled in a Bible college of one of these churches where I was trained by a person who had a doctorate from an accredited Association of Theological Schools and learned about such things as exegesis, systematic theology, etc. It was from this organization that I received a license to preach that, in addition to having developed a ministry within a business setting ad having serving in contextual ministry placements within two United Methodist denominations, that allowed me to enter into the candidacy process and to serve a church as a local licensed pastor.

I include all of this background primarily for third reasons. First, given the current status of the United Methodist denomination, I do not believe my story to be that unique in terms of how I came to be the persons primarily responsible for teaching the theology and practice of the liturgy. Second, I believe that as an "outsider" who eventually became an "insider," with regard to United Methodist theology, doctrine and polity I have a unique perspective in understanding what may actually be "happening on the ground" that affects our practice. Third, as a part of my doctoral studies, I conducted two congregational ethnographic studies with laypersons to ask them what their Christian formation process was and to see if what we thought we were communicating in the liturgy, theology, Bible and doctrinal studies was actually what people believed or was there something else shaping how they thought theologically and practiced the sacrament.[69] I offer the following as suggestions as to what happened to all of the good information provided by both study committees in *This Holy Mystery* and its counterpart for baptism, *By Water and The Spirit*.

Information, Incomplete Transformation

Although many denominational bodies, including seminaries, boards of ordained ministry and local congregations affirmed the work of *This Holy Mystery* and *By The Water and the Spirit* by including it in course curriculum, making it part of the doctrinal questions for commissioning and ordination, promoted it at annual conferences and offered as small group studies within local congregations, much of the theology and practice at many local churches did not change. While it is true that many churches increased the frequency of Holy Communion and/or began to make it

---

69. After conducting several interviews with my congregation, I embarked on a program of preaching on the Eucharist every time we offered it, as well as on baptism. I also reinstituted the *Reaffirmation of Baptism* services to help persons remember and reaffirm their commitments to Christ made at their baptism and reaffirmed at every communion feast. This, in addition to getting back to the basics of the Christian faith (i.e., "sin," "salvation," "evangelism," "mission") made the greatest contribution to the spiritual growth of the laity within my church, as well as those preparing for licensing and ordination, as well as those serving as Deaconesses and Home Missioners.

available, the sad truth is that the richness of the document in terms of theology, principal and practice did not totally transform the practice within congregations. This occurred for several reasons.

First, many congregations, while offering *This Holy Mystery* as a small group study or a study amongst church, primarily clergy, staff, did little to catechize the entire congregation. In particular, at both annual conference and local church levels, as well within seminary worship services, the desire to keep the worship services to a minimum, usually no more than one hour and fifteen minutes in length and the primacy of music and the preached word, allowed worship designers and presiders to truncate the service of the Eucharist. In many instances, this truncating of the service had a twofold effect. First, usually omitted in the service was the invitation, confession/pardon, passing of the peace and the offering of ourselves and our gifts to God. The issue with the omission of these critical pieces of worship mean that Wesley's primary motif of Christ's atoning sacrifice, our need for forgiveness and the united of our total being—mind, soul, body, spirit and possessions is omitted. The effect of this is that the *anamnesis* of the service can be viewed as pure memorialism with Christ doing the all the work and communicants receiving all the benefits without any concomitant requirement of sacrifice. Second, and as, if not more critical, was the bifurcation of the "word" and "table." Rather than see the entirety of the liturgy for worship as one congruent whole (i.e., the emphasis on the Service of Word *and* Table), many worship services treated the entirety of the service as leading up to the preached word, at best; or at worst a collective of disjointed aspects of worship having nothing to do with each other, with the Eucharist, again starting with the service of The Great Thanksgiving (i.e., "The Lord Be With You"). Even in those instances when there was either an altar call (i.e., a call to become a follower of Jesus Christ or to join the church), or an invitation to Christian discipleship which asked persons to considered how the preached word challenged them to grow in Christian maturity, little was done to relate the preached word, altar call/invitation to Christian discipleship, to the Eucharist. Again, having the effect of reducing the sacrament to mere memorialism.

In addition, rather than utilizing the rich legacy of hymns written for the Lord's Supper that emphasized various aspects of the Eucharist, many times in worship services at all levels of the denomination the emphasis was on either songs that highlighted the memorialist aspects of worship (i.e., "I knowed It Was the Blood") or those that without

catechesis could be interpreted that we together are not one body in service to the Lord together, but rather a collective of individuals each living
out their Christian faith in a similar fashion to social clubs or volunteer
organizations not as one body mutually interdependent and accountable
to one another (i.e., "One Bread, One Body"). This idea of a collective
versus a communion can also be seen what were utilized for communion
elements and how they were dispensed. Although many congregations
and denominational worship services utilized loafs of bread, singular
cups, and the method of intinction, many did not. There were quite a few
who used individual wafers and cups, either out continuing practice or
from the theological heritage of the laity or clergy. Many congregations
began to implement single-serve cup/wafer combinations so as to move
the service along faster. Furthermore, in some cases, to honor the request
by denominational leaders to offer the Eucharist more frequently and to
balance the need to keep services at a minimum, some churches, simply
placed consecrated elements in a room and told parishioners that they
were welcome to partake of the elements "as they wished" as they were
leaving service.

If it is true that liturgy, not in words or written down, actually
shapes belief (i.e., theology) and consequently behavior (i.e., ethics), we
must ask ourselves how has the mal-practiced liturgy, in the midst of the
wonderful resources provided within This Holy Mystery and the orders
of worship in the "Service of Word and Table" and "The Great Thanksgiving" convey to communicants who may or may not have read This Holy
Mystery? More importantly, we must ask if the creation of This Holy Mystery almost ten years ago really solved the problem that it so eloquently
sought to address as contained in its introductory: "United Methodists
recognize that grace and spiritual power are available to them in the sacrament, but too often they do not feel enabled to receive these gifts and
apply them in their lives. Many laypeople complain of sloppy practice,
questionable theology, and lack of teaching and guidance."[70]

I submit that This Holy Mystery for the most part has provided
information in that scores of denominational leaders can reiterate the
theology and polity with regard to the practice of the Eucharist, but it has
not led to the transformation of individual, congregational and denominational life intended because of how the Eucharist has been practiced in
actuality. Further, given the rapidity of decline within our churches and

70. Felton, This Holy Mystery, 7.

the lack of catechesis on the foundational elements of the Christian faith are now such that it is quite possible, given the evidence that I submitted above that there are many laity in our churches who even recognize that the practice is sloppy, the theology questionable or even know and/or desire more teaching and guidance with regard to the sacrament. Simply put, for those who do not know, tradition often trumps accuracy.

As our study of the legacy of both John and Charles Wesley describes the Wesleys utilized the Sunday services, in particular the preached word and the hymns to communicate and to catechize communicants with regard to the meaning of the Eucharist as both Sacrament and Sacrifice. Jam-packed in the 166 *Hymns of the Lord's Supper*, which included an abbreviated version of Brevint's *The Christian Sacrament and Sacrifice* were seeds of transformation set to memorable hymns which brought together theology and worship to aid in the spiritual formation of communicants. Not only does Wesley provide both the hymnbook and his sermon on the duty of constant communion, he modifies the Sunday service to address the concerns of those who are disturbed by its current length. Again, he and Charles address the subject of length by including the hymns which both Rattenbury and Stevick remark add an element of joy to the Eucharist. I submit part of the reason why we may practice the Eucharist so haphazardly is that our bifurcation of word and sacrament as I have described above has hindered such formation and transformation in many United Methodist congregations.

United Methodist Titles/Non-United Methodist Practices

As I mentioned in my lengthy introduction of this section, I was licensed as a local pastor and presided at many communion tables before I was ever trained in the theology and practice for the Eucharist as adopted by the denomination. Thus, if I am honest I conducted not only the Eucharist, but also baptismal services from how I had been spiritual formed and formally catechized in other denominations and by watching Christian television. What I found in my formal and informal interviews with clergy, local pastors and laity is that usually the basic theology functioning even though the practice might have changed to reflect the denomination's new orders of worship or disseminated information was that which they had brought with them either from their previous denomination or what they learned from so-called church leaders/innovators either via Christian television or non-United Methodist related seminars and conferences on church effectiveness. Whereas many of those preparing for ordination had to immerse themselves in understanding the theology and practice of the Eucharist in accordance with *This Holy Mystery*, there were many current and successful pastors who offered communion in accord with previous denominational affiliation. This was especially true of licensed local pastors and some clergy.[71] Furthermore, for those congregations in which the Eucharist had always been practiced more frequently, small group studies on *This Holy Mystery* were not offered and if offered, rarely attended because the people believed they knew all there was to know about the Eucharist.

At issue here is that while the "tent" of United Methodist theology and practice may be broad, there are boundaries—that is, denominational doctrine and polity, which as church leaders we vow to uphold. In preparing for ordination, those who serve at word and table (i.e., the Eucharist) are continually called to be able to articulate their theology and practice as they move thorough the ordination process. Furthermore, candidates for ordination are often required to submit the practical aspects of their ministries (i.e., Bible studies, sermons, bulletins and videos of entire worship services) to see if their theologies and practices are in harmony. As far as I know, no such formality exists for licensed local pastors. In addition, in many conferences with huge numbers of small congregations, as well as the high demands of conference work, it is hard for bishops, conference staff to determine whether or not licensed local pastors and clergy simply "went through the motions," by providing "right answers" for judicators or are they actually practicing from a Wesleyan, albeit, United Methodist, theological perspective as their ministries progress.

If we cannot trust that the official theology and practice of the sacraments are not being practiced at the local level, either by ordained or licensed clergy, then how can we expect the theology and practice of the Eucharist to transform and form persons as Christians that are Wesleyan, and specifically, United Methodist in their orientation? In both

71. A colleague of mine in being interviewed by her district Board of Ordained Ministry was critiqued for providing answers to sacramental questions as per *This Holy Mystery* and *By Water and the Spirit* by a seasoned and successful clergy member who, though ordained as a United Methodist elder, still holds fast to Baptist theology, doctrine, and polity. It took the Board Chair, another seasoned and successful clergyperson, to inform the first pastor that indeed my colleague had responded in line with the official theology, doctrine, and practice as outlined in these denominational resources.

his sermon *The Duty of Constant Communion* and in the Hymns on the Lord's Supper, with the abridged version of Brevint's *Christian Sacrament and Sacrifice,* John Wesley is defining for clergy and laity the difference between the Methodist theology and practice of the Eucharist and other popular theologies and practices of the day. Especially in "The Duty of Constant Community," Wesley is offering both critique and apologetics of the other practices by refuting such doctrines as not communing regularly, stillness and who is worthy to partake of the communion elements.[72]

Whereas often our colleagues who transfer from other denominations are welcome additions to our United Methodist family, the sad truth is that while we require them to take courses in United Methodist history, doctrine and polity, there currently is no mechanism to ensure what theology is practiced and convey in worship. Furthermore, with recent studies highlighting the economic impact of the low salaries associated with licensed local pastors, especially part-time local pastors, in spite of congregational desire and pressure for full time service, many of these dedicated, hardworking and effective church leaders simply do not have the time or inclination to study or lead Bible studies with regard to either *This Holy Mystery* or *By Water and the Spirit.* Many of them are simply too busy with other part-time or full-time work to supplement minimal pastor salaries, and/or engaged in conference and denominational training for church growth strategies which include little to no emphasis on the sacraments.[73]

72. Interestingly when I speak with my clergy colleagues who have been formed by *This Holy Mystery* and *By Water and the Spirit,* I often find that we share the common experience of having to justify our theology and practice of the sacraments in light of what previous pastors have or haven't done and in light of current "teaching" on the sacraments by popular televangelists. In fact, as I have been trying to prepare persons for the ministry process, I have noted that several candidates as they begin the process have either books and/or CDs of messages (i.e., televangelist Paula White's *The Meal That Heals,* which promises health and wealth if one partakes of the sacrament daily, even if alone). In addition, I know of several licensed local pastors who were ordained in other denominations who have not read *This Holy Mystery* or who are unfamiliar with our worship practices, who simply utilize the order of worship for The Great Thanksgiving IV, as the entire service. The primary issue with this, aside from the points I make with regard to problems of bifurcating the service of word and table, and omitting the invitation, confession/pardon, passing of the peace and offering, is that this order of worship is designed for persons to tailor the order of worship for specific days and to end with these words of blessings. My colleague simply utilizes this with no explanation at all (i.e., even the *anamnesis*—the remembering how and why Jesus instituted the sacrament is removed from the practice of it.).

73. For more on this, see Choi and Blue, "The Clergy Women's Retention Study II, Summary, 2013" and LaBoy, "Women by the Numbers."

The Effects of the Seeker-Service Church Growth Strategies Promulgated by Megachurches in the Midst of Declining Denominational Membership

Coming of age in the late 1980s and early 1990s, several prominent churches began to share with the American church and with the world the reason for their astronomical growth—they began to offer what they named "seeker services" in addition to traditional worship services in order to "turn irreligious people into fully devoted followers of Jesus Christ."[74] Targeted to "unchurched Harry and Mary," these services were designed to attract not only unchurched, but dechurched, and mostly post-moderns who were disenfranchised with the traditional Christian church service. Thus, the "seeker service" model was seen primarily as an evangelism tool to assist churches in reaching new people groups.

In addition to the "seeker service," which typically included more contemporary music, the removal of traditional "Christian" items (i.e., crosses, altars, pulpits, sacraments), and a slew of services designed to help seekers get comfortable with the church before making a commitment. For those wanting to grow in their relationship to Christ, these churches offered small groups based on differing interests, as well as a worship service aimed at those who were interested in becoming and/or growing as Christians. This service was usually offered on a different night and usually was aimed at getting congregants to agreed to a higher level of participation in the life of the church.

To clarify and to simply our definition for "seeker service," we will utilize the one developed by Lester Ruth. According to Ruth, the definition of seeker service can be devised by understanding exactly what these churches meant in defining the terms "seeker" and "service." Extracting from the Willow Creek materials, inarguably the most influential church of the "seeker service" movement, Ruth writes:

> As used by seeker service practitioners "seeker" designates those adults searching to make Christianity part of their lives. These adults include both those who had no previous formal relationship to a church and those who are in some lapsed state. . .Seekers are "people who are in the process of making a decision for Christ or evaluating Christianity . . .

---

74. Willow Creek Community Church, *What Willow Believes.*

... Perhaps it is safest to give the word "service" the most generic meaning possible: a communal meeting sponsored by a church with some context of speaking about God.

Combined with the previous definition of "seeker," the definition of "seeker service" . . . [is] a church-sponsored meeting characterized by its high level adaptation to the targeted seeker's culture, desired, perceived needs, within some context of speaking about God.[75]

In addition to adapting the traditional worship service to meet the "felt needs" of seekers, these innovators also dramatically changed the architecture of their churches. Retooling strategies of evangelistic churches from the 1870s and 1880s which emphasized both an amphitheater plan for the worship space and technological innovations, these churches brought a wide variety of dramatic and multi-media tools to worship environments. Not only were worship spaces revamped so that "seekers" might be comfortable in these spaces, but most of the floor plans of the entire buildings were designed almost as mini-malls. While some of the key pastors of the "seeker service" movement contend that this was done because previous church architecture made it hard for persons to see or hear what was going on, some critics argue that "'the church home is no longer relevant, but the mall provides the feeling of worry-free comfort for which the mega-church strives.' Most mega-church designs resemble shopping malls since these are locations in which particularly American Christians feel comfortable and familiar. While an effective strategy for attracting and accommodating large crowds, such rationale is anthropologically rather than theologically based."[76]

At the time so influential were these innovations that other churches, who did not have the capacity or who did not wish to separate the "seeker service" from the worship service, began to create "seeker sensitive" services. In these services, traditional worship services were altered with seekers in mind. Many others, in order to appeal to a wide range of persons, offered a spectrum of services which "have varying degrees of adaptation to the targeted seekers and varying degrees of reliance on previous liturgical tradition."[77]

75. Ruth, "Lex Agendi, Lex Orandi," 386–87.

76. Warner, "Mega-Churches," 26.

77. Ruth, "Lex Agendi, Lex Orandi," 391.

A primary factor in the creation of these services was the "Church Growth" model developed by Donald McGavran and C. Peter Wagner which sought to define the social factors which determined numerical success or failure in evangelism. McGavaran's model has been critiqued because of his "homogenous unit principle" in which he argued that "People like to become Christian without crossing any racial, linguistic, or class barriers," for systematizing racial segregation and privilege within the ethos of those churches following the church growth methodology.[78] Although highly pragmatic, McGavran's model did have a theological foundation, an understanding that the central work of church mission was that "it was God's will that lost men and women be found, reconciled to himself, and brought into responsible *membership* in Christian churches."[79]

The effect of the "seeker service" or "seeker sensitive" model is still affecting the Protestant Christian church landscape today. In 2008, John Vaughn reported that a mega-church, one that is more likely than not to follow either the seeker service, or seeker sensitive worship model, is emerging, on average, every one to three days. Further in their 2007 study of mega-churches, Thumma and Travis contend that "mega-churches, their practices and their leaders are the most influential contemporary dynamic in American religion. They have superseded formerly key influences such as denominations, seminaries, and religious presses and publishing."[80]

With all of the critique of the churches that adopted these modes, there are many gifts these churches bring to the contemporary landscape. As Warner asserts, "At their best, mega-churches demonstrate meaningful worship, comprehensive Bible study, and impactful outreach ministries." But there are challenges which include a preoccupation with numbers and size and a tendency towards nominal Christianity for those who attend such services.[81]

---

78. Rah, *Next Evangelicalism*, 83–84. In this book, Rah reports that Willow Creek founding pastor, and inarguably the most influential in the "seeker service" movement, Bill Hybels as confessing that during the early years of the church-growth movement, they were advised to not spend any time dealing with "race issues" but to focus solely on evangelism. This policy as Rah asserts, and as Hybel admitted, systematized racial segregation and privilege within the ethos of the church.

79. Wagner, Preface to *Understanding Church Growth*, ix.

80. Thumma and Travis, *Megachurch Myths*, 4.

81. Warner, "Mega Churches," 24.

Arguing that these churches will continue to grow rapidly, scholars also offer that the reason for their growth is that these church continue to fit in with American culture, especially in terms of its individualistic and consumeristic modes. Further, since American society is more casual, detached and mobile, these researchers maintain that persons do not mind driving distances to a mega-churches that offer them the type of worship services, and/or child services, they desire.[82] In addition, as the entertainment industry booms, the style of these services also are appealing. Noted theologian and pastor Elmer Towns summarized the views of "experts" of this movement regarding what the 1990s "churchgoing consumer" is looking for when he wrote,

> American's Protestants choose churches on the basis of what affirms us, entertains us, satisfies us or makes us feel good about God and ourselves. If we recognize church worshippers as consumers, we will recognize church programs as menus, and types of worship as the main entrees in the restaurant . . . consumers go where the menus fit their taste . . . the church menus Americans seek are not filled with doctrinal options but with a variety of worship options. Americans go where they feel comfortable with the style of worship that best reflects their inclinations and temperament.[83]

In terms of our discussion with regard to the implications for how persons understand the theological importance of both the sacraments, in particular, the Eucharist and the importance of their practice in terms of Christian discipleship and spiritual growth the effects of this model has had significant effects. First, given this seeker model's emphasis on pragmaticism, several scholars and pastors argue that business pragmaticism has become the "defining ecclesiological concept," which in turn treats the attenders as liturgical consumers whose desires drive worship design. Thus, in many services little is expected of those who attend. For the regular members, except for those who are "delivering" services (i.e., worship/praise bands, ushers, greeters, etc.), there is no little to no demonstration of the services or offering that they present in that much of this is done "off-line" so as to not offend the persons that are seekers.[84]

82. Drane, *McDonaldization of the Church*, Kindle locations 133–37.

83. Towns, *Inside Look at Ten of Today's Most Innovative Churches*, as quoted in Morgenthaler, *Worship Evangelism*, 19.

84. John Lester Ruth, Sally Morgenthaler, and John Drane all reference this consumeristic attitude within these services.

Furthermore, the sermons are utilitarian in that they function primarily to demonstrate some key moral premise or serve as a primary way to help participants become more self-actualized human beings.

All of this has devastating consequences for an theological understanding and practice of the sacraments as handed down through early church history, as well as for how it is practiced in a Wesley, albeit United Methodist, fashion. Furthermore, because of the lackadaisical manner by which the sacraments are offered (at the desire of the people), the people participate in the Eucharist, not because Christ has commanded it, but because they desire to do so either out of a sense of peer pressure (i.e., everyone else is, so they might as well) or because they think it is important to do this to demonstrate their support for what Christ has done, which Kyle Idleman likens to the behavior of being a fan and not a disciple.[85] More importantly, Wesley's understanding of the potential of the Eucharist/Holy Communion to be a converting ordinance is lost because for it to be a converting ordinance, the presider would actually have to talk about sin and Christ's atoning death, and how we ought to offer ourselves as a living sacrifice in gratitude for what Christ has done, which would seem highly problematic in a consumeristic environment. In this way, rather than serving as instrument of justifying and sanctifying grace, the Eucharist, further serves to make nominal Christians, whom Wesley understood as primary focus of his evangelistic work.

The second consequence of the seeker model on church services is that it creates a new type of liturgy that privileges pragmatism and allows for little mystery within the worship service. Lester Ruth describes this as exchanging the age-old adage for worship *lex orandi, lex credenda*—the order of prayer/worship is the order of believing—with *lex agenda, lex orandi*—the order of the agenda is the order of prayer/worship. In this scenario, again those who are not mature in the Christian faith are those who are setting the agenda, the worship and arguably the ethics/service of the majority of those gathered. In this way, the entire Christian definition, theology and practice of liturgy is undermined. Ruth explains this truncation of the liturgical life of the church when he writes,

> Typical definitions of "liturgy" emphasize two elements: the activity of Christ on behalf of others, particularly as seen in priestly terms, and the Church's participation in this activity. . .the

85. For more on the idea of creating "fans" of Jesus rather than disciples, see Idleman, *Not a Fan*.

liturgy "is considered as an exercise of the priestly office of Jesus Christ" in which "the whole public worship is performed by the Mystical Body of Jesus Christ, that is by the Head and his members." Such a definition of liturgy assumes a certain doctrinal background. . ..orthodox Christian worship is explicitly Trinitarian in character. Consequently, the object of worship is commonly portrayed as the "Father," the glorifying of whom the Church participates in through the power of the Holy Spirit. Simply stated, traditional "liturgy" assumes the dynamics of relationships between the persons of the Trinity (and, by extension, the interaction of the Trinity with the whole of creation). "Liturgy" in a technical sense is the Church's participation in the dynamics of this relationship.[86]

From our review of both the Wesleys and Brevints theology and practice of the Eucharist as both Sacrament and Sacrifice, Ruth's definition above can be described as simply a restatement of the priestly function of Christ in the Eucharist and the church, collectively and individually as participants in it. Given that participation of the Eucharist is decided upon by those in attendance, and that there is even little value given to it in terms of the spiritual nourishment it provides for communicants to withstand evil and grow in Christian maturity, it can be argued that in this way the Eucharist is reduced to pure memorialism, again which leads to nominal and/or immature faith.

The final and most devastating critique is that research is demonstrating by taking a more marketing oriented approach by giving seekers what they want, proponents of these models in affect are in danger of losing them, especially as more and more persons gravitate to the "spiritual, but not religious category." Sally Morgenthaler reported almost ten years ago that seekers were dissatisfied by what they found in these seeker services in that they came to the church because they wanted more than left-brain information about how to utilize the Bible as a spiritual how-to book. Morgenthaler reports that really what persons wanted was an encounter with the Holy and what they received was more of what they had encountered outside of the church in terms of consumer, entertainment and motivational venues.[87]

Not only have scholars and religious researchers found this to indeed be the case, that seekers are dissatisfied with the "thinness" of their

86. Ruth, "Lex Agendi, Lex Orandi," 402–3.

87. Morgenthaler, *Worship Evangelism*, 17–31.

worship experience, innovators of the seeker model, such as Hybels, find themselves in agreement with these critics as well. As reported in a June 2008 *Christianity Today* article, Hybels announced that Willow Creek would be moving toward gearing its weekend services toward helping persons growing in the faith. In addition, they planned to exchange its midweek service for classes in theology and the Bible.

The reason for the change—Willow Creek's self-assessed research that reported that the evangelistic impact of the church was greater from those who reported a closer relationship to Christ, rather than the seekers, which was completely opposite of what church leaders supposed. The main reason for creating seeker services, they and McGavran maintained was that people would be in groups, not individually. As individuals were "experimenting with Christianity, they would invite others to experiment and they would make a group decision for Christ. In addition, the survey revealed that over a quarter of those persons who reported a closer relationship to Christ described themselves as "spiritually stalled" or "dissatisfied" with the role of the church for their spiritual growth. Even more devastating, about 25 percent of the "spiritually stalled" and 63 percent of the "dissatisfied" had contemplated leaving the church for greener pastures. Although they recognize that their methodology must change, Greg Pritchard, author of *Willow Creek Seeker Services*, maintain that really what is shifting is not the pragmatic church model paradigm of the past, but rather the target market which Willow Creek is now focusing on.[88]

If Pritchard is correct in his assessment of the shifts at Willow Creek, then we have to consider if they will be doomed to repeat the same mistake as the traditional congregations that they so heavily critiqued. Also, if Pritchard is correct, this again is simply another strain of *lex agenda, lex orandi*. In the Wesleys' understanding of the nature of God at work in the sacrament, the very encounter that people are hungering for and the spiritual nourishment whereby to grow into a relationship with God cannot be devised by marketing techniques. As Welsey asserts, to grow in love of God and neighbor (i.e., to experience holiness) will mean the practice of spiritual disciplines that emphasize the fact that we are creatures who stand by God's Grace in the presence of a holy and righteous God who is both known and unknown, and who has chosen to communion with us in the sacraments. Willow Creek and others like them will have to

88. Branaugh, "Willow Creek's 'Huge Shift,'" 13.

recover the mystery of the presence of God, something that the latest Pew Research is telling us, that American Christians have made an exodus out of the church for. They will have to admit that the formation of Christians is the work of the triune God that we participate in, not orchestrate. And they and we, will have to understand in an American society which is dominated by rugged individualism and hyper-consumerism, the church will never stand as a viable alternative to it by subordinating our worship and the means of grace, especially those instituted means of grace, baptism and Eucharist, to societal norms.

Eucharistic Theology and Practice: A Question of Identity

Overall, the main issue with the poor theology and poor practice of the Eucharist is comes down to understanding claiming and reclaiming continually our identity. Just as the identity of the young woman in the introduction of this text was formed through the ritual of roast-making, we as Christians are formed in our rituals, specifically in our liturgical ones, especially the sacraments—Baptism and Eucharist. Whereas in baptism we are initiated into the life of God, receive our identity and mission as Christians, the Eucharist is the sacrament that is designed to sustain and nourish us. The constant practice of it, reminds us of who we are, whose we are and the great grace of the triune God who invites and empowers us to join this God in reconciling the world to God, and in reconciling us to each other. In a Wesleyan framework, the Eucharist extends not only justifying but sanctifying grace as well so that we might be equipped for the journey and the work ahead. A truncated theology and practice of the Eucharist, means that we are like the man who believing in the great promise of America, purchased a steamship ticket with the last of all he had. Once on the boat, he survived on cheese and crackers, because he did not know that all of his meals were provided for in the purchase of his ticket. A truncated theology and practice of the Eucharist leads only to a memorialist understanding of Christ's atoning work in and for us, and leads us to believe that the benefits of our salvation are only to be found in heavenly realms at the end of our lives. Thus, we survive on "cheese and crackers," rather than taken in the nourishment provided in the Eucharist for the ministry we are called to in the world. The sacraments, in particular the Eucharist makes us response-able by the power of the Holy

Spirit to enter into Christ's sacrifice in and for the world now and to invite others to participate in the love we have found in the Christian God.

Worship, evangelism, and ethics work in tandem with one another, with worship serving as the pinnacle. As demonstrated above, in our analysis of both the Wesleys' and Brevint's theology of the Eucharist, evangelism and ethics or social justice are the byproducts of our participation with the triune God in the sacrament. We will now turn our attention specifically to how the sacraments, in particular the Eucharist, affect personal holiness, evangelism and social justice.

Questions for Consideration

1. What are the different ways Methodists in general and United Methodists in particular have identified or named Holy Communion, or the Eucharist?

2. What is the Eucharist, or Holy Communion? What does it represent?

3. What two theological resources play a large role in shaping Wesleyan theology and practice of Holy Communion?

4. What role does the Eucharist play as a means of grace in the Wesleyan view of salvation as a key to the life of holiness?

5. How does Wesley's emphasis on the practice of "constant communion" adhere among followers in the Methodist theological tradition today?

6. What are the strengths and weaknesses of viewing Holy Communion or the Eucharist as a "converting ordinance"? What does such a view assume?

7. What liturgical importance did the hymns of Charles Wesley have in the preparation of receiving Holy Communion in worship?

8. What are the dangers of "solitary" communion? Is this a contradiction in terms? What obstacles does the church currently face in practicing communion in a consumeristic and hyper-individualistic culture?

9. How did John and Charles Wesley understand Christ's atoning work on the cross and the role of the Holy Spirit in relation to the presence of God in the Eucharist? How is such a view different than other Christian communions?

10. How does the "outlining" of the Eucharistic hymns in terms of Memorial, Means of Grace, Pledge of Heaven, and Sacrifice help to enter into the mystery of God's Grace in Holy Communion?

11. What dangers do the "mega-church," "seeker-sensitive" models of church pose to Wesleyan identity and to the theology and practice of the Eucharist? Are such dangers avoidable? How can they be resisted?

12. How are the practices of the Eucharist truncated when consumerism and pragmatism become dominant criteria in the church and culture? How does a "cheese and cracker" approach to treating the Eucharist play into the hyper-individualism of Western culture?

four

Understanding Holiness, Evangelism, and Social Justice in the Midst of Contemporary Challenges

Introduction

Before we can discuss how a more faithful theology and practice of the sacraments might assist us with evangelism and social justice, we will need to define not only what we mean by the words *evangelism* and *social justice*; but we will have to determine as well what the Wesleys meant with regard to these concepts theologically. In particular, we will analyze the implications of holiness on evangelism, charity, and social justice. Finally, we will look at contemporary challenges to current practices of evangelism so as to determine if a more robust practice and education of the laity regarding the sacraments might prove fruitful with regard to the church's evangelistic efforts.

Personal Holiness, Social Holiness, Charity, and Social Justice

As Andrew C. Thompson maintains in his essay "From Societies to Society: The Shift from Holiness to Justice in the Wesleyan Tradition," many contemporary Methodists simply confuse and conflate the terms social holiness and social justice, equating them with one another. The problem with conflating and confusing the terms is two-fold in that first and foremost, this misunderstanding of the term social holiness creates a distortion of how Wesley understood social holiness to function in the process of sanctification.[1] It also nullifies the importance of social holiness as a catalyst for social justice which is not only concerned with the needs and contemporary issues of the disenfranchised, but which also confronts the benevolent paternalistic attitudes with those who may engaged in social justice and/or missions work.

Thompson also emphasizes the error of pairing social holiness with personal holiness, as in "personal and social holiness." This error also conflates the idea of social justice with social holiness by focusing on the difference between the adjectives "social" and "personal" to describe the difference between communal or society and individual effort.[2] This conflation results in a loss of how we understand the role of the church in effecting holiness amongst its congregants and the greater society at large.

So that we might be better equipped to understand what a more robust practice of baptism and Eucharist might mean for our churches in terms of personal holiness, social holiness and social justice, we will define each of these terms now in light of their contextual and cultural understanding at the time of their institution. Thus, we will define both personal holiness and social holiness in terms of how John and Charles Wesley would have understood them. We will then define social justice, by referring to Luigi Taparelli D'Azeglio, who is credited with first introducing the term in 1840.[3]

Personal Holiness

Holiness or Christian perfection was central to Wesley's theology and practice. For Wesley, holiness is the "moral attribute of God that is

---

1. Thompson, "From Societies to Society," 141–72.
2. Ibid., 143–44, 155–57.
3. Ibid., 143.

expressive of divine love." Since holiness is an attribute of God, it is an attribute that humans are meant to share as creatures created in the image of God. Humans cannot attain holiness based on their own initiative because of the power and penalty of sin. Thus, only God can make holiness attainable to humans by God's Grace. This is done through the person and work of Jesus Christ and by the power of the Holy Spirit. God's prevenient grace makes persons aware of their sinful nature and the need to be born again (i.e., the New Birth). Justifying grace mediates pardon from sin through the finished and atoning work of Christ such that one's life before God is made righteous (i.e., forgiven and reconciled to God). Sanctifying grace is the working of the Holy Spirit in the life of one who has been transformed by justifying grace such that their outward lives reflect the inward change that has been made possible through justification. Simply put, justification effects a real change in the life of the believer (i.e., the change of one's status before God), while sanctification is the process by which real change occurs (i.e., how one's life is systematically changed because of the change in one's status before God). Wesley defined this progressive transformation of believers as "holiness of heart and life." He explains this transformation in the life of the believer in his sermon "The New Birth":

> From hence it manifestly appears, what is the nature of the new birth. It is that great change which God works in the soul when he brings it into life; when he raises it from the death of sin to the life of righteousness. It is the change wrought in the whole soul by the almighty Spirit of God when it is "created anew in Christ Jesus;" when it is "renewed after the image of God, in righteousness and true holiness;" when the love of the world is changed into the love of God; pride into humility; passion into meekness; hatred, envy, malice, into a sincere, tender, disinterested love for all mankind. In a word, it is that change whereby the earthly, sensual, devilish mind is turned into the "mind which was in Christ Jesus."[4]

In this schema, it can be said that the terms "holiness" and "sanctification" are synonymous and point to the culmination of the Christian life—Christian perfection. According to Wesley, Christian perfection is that state wherein both the power and the penalty of sin are overcome in the believer's life. While Wesley believes that this is a possibility in the life of the believer, he also allows for the fact that persons might "fall from it

---

4. John Wesley, Sermon 45, "The New Birth."

in part or in whole," and that perfection is an ongoing process that can continue on "to all eternity."[5]

According to Thompson, although Wesley does use the term "personal holiness" a few times, he never uses it paired with social holiness as in "personal and social holiness."[6] When Wesley utilizes the term "personal holiness," he does so to describe the linking of sanctification with justification in the lives of individual believers such that holiness of heart and life is occurring. Wesley further utilizes the term "personal holiness" to emphasize first and foremost that there is a difference between the holiness of humans and God. Second, Wesley uses the term "personal holiness" to signify that justification (i.e., the imputed righteousness from Christ's atoning work) is insufficient for believers to attain the holiness required to see God (Heb 12:14). Wesley makes this point well in his sermon "On the Wedding Garment" when he writes,

> The righteousness of Christ is doubtless necessary for any soul that enters into glory: But so is personal holiness too, for every child of man. But it is highly needful to be observed, that they are necessary in different respects. The former is necessary to entitle us to heaven; the latter to qualify us for it. Without the righteousness of Christ, we could have no claim to glory; without holiness we could have no fitness for it. By the former we become members of Christ, children of God, and heirs of the kingdom of heaven. By the latter "we are made meet to be partakers of the inheritance of the saints in light."[7]

Social Holiness

Although it is inaccurate to pair personal holiness with social holiness as in "personal and social holiness," the two are related in Wesleyan theology and practice in that Wesley is clear that "there is no personal holiness without social holiness." But what exactly does this mean? Did Wesley mean to infer as modern heirs of the Wesleyan tradition, United Methodists do, when they describe social holiness as referring to that aspect of holiness that is not focused on the holiness of heart and life of the

5. John Wesley, *A Plain Account of Christian Perfection*, and Sermon 40, "Christian Perfection."

6. Thompson, "From Societies to Society," 156.

7. John Wesley, "On the Wedding Garment," as quoted in Thompson, "From Societies to Society," 157.

individual, but rather describes the transformation (i.e., sanctification) of society. Simply put, does Wesley in his phrase "no personal holiness without social holiness" mean to infer that the transformation of society (i.e., social holiness) is the fruit of personal holiness?

According to Thompson, to respond to this question in the affirmative is to miss definitively Wesley's understanding of social holiness and how this affected the development of his particular process of Christian formation that utilized classes and bands. Wesley utilizes the term only once in his corpus of writings and that in the Preface to *Hymns and Sacred Poems*, which he published jointly with his brother Charles in 1739. The purpose of Wesley's Preface to *Hymns and Sacred Poems* was twofold. Wesley sought first of all to convey his theology of salvation, and second to establish the "context in which salvation should be understood to be manifest in present life." It can be surmised that Wesley's overall intent was to address his specific concerns regarding the mysticism of his day, specifically that of the "Mystic Divines." The Mystic Divines emphasized union with God and internal piety and denied the necessity of church doctrine as having any bearing on humans' acceptance before God.[8]

In Article 2 of the Preface, Wesley reaffirms the Reformers theological position that justification is by faith alone. Thus justification is neither the product of good works or inner witness. We are justified and made righteous because of the sole salvific work of Christ's atonement. As Wesley contends,

> For neither our own Inward nor Outward Righteousness, is the Ground of our Justification. Holiness of Heart, as well as Holiness of Life, is not the Cause, but the Effect of it. The Sole Cause of our Acceptance with GOD (or, that for the Sake of which on the Account of which we are accepted) is the Righteousness and the Death of CHRIST, who fulfilled GOD's Law, and died in our Stead. And even the Condition of it, is not (as they suppose) our Holiness either of Heart or Life: But our Faith Alone; Faith contradistinguish'd [sic] from Holiness as well as from Good Works.[9]

To grow in holiness, individuals must be engaged in a community of faith that is mutually accountable and designed to help persons in the process of sanctification. While Wesley is sensitive to the need believers to

---

8. Thompson, "From Societies to Society," 157–58.

9. John Wesley, "The Preface, Article 2," in *Hymns and Sacred Poems* (1739).

engage in periodic disengagement from the world for prayer and spiritual renewal, he is clear that this is very different from the suggested practice of the Mystic Divines. In the Preface, Wesley is clear that sanctification occurs, not from personal piety alone, but instead

> Whereas, according to the Judgment of our Lord, and the Writings of his Apostles, it is only when we are *knit together*, that we *have Nourishment from Him, and increase with the Increase of GOD*. Neither is there any time, when the weakest Member can say to the strongest, or the strongest to the weakest, "*I have no need of Thee*." Accordingly, our Blessed Lord, when his Disciples were in their weakest State, sent them forth, not alone, but *Two by Two*. When they were strengthen›d a little, not by Solitude, but by abiding with him and one another, he commanded them to *wait*, not separate but *being assembled together, for the Promise of the Father*. And *they were all with one Accord in one Place*, when they received the Gift of the Holy Ghost. Express mention is made in the same Chapter, that when *there were added unto them Three Thousand Souls, all that believed were together, and continued stedfastly* not only *in the Apostles Doctrine* but also *in fellowship and in breaking of Bread* and in praying *with one Accord*.[10]

It is after this that Wesley makes the phrase that many have inferred as the foundation of Wesley's program of social justice:

> Directly opposite to this is the Gospel of CHRIST. Solitary Religion is not to be found there. *"Holy Solitaries" is a Phrase no more consistent with the Gospel than Holy Adulterers. The Gospel of CHRIST knows of no Religion, but Social; no Holiness but Social Holiness. Faith working by Love*, is the length and breadth and depth and height of Christian Perfection. *This Commandment have we from CHRIST, that he who love GOD, love his Brother also*: And that we manifest our Love, *by doing good unto all Men; especially to them that are of the Household of Faith*. And in truth, whosoever loveth his Brethren not in Word only, but as CHRIST loved him, cannot but be *zealous of Good Works*. He feels in his Soul a burning, restless Desire, of spending and being spent for them. *My Father*, will he say, *worketh hitherto and I work*, And at all possible Opportunities, he is, like his Master, *going about doing good* [emphasis mine].[11]

---

10. John Wesley, "The Preface, Article 3" in *Hymns and Sacred Poems* (1739).
11. John Wesley, "The Preface, Article 5" in *Hymns and Sacred Poems* (1739).

That Wesley was a social reformer cannot be denied. But as demonstrated in his Preface to *Hymns and Sacred Poems*, Christians have been justified and are in the process of sanctification within Christian community who are most equipped to work on the transformation of society. Thus, societal transformation, or what we in this modern era refer to as social justice (i.e., the "going about doing good") is the "fruit" of Christian life, indeed of holiness of heart and life in the context of a faith community in which there is mutual accountability. But what does Wesley mean when he admonishes his readers that one of the marks of Christian growth is to "go about doing good?" To understand this, we will now turn our attention to Wesley's understanding of social justice.

Charity and Social Justice

Wesley's system of "going about doing good" was indeed comprehensive and well organized. As is implied above, it was a critical component of his *via salutis* (way of salvation). For Wesley holiness involved both love of God and love of neighbor. In fact, for Wesley, true religion (i.e., holiness) and true happiness is "in two words, gratitude and benevolence, gratitude to our Creator and supreme Benefactor, and benevolence to our fellow creatures."[12]

So convinced was Wesley that love of neighbor was critical to one's growth in holiness, he organized societies and mandated their observance of the General Rules. The General Rules, which admonished persons to (1) do no harm/avoid evil, (2) do good, and (3) attend to the ordinances, were designed to provide Methodists with a systematized way of growing in the love of both God and of neighbor. So mandatory was the observance of the General Rules that the last paragraph of the General Rules contained severe consequences for those of the early Methodist societies who did not follow them, including expulsions and penitential bands for those removed. As Rebekah Miles notes, the removal of those not following the rules were not for the rules' sake, but rather so that one would grow in holiness.[13]

Wesley's system of doing good to one's neighbor was quite comprehensive in that it not only provided charity, in the form of direct aid, but also included the edification of others in the term of assisting persons

12. John Wesley, "The Unity of Divine Being," as quoted in Miles, "Happiness, Holiness, and the Moral Life," 207.

13. Miles, "Happiness, Holiness, and the Moral Life," 211–15.

in increasing their ability to live better lives, especially economically.[14] In addition, Wesley's system of doing good to one's neighbor included a justice component. Wesley regularly spoke out against the injustices endured by the poor, marginalized and disenfranchised in his sermons and in his writings. In fact, Wesley's form of social justice included systematic initiatives that worked to dismantle the very systems that caused persons to be poor and disenfranchised in the first place. As many scholars have noted, Wesley not only spoke out against the institution of slavery at a time when slavery was key to the economic success of Europe, but he also "decreed miscarriages of justices in the court systems, corrupt election practices, and government policies that adversely affected the nation, especially the poor" and wrote vigorously on behalf of better prison conditions."[15]

It is interesting to note that Wesley's system of social justice, which included charity, betterment, and justice/advocacy was not one sided in that Wesley was not only concerned about the effects of need and injustice on the poor and marginalized. He was also quite concerned about the effects that these systems had on those who were privileged in terms of their ability to grow in holiness. For example, in his writings against the slave trade, Wesley not only maintains that slavery is horrible to the bodies and souls of those enslaved, and detrimental to their native cultures, he is clear that any person who engages in the slave trade, including slave traders, merchants, and slaveholders, is in danger of hellfire.[16] So scathing was Wesley's critique of the slave trade and those who benefited from it, that an escape route was constructed from the pulpit of a church within blocks of a slave auction for Wesley to escape from parishioners angry at his sermons that critiqued their privileged status, due in large part to the revenue made from slavery.[17] In another instance, Wesley is particularly frank with admonishing parents in steering their child to view holiness as their life pursuit over riches and honor.[18]

Wesley's system of charity, economic empowerment, and justice/advocacy was the direct result of his understanding of the means of grace,

14. For more on Wesley's "Evangelical economics," see Jennings, *Good News to the Poor.*

15. Keefer, "Methodists and Social Reform in England," 8.

16. For more on this, see John Wesley, *Thoughts Upon Slavery,* and Miles, "Happiness, Holiness, and the Moral Life," 215–18.

17. Tuttle, Review of *Social Justice through the Eyes of Wesley,* 221.

18. Miles, "Happiness, Holiness, and the Moral Life In John Wesley," 223.

and his privileging of works of mercy over works of piety.[19] In fact, Jennings argues that even before the terms "preferential option for the poor" or "social justice" were utilized, Wesley is concerned with demystifying the dangers of wealth and power to those who are pursuing a life of holiness. Wesley's system is designed to create a new ethic, an ethic of the kingdom of God for those who are a part of the Methodist societies and in pursuit of holiness of heart and life. Jennings describes this ethic when he writes,

> But Wesley is not content merely to condemn injustice. He is also concerned to develop a positive ethic that will alter the given socioeconomic reality. Thus he proposes a view of stewardship that breaks the spell of "private property" and leads to a redistribution of wealth whose criterion is the welfare of the poor. This goes far to lead Wesley to an acceptance of the economic model of the Pentecostal community of Acts 2–4, which "had all things in common" and "made distribution to the poor," as the proper expression of Christian faith that works in love.[20]

Whereas Luigi Taparelli, a nineteenth-century Jesuit priest and political theorist, first used the term *social justice* to define a virtue concept based on natural law utilizing concepts from political theory, Wesley based his system on his understanding of the necessity of doing good for one's neighbor and—as a logical progression—in the pursuit of holiness. For Taparelli, "Social justice is both a norm and a habit—a social virtue embodied in the political, legal, and cultural institutional conditions obtaining in a given society—of promoting the common good by encouraging *the free exercise of the rights of persons and particularly of the intermediary associations they freely form to pursue their own good*, according to the complimentary principles of solidarity and subsidiarity [emphasis mine]."[21]

For Taparelli, social justice stood somewhere between commutative justice, "the virtue that regulates those actions which involve the rights between one individual and another individual," and distributive justice,

---

19. Tuttle, Review of *Social Justice through the Eyes of Wesley*, 221.

20. Jennings, *Good News to the Poor*, 25.

21. Thomas C. Behr, "Luigi Taparelli and Social Justice," as quoted in Thompson, "From Societies to Society," 149. Taparelli defines subsidiarity as "the rights of social groupings, with their just relationship organized toward the common good." Solidarity refers to the "natural duty" of these groups to act for not only their own good, but for the good of society. Taparelli originally used the term *sociality* to describe solidarity.

"the virtue that regulates those actions which involve the rights that an individual may claim from society."[22] By basing his definition of social justice on rights, duties and free exercise, Taparelli leaves open the question of whether or not one will follow his proposal of social justice. For Wesley, for those who are in pursuit of holiness, there is a mandate, born not of "rights, duties, and free exercise, "but rather out of the recognition of the fallen state of all humanity before a holy and righteous God and the gratitude for the prevenient, justifying and sanctifying grace of God that makes salvation possible. Further, as we will expound upon later, Wesley understands that the life of believers is bound in Christ such that when they participate in the sacraments, in particular the Eucharist, they are meant to sacrifice themselves on behalf of others in the same manner that Christ sacrificed himself for them, which undoubtedly will mean suffering.

Mission, Missions, and Evangelism

To be able to adequately discuss how the practice of the sacraments might yield a more fruitful practice of evangelism, it will be necessary to define exactly what we mean by the terms "mission," "missions," and "evangelism" and how these relate to one another, theologically and practically. To define these terms theologically will also be critical in that we might provide practitioners with a theological rubric whereby to assess if current practices are in actuality evangelism and/or mission/missions, or if they are rather practices that have been sacralized from other disciplines (i.e., marketing). We will begin our discussion by understanding the distinction between "mission" and "missions." Then we will define what we mean by evangelism, especially in terms of a decidedly Wesleyan—albeit United Methodist—theological and biblical framework. Once defined, we will finally discuss how these terms relate to one another.

Mission, Missional, and Missions

In 1998, Darrell Guder introduced the church world to the term "missional" with regard to *telos* of the church in his book *Missional Church: A Vision for the Sending of the Church in North America*. In this book Guder, a professor of evangelism and church growth at Columbia Theological

22. Ziegler, "What Is Social Justice? From Taparelli to John Paul XXIII."

Seminary, argued that for the most part churches in the North American context operated more like secular nonprofits that at best served as chaplains to society and at worse operated more like vendors of religious goods and services. As sacralized pseudo-nonprofits, Guder charged that for the most part churches began to function like other North American volunteer organizations that survive by their ability to keep members. Guder further argued that these churches were also influenced heavily by the development or rational social organizations and economic developments in the country that caused churches to organize as business organizations. The influence of the development of rational social organizations led churches to function such that "the individual was both a manipulative part and capable master, and managing the organization became the equivalent of being the church."[23] Citing research by Finke and Starksy, Guder described how North American churches began the progression to become vendors of religion with stark consequences. Finke and Starsky contend that the commodification of the church is a natural consequence of there being no state-sponsored religion in the U.S. In this "free market" of religious choice, religious organizations must now begin to "compete" for members. Given the unimaginable, overreaching influence of capitalism and free market enterprise on every aspect of human life in the U.S., it is easy to see how churches begin to sacrilize corporate values as a means to gain both members and consequently, income, as well as to grow into large "religious corporations" (i.e., describe the use of marketing techniques as evangelism; or to define Jesus as "CEO").[24] One also has to keep in mind that this link between economics, evangelism, and mission dates even further back in that early colonialistic practices often cloaked consumeristic intent in religious— primarily evangelistic—terms.

The net effect for many contemporary churches is that now church members become volunteers, the clergy become salespersons and the church doctrine and practice become the product, and churches function like large corporations, even while maintaining the language of church. In this way, the church is concentrated mostly on itself and "does missions," perhaps; but has lost the focus of the mission (i.e., the *telos*—the end for which God created and intended the church). Although Guder wrote his book almost twenty years ago, a simple review of many churches in

---

23. Guder, *Missional Church*, 84.
24. Ibid. See also Finke and Stark, *Churching of America*.

mainline denominations, as well as those that are independent and non-denominational, can also be described as fitting into this model. Further, although there were churches who took seriously his critique to become more missional, there are those who critique some within the missional movement as treating "missional" as the "trend de jure" and the utilization of Guder's critique and recommendations as the latest marketing technique.[25]

So exactly how does Guder distinguish between "mission/missional" and "missions?" First, Guder maintains that the result of the church becoming a vendor of religious services had the next effect of helping persons, whether members of a church or not, to define church as a place rather than a people (i.e., the *ekklesia*). Utilizing research from mission theologian David Bosch of South Africa, Guder explains that for the most part, churches shaped by the Reformation were left with an understanding of church that was unintended by the Reformers in that church became a place where certain things happen (i.e., wherever the gospel is rightly preached, the sacraments rightly administered; and church discipline exercised). By focusing on the idea of the church as a "place where," Bosch argued that these churches essentially became places where the Christianized society gathers for worship and where Christian character is cultivated. As Europeans began to encounter persons who had never heard the gospel and voluntary missionary societies emerged, missions in the nineteenth century came to be defined as "something that happens at a great physical or social distance." Therefore, many U.S. churches are continuing this historical understanding of themselves as the center of everything, localized evangelism becomes passive (i.e., society provides support for persons to attend church) and missions is what occurs, usually out of the local context.

Bosch further argued that beginning in the mid-twentieth century, from the dismantling of colonialism and the emerging of new independent churches from the global south who "now pressed toward their own independence from the missions and the churches of the West," the new global church community has now been shifting to an understanding of mission as being *ecclesiocentric* (church-centered) to *theocentric* (God-centered). Thus, the church reorienting its understanding of mission as something the church does with "an aim to extend the church or plant it

25. See McCraken, "The Church in a Missional Age"; Billings, "What Makes a Church Missional?"; Canty, "A Black Missional Critique of the Missional Movement"; or Cleveland, "Urban Church Planting Plantations."

(in all of its cultural norms) in new places" by sending "the mission out and defining its character" to redefining itself as "a community spawned by the mission of God and gathered up into that mission." In this way, mission is not what the church does or a part of its total program, mission, as in the mission of God (*missio Dei*) is the essence of who the church is.[26]

By grounding the concept of "mission" in the very life of the Triune God, "mission" must now be understood as "our participation in the Father's mission of sending the Son and the sending of the Holy Spirit by the Father and the Son."[27] We participate in the mission of the Triune God because when we accept Christ as our Lord and Savior and are baptized into his body, the church. Therefore, we mystically are incorporated into the life of the triune God through Jesus Christ by the power of the Holy Spirit. Thus, mission cannot be separated from soteriology, pneumatology or ecclesiology, which is often the case with regard to theologies of evangelism that privilege individual conversions and personal piety. In this way the church fulfills its mission as defined by the Nicene Creed of being "one, holy, catholic and apostolic church" in that it is apostolic, not only because it continues the apostles' teaching, but that like the early church it re-presents Christ as it witnesses to the triune God and as it participates in God's mission in the world. Jürgen Moltmann describes how the apostolicity of the church when he writes, "The historical church must be called 'apostolic' in a double sense: its gospel and its doctrine are founded on the testimony of the first apostles, the eyewitnesses of the risen Christ, and it exists in the carrying out of the apostolic proclamation, the missionary charge. The expression 'apostolic' therefore denotes both the church's foundation and its commission."[28]

From this standpoint of understanding that the foundation of the church's life is missional in that "central to a biblical vision of God's mission is that God does, in fact, work in and through [God's] church and that it is central, not ancillary to [God's] mission. Indeed, the church is the only community Jesus Christ has specifically instituted to reflect the Trinity and to participate in His mission in the world."[29] Given that this

26. Guder, *Missional Church*, 81–82.

27. Vicedom, *The Mission of God*, as quoted in Tennent, *Invitation to World Missions*, 55.

28. Moltmann, *Church in the Power of the Spirit*, as quoted in Guder, *Missional Church*, 83.

29. Tennent, *Invitation to World Missions*, 58–59; emphasis in original. See also Lohfink, *Does God Need the Church?*

idea of mission is to foundational to the church's life, then Wright and others argue that it is the hermeneutic that we should utilize to understand the entirety of the church's life, including how we read and interpret the Bible, how we practice the sacraments, and how we should understand such theological concepts as ecclesiology and soteriology. Therefore, for the purposes of this document, we will define and distinguish between "mission" and "missions" by utilizing the definition for these terms provided by Tennent:

> *mission* refers to *God's redemptive, historical initiative on behalf of His creation.* In contrast, *missions* refer to *all the specific and varied ways in which the church crosses cultural boundaries to reflect the life of the triune God in the world and, through that identity, participates in His mission, celebrating through word and deed the inbreaking of the New Creation* [i.e., the reign of God]. [30]

In essence what this means is that everything the church does must be oriented toward *mission* (i.e., *missio Dei*) and missions—worship, discipleship, evangelism, social justice work, etc. If this is so, then it can be said that the church must now understand itself as a continuation of the life of Christ in the power of the Holy Spirit. Therefore, the church must orient and model its entire life on the person and work of Christ in a holistic way. This is to say that the church must take seriously Christ's words to the disciples, "As the Father has sent me, I am sending you" (John 20:21). As the person of Christ was not separated from Christ's work, neither can the church separate worship from either evangelism or ethics. As we are incorporated into the body of Christ (i.e., the church) through our baptism, we are to be continually reminded that as our maturity comes within the context of mutually accountable community that cares for one another and understands itself to be in ministry with one another to all the world in the power of the Holy Spirit until Christ comes in final victory and we feast at with him and all of the church triumphant at the heavenly banquet. In this way, then the church serves as a sign and foretaste of the reign of God and witnesses to the love and grace of the triune God.

Now that we have a working definition and theology of mission and missions, we will now move to defining evangelism and expound on its relation to mission and missions.

---

30. Ibid., 59.

Evangelism, Mission and Missions

Usually, when someone is asked to define the word *evangelism*, they give an answer that has something to do with heaven, hell, souls, and sin. Most often, persons contend that evangelism occurs when the church goes out to "save souls" from hell and for heaven. This way of discussing evangelism is problematic for several reasons. First, in the cultural climate of today's world, "hell" is not as frightening as one would have once thought. Persons are either unafraid of hell because of their current conditions on earth, whether hellish or prosperous, or because they are not so certain that Christian story is the most accurate one in terms of understanding how persons get to heaven. In a pluralistic, interreligious, and secularized society, there are many options to heaven, or so it would seem. In some cases, the current rise of the "spiritual but not religious" has given rise to this idea that either all humans will go to heaven, or that all humans will reach a heavenly state in this world and in the hereafter. Even more troubling is that younger generations increasingly perceive that "getting saved" (i.e., conversion), is simply a tactic for getting more members (i.e., "customers") and that those who engage in evangelism are not concerned with them as people at all. In this way, evangelism is at best a marketing technique, at worst pushy, bait and switch salesmanship.[31]

The second issue with understanding evangelism only in the context of "saving souls," is that it does concern itself with the human subject in existential reality of their life on earth. This type of thinking is not only antithetical to primary Christian doctrines and the importance of such themes as creation, incarnation, and resurrection. Further, an overemphasis on "soul salvation" can lead to the oppression, enslavement, brutalization and mutilation of bodies as a means to save souls. The tendency for this can be easily demonstrated when one considers the colonization of the Americas, Africa, and Asia. It also well documented in the numerous books on American slavery.[32]

Given that we have established the reign of God (i.e., *missio Dei*) as the central theme for understanding the content of the Christian faith, it seems reasonable that we would define evangelism within this same rubric. Building on the work of Mortimar Arias and William Abraham, Scott Jones writes that simple etymology of the word evangelism

31. Kinnaman and Lyons, "Get Saved!," 67–90.

32. Two important works on this point are Douglas, *What's Faith Got to Do With It*, and Carter, *Race*.

reinforces the fact that evangelism must be centered on the theme of the reign of God because it was central to Jesus' ministry and the preaching and teaching of the apostles. Thus, "our witness today should still focus on how it is 'at hand' in the world and how it is to be anticipated as coming fully in the future."[33]

Therefore, if the reign of God is the church's primary mission, then it would seem to reason that the summary of the "law" of the reign of God is as it is described in Luke 10:27 and can be summed up as love of God and love of neighbor. Growth in love of God and neighbor is precisely what both John and Charles Wesleys affirmed as growth in holiness and what is the goal for the life of every believer. If, the reign of God which has as its central tenets love of God and love of neighbor, then we must take into account the insights from liberation theology and other social justice movements beyond charity and make them central to our theology and practice of evangelism. Beyond personal piety that is a "personalized, privatized transaction between God and the soul" and that focuses solely on heaven and the coming fulfillment of the reign of God, evangelism that is defined by our participation in the life of the triune God must be modeled after the ministry of Jesus and the early church. To practice evangelism in this manner, means that one understands that all evangelism efforts must be not only be grounded in the evangelistic love of God, but also must be "biblical, evangelical, holistic, humanizing, conscientizing, liberating, contextual, engaged, incarnational and conflictive."[34]

In this way, the Gospel message announces the present and future hope of the reign of God, it must also denounce all that is destructive to human flourishing and that opposes God vision for humanity. Evangelism that is consistent with the biblical message and with the ministry of Jesus then must side with the poor, marginalized and powerless in their struggle for freedom from the demonic powers of this world. Although this kingdom evangelization has preference for the poor, marginalized and powerless, it does not only focus on these persons without concomitant concern and love for those who participate in the systems that help create the oppression. This is a *kingdom evangelization* that invites Christian disciples not to focus solely on the benefits of salvation; but to participate in the suffering and sacrifice of Christ that secured our own.

---

33. Jones, *Evangelistic Love of God*, 27.

34. Arias, *Announcing the Reign of God*, xiii–vi.

In this way, we are invited into a costly discipleship that mandates our participation in the challenges, demands and tasks of the kingdom and an with the powers and principalities, the so-called "anti-gods" of this world.[35]

Simply put, to apply a missional hermeneutic to evangelism implies that we have to relate evangelism to discipleship, by maintaining is the entry point into a process of lifelong Christian discipleship that has as its ultimate goal to make us Christ-like. This link between evangelism and discipleship is exactly the same link that John and Charles Wesley make between justification and sanctification. Whereas evangelism is the portal by which one enters into the body of Christ (i.e., the church) and the life of the Triune God, as signified through our baptism, sanctification from a historical Wesleyan understanding occurs within Christian community. This is what John Wesley meant by social holiness and what is at the heart of the Wesleyan class system.

From this missional hermeneutics we can concur with Paul Chilcote and Laceye Warner's six propositions which provide a framework in understanding and defining evangelism:

1. Evangelism is a *part* of the *missio Dei* (i.e., the mission of God in the world).

2. Evangelism is not a one-time event, but a process in that not only do outsiders need to be invited to enter into the reign of God and make the biblical narrative their own, but that insiders (i.e., current Christians) need this reminder as well so as to not stray away.[36]

3. The goal of evangelism is discipleship and holiness, not growing churches or membership recruitment. As such, evangelism invites persons beyond mere mental consent of the Christian faith or a superficial prayer of commitment. Evangelism invites persons to a "radical trust of the whole person in God and a commitment of one's whole life to loving God and to loving all whom God loves"[37] in the way that God loves—holistically, radically and sacrificially.

---

35. Ibid., 105–6.

36. For more on this theme of evangelism being a process for outsiders, insiders and for children who grow up in Christian faith communities, see Brueggemann, *Biblical Perspectives on Evangelism*.

37. Jones, *The Evangelistic Love of God and Neighbor*, 49.

4. Evangelism must be oriented toward the reign of God which includes personal piety and social justice marked by charity and
   justice which has at its center a preferential option for the poor,
   marginalized and oppressed and which is also concerned with how
   systems of oppression oppress persons who benefit from such systems of oppression whether they recognize it or not.

5. Evangelism is more than the isolated work of a particular committee or group of persons in the church. "Evangelism is a missional
   practice of the whole people of God . . . It is a set of practices—a
   habituated way of being in community."

6. Evangelism must be contextual and contextual in such a way that
   allows for the mutual transformation of culture in both the ones being evangelized and the ones evangelizing. In this way, evangelism is
   not about making Christians according to our cultural norms (i.e.,
   proselytes), but is concerned with initiating persons into Christian
   discipleship such that the message is transformed and is transforming to their culture.[38]

7. Evangelism is grounded in the evangelistic love of God that is concerned with helping persons grow in the love of God and neighbor
   (i.e., holiness).

8. Evangelism is the work of the whole people of God who experience
   and enabled by power and presence of the Holy Spirit in their midst
   to give witness to the reign of God and to invite others to participate
   in the present and not yet coming kingdom of God as inaugurated
   by Jesus Christ. Thus, evangelism is the church's participation in the
   life of the Triune God by the power of the Holy Spirit to continue as
   the body of Christ, Jesus' ministry in the world.[39]

Given that these are our foundational propositions for understanding the theology and practice of evangelism, we can now define evangelism as

> That set of loving, intentional activities guided and graced
> by the power of the Holy Spirit, and governed by the goal of

38. For more on this idea that culture is a gift from God that helps us get a better
perspective of who God is and the need for making converts not proselytes, see Walls,
"Converts or Proselytes?"; Rieger, "Theology and Mission between Neocolonialism
and Postcolonialism"; Russell, "God, Gold and Gender"; and Newbigin, "Foolishness
to the Greeks."

39. Chilcote and Warner, introduction to *Study of Evangelism*, xxvi–xxvii.

initiating persons into entire process of Christian discipleship" which includes both justification and sanctification within a specific Christian community in response to the reign of God that takes seriously their socio-economic and cultural contexts, not as something to be colonized, but rather as a gift to provide the entire body of Christ with a richer understanding of the Triune God.

Evangelism that is defined and practiced in this manner meets the criteria for "kingdom evangelization" which is "biblical, evangelical, holistic, humanizing, conscientizing, liberating, contextual, engaged, incarnational and conflictive."[40] Further, evangelism practiced in this way is be understood as the outflowing of our collective participation in the life of Triune God in the power of the Holy Spirit to continue the ministry of Christ in the world, not as the result of human initiative.

In this way, practices borrowed from other disciplines (i.e., business, marketing, etc.) will be subordinated to the theology of the reign of God to determine if they communicate the theology, ethics, and practices of the kingdom of God as practiced by Jesus and the early church. This subordination of our evangelistic practices takes seriously our baptismal vow to denounce all powers, principalities and spiritual forces of wickedness in this world and ensures human flourishing. This subordination also takes seriously the powers and principalities of this world, even those that appear to be good but are deceptive in that they destroy the mutual accountability and relationality of those evangelizing and those being evangelized. Rather, the goal of evangelism is not to subsume persons into our culture through a modern day practice of Judaizing by converting persons to our cultural norms (i.e., proselytizing), but to make converts of Jesus Christ that are able to provide a helpful lens by which our own cultures, whether racial, ethnic, socio-economic, gender- or sexed-based, might be examined and critiqued. Thus, practices will flow from Scripture, theology and history; as well as be in conversation with them so as to offer a corrective to contemporary and historical forms of evangelization and mission.

---

40. Arias, *Announcing the Reign of God*, xiii–vi. See also Arias, "Contextual Evangelization in Latin America," 345–51.

Contemporary Challenges to Evangelism, Missions, and Church Growth

Now with a robust definition of evangelism and mission, we must consider our current North American context to see what factors must be taken into account as we seek a faithful practice of the sacraments, evangelism and social justice. We also consider these because in 2016 it is no surprise that many mainline, as well as many evangelical and nondenominational churches are experiencing declines in terms of membership, volunteerism, offerings, and practices of Christian formation. For example, a 2014 Barna Group study found that when asked what things are important to spiritual growth and formation, church attendance was not listed among even the top ten practices. This study also found that for adults overall 51 percent stated that church was "not too important" or "not important at all" for spiritual formation. Whereas regular church attendance was once defined as attending church three or more times per month, many persons survey consider regular church attendance to be once every four to six weeks.

While these numbers are startling, to say the least, what is even more dramatic is that when one considers age, this same study found that only 20 percent of Millennials (those thirty and under) believe that church is important, and that almost one-third take an anti-church stance. Even more startling, the study found that 59 percent of Millennials who grew up in church have dropped out, with more than 50 percent not having attended church in six months or more. While more elders (those over sixty-eight) are more favorable toward church and the importance of church attendance, almost half of those in between, Boomers and Gen-Xers, are divided about the need for the church at all. These facts are startling to say the least and point to the fact that if the church does not consider carefully its theology and practices, especially as they pertain to worship, evangelism and social justice, church as we know it may cease to exist.[41] Furthermore, these statistics also provide much in the form of critique for those churches who only wish to focus their evangelistic efforts on young adults and families as a means to take them back to the church's glory days and/or to maintain the churches in terms of volunteerism and revenue.

Whereas there are numerous challenges to evangelism in the current North American context, we will focus our attention on the following

41. Barna Group, "Americans Divided on the Importance of Church."

eight as those representative of the most significant challenges faced by the church in the second decade of the new millennium:

1. the collapse of Christendom;

2. the shift from modernity to postmodernity;

3. rising North American pluralism and multiculturalism and the North Americans church's inability to effectively deal with multi-culturalism and diversity;

4. technological shifts—moving from a Gutenberg (book/paper-based) society to a Twitter, Google, Tablet, Facebook (technology-based) society;

5. rapidity of and discontinuity of change and the ability to respond effectively;

6. generational differences in terms of the Media Matrix (how others learn and interact with others);

7. the growing divide between the haves and have-nots;

8. the Rise of the "Nones" and the "spiritual but not religious"; and

9. nominal Christianity that is influencing Boomers, Gen-Xers, and Millennials.

We will now look at each of these challenges independently.

The Collapse of Christendom

In previous generations, and although the Constitution stated that there was a separation between church and state, North American society would have been characterized as a Christian society. In this way, while arguing that there should be no official state church, there was a special relationship between church and state that created in the United States a system that can be described as Christendom. In Christendom, the state and the church are in a special arrangement such that the state through official and nonofficial policies "promotes Christian hegemony over the religious and cultural life of its citizens. In turn, the church gives legitimacy to the state by supporting the political establishment and tacitly granting divine sanction to the actions of the state."[42]

---

42. Tennent, *Invitation to World Missions*, 18.

In a classic understanding of the term *Christendom*, it is assumed that the faith of the leader is the faith of the realm. In the United States, with its supposed stance on the division between church and state, it can be said that a sort of civil religion that privileged Protestantism has existed since the inception of the country. This civil religion utilized the moral tenets of the Christian faith so as to provide sense of unity and moral fiber to the overall society. The way that Christianity has been privileged is easily seen in the fact that religious beliefs of presidential candidates are considered paramount with regard to the eligibility for office; governmental officials take the oaths of office with their hands on the Bible; governmental holidays are most those of Christian high holy days (i.e., Christmas, Easter, etc.). In Christendom-oriented societies, societal structures, both formal and informal support a so-called Christian lifestyle. In Christendom societies the basic Christian narratives are taught in non-church arenas, and it would never occur to persons that people did not attend a Christian church.[43] Any inquiries would refer only to denominational differences. Persons outside of Christianity would be considered persons with misguided belief systems who now needed to be converted to the "correct" way of living, which they are subtly conditioned to do so through governmental, school, and work policies.[44] In this scenario, evangelism happens passively. Persons come to church, because "they know that this is what they should do." Spiritual formation becomes centered around making congregants more self-actualized persons with God. Clergy and congregations are now designed to care for the needs of those who attend and those who need supportive services beyond the church.

Under Christendom, North American churches can function more like volunteer/pseudo-business organizations who sole mission is to keep its constituents content because of the services they provided to them and to the causes they deem important. In many Christendom-based churches, little is said or done that challenges state/societal policies that support marginalization and oppression. Rather, cultural policies and practices are seen as the "norm" with marginalized and disenfranchised person out of step with society because of personal deficiencies or the

43. What I have in mind here is the once numerous Christmas children's specials that highlighted the birth of Christ or school activities that privileged Christmas over other religious holidays such as Hanukah or Milad un Nabi.

44. In addition to Tennent, *Invitation to World Missions*, see Moore, *Touchdown Jesus*.

deficiencies of their parents. In such societies, mission is what happens "over there," most often in a "foreign" place, with foreign describing location (i.e., "urban"), race/ethnicity and/or socio-economic condition. In this environment, Christians do not have to have a robust faith that can not only able to defend itself against some alternative religion, but can also withstand secular humanism.

That Christianity has shifted from this position of centrality in the religious and cultural life in the United States, as it has in much of North America, is of no surprise to anyone. With rising disenchantment with Christianity, the increase in the number of person who identify as "spiritual, but not religious," and increased tolerance of persons of different faiths as Christianity shifts from being the primary religion practiced in the United States and North America. Christianity has now moved to being on the periphery with the United States and much of North America and Europe now being seen as mission fields by the very persons from the global south they once sent missionaries to.

With the collapse of Christianity, the challenge that most churches now face is that the evangelism strategy that served them under Christendom and to which they are most attached to will not work in the current environment in which Christianity no longer has a privileged position. In this era, evangelism cannot be passive nor colonial-/neocolonialistic. Whereas churches could once rely on society to assist with getting persons to church and in helping them to at least be somewhat familiar with the basic stories of the Christian faith, this is no longer the case. Further, whereas society once accommodated itself to a church calendar (i.e., "blue laws" kept retail establishments from being open on Sundays and schools did not schedule activities for Sundays or Wednesdays after a certain hour), this is no longer the case. Sunday mornings, once thought sacred are now fodder for retail establishments and for school sporting activities. In fact, Sunday sports have such an impact on the church, that many churches plan worship services and activities around major sporting events such as the Super Bowl.

These post-Christendom churches are also caught in a spiritual malaise in that not only do they not have financial and human resources they once had to spur growth and activity, the very persons they are interested in, that is, Millennials and Gen-Xers, are not interested in them as evidenced by the Barna Study cited above. Simply put, many churches that are in decline fail to see that with the collapse of Christendom, their desire to return to the evangelistic and mission practices of their heyday, is a recipe for disaster.

The Shift from Modernity to Postmodernity

Not only has the collapse of Christendom affected the church with re- 7
gard to evangelism and social justice, so has the shift from modernity
to postmodernity. According to the French philosopher Jean-Francois ,
Lyotard, the twin forces of Christendom and the Enlightenment gave rise
to modern Western societies. This era, defined by scholars as modernity,
provided the following foundational beliefs that undergirded much of
how humans in Western society approached all of life—religious, cultural, and political:

1. Generic individualism in which the individual is prior to and privileged over the group. Thus groups are simply sums of individuals
   and real action happens at the level of the individual, not the group.

2. Language describes the world at large.

3. Beliefs are nothing but assertion about reality and therefore can and
   should be tested.

4. Progress is inevitable.

5. Human reasoning is reliable.

6. Truth is objective and absolute.[45]

With the rise of relativistic pluralism and the loss of faith in the inevitability of human progress and in the ability of humans to know truth
absolutely and objectively, society entered into a cultural and theological
"crisis" that Lyotard described as postmodernism. Contrary to the claims
made under modernity, postmodernism contends the following:

1. Although the individual is important, the group is prior to and larger than the sum of its individual members, implying that the group
   has a greater possibility to affect and influence individual members.

2. Language is performative, not descriptive, meaning that language
   creates our world and trains us into a communal form of living. In
   this way language trains us to think in a particular fashion.

45. See Tennent, *Invitation to World Missions*, 25. See also Smith, *Who's Afraid of Postmodernism?* and Kallenberg, *Live to Tell*, especially 15–29.

3. Beliefs are social as they are rational which means that there must be some recognition that beliefs are contextually constructed. Thus, whereas there may be some larger notion of an absolute Truth, my claim to be in position of the absolute and objective truth is fallible because it is conditioned by one's rationality and context.

4. Because truth is contextually constructed, there is a skepticism of truth and a cynicism toward those in power. James K. A. Smith describes the dangers of asserting objective truth in a subjective world when writes, "To assert that our interpretation is not an interpretation but objectively true often translates into the worse kinds of imperial and colonial agendas, even within a pluralistic culture."[46]

Under modernity, conversion is all about getting persons to accept a particular set of truth claims that can be "proved" and individual conversion is paramount. Under postmodernity, conversion is a paradigmatic change in social identity and is paramount to being immersed in a new culture. Conversion under postmodernity is now all about how does one fit into the overarching metanarrative of this new context, utilizing new language and having a new worldview as constructed by the new language. One learns how to be a part of this new society, by living with those who are more experienced at it. A good example of the shift between modernity and postmodernity would be to think of moving from email to Facebook. While both systems offer a way to communicate with colleagues and friends, the systems are radically different. Email, it can argued, is simply another way of writing letters or memos. In addition, emails are driven by individuals. On the other hand, Facebook requires understanding of a whole new language and paradigm. Under Facebook's rubric, friend, which used to be defined as a "noun," is now a verb which describes how one associates with another person. Persons usually participate on Facebook because someone who is already a part of the Facebook culture invites them to do so. Proficiency is gained by communal living within the Facebook domain.

The challenge of the shift from modernity to postmodernity for the church in terms of worship, evangelism, and social justice is that in the past under Christendom, the church did not have to have a robust understanding of the gospel or be able to discuss secular humanism and/or other faith traditions in a respectful way. For many of these churches, the claims of the gospel are "black or white"—objective and absolute. There

46. Smith, *Who's Afraid of Postmodernism?* 51.

is no room for the grey areas of life, including both mystery and doubt. Further, for those churches who utilized the gospel message to support the idea of inevitability of human progress which finds its culmination in material prosperity, the current downward economic trends in society, the escalation of war and our inability to stop disease and hunger, the simple formulaic patterns provided as spiritual antidotes have proven themselves ineffective in current human experience.

Finally, two recent religious studies—"Americans Divided on the Importance of Church," by the Barna Group (2014), and "'Nones' on the Rise," by the Pew Forum on Religion and Public Life (2012)—cite that the reason most Americans want little to do with the church is that they see little to no evidence of the so-called absolute truth claims of Christians making a difference in the lives of its adherents.[47] In fact, Ronald Sider citing studies from both Gallup and Barna, report that for the most part many American Christians live no better than, and in some cases are as or more xenophobic, materialistic, self-centered and sexually immoral as than their non-Christian counterparts. On the scandal of American "Christian" behavior, Sider reports,

> Scandalous behavior is rapidly destroying American Christian-ity. By their daily activity, most "Christians" regularly commit treason. With their mouths they claim that Jesus is Lord, but with their actions they demonstrate allegiance to money, sex, and self-fulfillment . . .
>
> . . . If Christians do not live what they preach, the whole thing is a farce. "American Christianity has largely failed since the middle of the twentieth century," Barna concludes, "because Je-sus' modern-day disciples do not act like Jesus." This scandalous behavior mocks Christ, undermines evangelism, and destroys Christian credibility.[48]

The problem with churches that were constituted under modernity and which operate all facets of worship, evangelism and social justice ministry according to its philosophy is that their churches provide little to no evidence of the Gospel's power to transform the lives of its adher-ents for a postmodern age that is more interested in seeing a lived version of Gospel/reign of God living. Simply put, in a pluralistic society, persons

---

47. See Barna Group, "Americans Divided on the Importance of Church," and Pew Forum on Religion and Public Life, "'Nones' on the Rise."

48. Sider, *Scandal of the Evangelical Conscience*, 12–15.

are more interested in seeing the effects (i.e., the being or witness) of the transforming power of Christianity, not being bombarded with lectures of supposed "truth claims" of the gospel or "fire and brimstone" messages of going to hell. If Christians do not display individually or collectively the reign of God that they say they adhere to, then it is easy in a post-modern culture for persons to assume that Christianity is simply another philosophy that can be sampled rather than something one would give one's life to.

In addition, in a society that is skeptical about absolute truth claims and cynical toward those in power, Christian's seemingly collusion with power, especially political and financial power, as well as the sometimes virulent attacks on issues of social justice and the lack of advocacy for those who are marginalized, disenfranchised and poor only add more contempt to how the church is perceived. Further, the embrace of some factions within the church of the prosperity gospel, and even the per-ceived opulence of churches and of their clergy in an era of economic instability, especially as it pertains to Millennials and Gen-Xers, seems to fly in the face of the church exhortations to stewardship which only seem to support the church and those in authority.[49] For example, one has only to review the church's response to the Occupy Movement or to see how Pope Francis' agenda of social advocacy and compassion, especially for the poor and those in prison, as well as his swift action against those priests who embrace a materialistic lifestyle at the expense of congregants has engendered new interest in Catholicism.

Generational Differences in Terms of the Media Matrix

The shift to postmodernity as suggested above also coincides with a shift in how persons learn and are inculcated into various cultures. In addition to the philosophical shift from modernity to postmodernity, media also shapes how persons incorporated into society and how they expect to glean information from that society. As such, different media can be said to produce different cultures of people who have differing worldviews. For example, JR Woodward suggests that "print media causes humans to

---

49. For more on this idea about how the church has sacralized the American dream, see Platt, *Radical*.

become more detached and logical, while the Internet causes people to become more involved and participatory."[50]

Building on this idea that not only does the "medium shape the message," but that it also shapes the people, M. Rex Miller found that when the primary ways of sharing, storing and receiving information changes, people's worldview changes. He also discovered that the primary media utilized by various generations could also serve as a way to delineate how various groups of people communicate, build relationships, work and develop culture. Thus, Miller defined four primary media ages as the Oral Age (? bc–1500 ad), the Print Age (1500–1950), the Broadcast Age (1950–2010) and the Digital Age (2010–). Whereas in the past, one media predominated the structuring of most of society for the time period, because of the rapidity of technology, especially in the last twenty years, this is the first time that leaders have to deal with people who have been predominantly formed by three different media—print, broadcast, and digital—and who have very different styles when it comes to learning, community and culture which are described in the following chart:[51]

	Print Age 1500—1950	Broadcast Age 1950—2010	Digital Age 2010 -
Kinds of Leaders	Intellectual	Motivational	Impartational
Kinds of structure	• Division of Labor • Hierarchical • Living Machine	• Purpose-Driven • Empowerment • Buildings/ Programs	• Collaborative • Grass-roots • Dispersed Authority • Open Source
How Cohesion Maintained	• Structure • Inertia	• Psychological Stimulation • Sense of Mission	• Relationships • Collaboration
Focus of Leadership	• Like Field Generals • Achievement and Efficiency; • Teach by Instruction	• Like Motivational Speakers • Harness potential around mission • Teach by Exhortation	• Like Gardeners • Cultivate a collaborative approach to current situation • Teach by Example

50. Woodward, *Creating a Missional Culture*, 67.
51. Ibid., 68.

Nature of Relationships with Others	• Hierarchical	• Appointment • Functional to meet mission	• Unscripted • Personal/Familial • Mutual Benefit
Approach to Discipleship	• Takes place in Classroom • Logical Presentation	• Takes place in sanctuary • Programmatic • Seminar-oriented	• Takes place in living room/streets • Relational • Interactive • Mentorship
Qualities and Skills Needed	• Intellectual expertise • Maintaining predictability • Achieving stability	"Typical Leadership Model"	• Approachable/Agile • Networker/Advocate • Touchable • Collective Achievement • Transparent/Vulnerable • Storytelling • Resilient
"Typical Leadership Model"	• Senior Pastor/CEO • Servant Leader	• Lead Pastor • Team	• Equipper/Coach • Polycentric/ 5-Fold • Diverse

What this chart demonstrates so eloquently that our current models of evangelism, which only change methodology, but are based on the same modern philosophy of salvation, church and evangelism, will be ineffective for different groups of persons as formed under a different media age. For example, many churches distribute flyers inviting persons to participate in church activities and see this as a means of evangelism in communities in which they have built no relationships. Once persons come to the events, there is no follow up other than by providing information for future activities. In this way, the church communicates to persons looking for and shaped by relationship that the church is simply a vendor of religious goods or services. Another example can be seen when older persons lament that if only persons would come to Bible study or Sunday school, then they would grow in their faith, not recognizing that many more people are learning online and that work and school requirement may prohibit their attendance at traditional church times. For those who are oriented more towards a broadcast culture, who are preoccupied with efficiency, they may fail to relate to either those of the print or digital culture who want to have certain issues explained or who may want to see principles lived out before they will adhere to them. For those churches who do everything by committee or according to Roberts Rules, they may be seen as being unfriendly to those who know how to organize toward a "flash mob" concept to get things done.

Congregational analysis utilizing this research on the effect of the media matrix on members of the congregation, which is often comprised of a variety of media age groups; as well as honest assessment that the media age of one generation may make it difficult to evangelize and disciple others of a different age (i.e., older congregation trying to reach younger constituencies) yields some important facts with regard to evangelism and disciple-making. Namely, the "one size fits all strategy," or the "buy-it-in-a-box," will probably prove to be ineffective with regard to evangelism and/or disciple-making strategies. Further, for those congregations that have prided themselves on their efficiency in worship which allows no interaction, either via questions and discussions that occur when the faith community is gathered together, or socialization that is radically welcoming to outsiders at worship times, they will prove to be ineffective for those whose approach to discipleship happens in "the living room and on the street," no matter how slick their worship or evangelism materials. This is easily demonstrated in the results of the Barna Group study, "American's Divided on The Importance of Church," that found in the midst of a growing epidemic of loneliness, only one in ten persons reported that they went to church to find community.[52]

Technological Shifts: Moving from a Gutenberg (Print-Based) Society to a Twitter, Google, Tablet, Facebook (Technology-Based) Society

Almost three billion people, or about 40 percent of the world's population, are on the Internet. Within the last five years alone, Internet use has increased from 1.7 billion to 2.9 billion persons online, and it is expected to top 3 billion people by the end of 2014. The rapid rise of the Internet can be easily attributed to the fact that the web can be accessed from virtually anywhere around the globe via handheld smartphone and tablet devices which utilize satellite technology. Currently, the top ten countries with the highest number of people online are China (over 641 million),

52. Barna Group, "Americans Divided on the Importance of Church."

the United States (almost 280 million), India (243 million), Japan (109 million), Brazil (108 million), Russia (84 million), Germany (71 million), Nigeria (67 million), United Kingdom (57 million) and France (55 million).[53] In addition to the large number of users online, there are more than one billion websites, with almost 30 percent of them or created in the year 2013. Of the one billion websites, at the end of 2013, 180 million of them were active.[54] In addition, there are 1.3 billion active Facebook users, over 544 million Google+ users, almost 283 million Twitter users, and 42 million Pinterest users. Global Media Outreach reports that more than two million people per day search the Internet to find information for God, meaning, and hope. They also report that 76 million Americans report that they have no one to confide their deepest secrets to.[55] Also, Internet evangelists are reporting that thousands of persons are making commitments to Christ and are being discipled online daily.

- If the "world is indeed our parish," then traditional churches had better understand that our world is virtual and that if we are going to operate in a virtual world, we cannot operate virtually utilizing philosophy and strategies grounded in modernity without understanding the ramifications for our brick-and-mortar churches. In his lecture at the 2013 Biola University Digital Ministry Conference, missionary and theologian John Edmiston demonstrated that what persons once came to the church for are now available online. For example, online people can now

- make a faith commitment;

- make Christian friends on Facebook;

- read and study the Bible from a website or mobile app;

- hear first-class preaching on YouTube;

- get worship music to their liking on Spotify or iTunes;

- volunteer for a local or global mission or find an internship, job or an organization with which to work out your social justice ministry via ChristianVolunteering.org;

53. Internet Live Stats, "Internet Users by Country (2014)," http://www.internetlivestats.com/internet-users-by-country/.

54. Internet Live Stats, "Total Number of Websites," http://www.internetlivestats.com/total-number-of-websites/#trend.

55. Global Media Outreach, "How Can I Reach the World for Christ?"

- send out prayer requests via Twitter or text messages; and

- find a Christian spouse on ChristianMingle.com (or some other dating site).[56]

For many persons who are steeped in digital culture, the current way that the church operates does not work primarily because they either want to define their own theologies, or at least posit questions; do not understand the need to pay for the expenses of a physical place that they probably never utilize; have work and family life schedules that do not conform to the church's current operational practices; and do not want to get caught up in the church politics, gossip or administrative practices (i.e., the numerous meetings) required to get something done. In addition, in this current age where privacy is held at a premium, especially by younger generations who invite persons to be in relationship, strategies that seem imposing (i.e., door-to-door evangelism, contacting young persons without their parents' permission) inhibit current evangelism strategies. Simply put, persons do not want to come to a "place" (i.e., church) to receive what they perceive they can have online and that fits within their own life choices. In addition, perhaps more to the point, they do not want to be disturbed by those they have not invited into their private spaces in either the real or virtual world. This fact alone has many implications for those congregations who utilize "door-knocking" as their primary evangelistic efforts.

As many Bible colleges begin to offer courses not only online but also via mobile technology, the cost of Christian education is dropping such that current online internet evangelism organizations are trying to determine how to provide clergy in impoverished areas with education for approximately $300 per year, or one-tenth their annual incomes. In addition, these persons report that currently they can reach many more persons with their evangelistic outreach for approximately ten cents per person. Thus, the fact that the average lay person can now be as theologically educated as clergy, especially those who are offering simplistic messages, further challenges the need for brick and mortar churches.

With the Lily Foundation reporting that only 40 percent of churches with less than 150 members have a website, it would seem that in the digital age, many brick-and-mortar churches are destined for distinction. But does this have to be the case? Edmiston would argue that there is a possibility for evangelistic growth, but it is not in being the church

---

56. Edmiston, "The Ubiquitous Gospel."

that understands itself and functions as a vendor of religious goods and services. The advantage that traditional brick-and-mortar churches have over digital churches is that they can be intentional faith communities that demonstrate the love of Christ in the power of the Holy Spirit fully active and present in their midst. They can do this by providing regular services of healing and deliverance, meaningful worship, intergenerational family-like experiences, and by creating deliberate community and spiritual relationships in which persons have the opportunity to be ask questions, be accountable, and be loved. Edmiston says this is possible because

> the meaning of church is deeply connected with the meaning of human persons and also with what it means to be a Christian who is in the process of becoming like Jesus. If we are just biological computers with finite life-spans then information is enough and we can do church in cyberspace. If we are relational and eternal spiritual beings meant to share agape love in the presence of Jesus Christ, in the power of the Holy Ghost, then we need truly church, other believers and spiritual authority. [The] church needs to treat Christians as if they are important relational and spiritual beings and not just as brains in a pew![57]

Edmiston makes an important point about who the church is and how we are to relate to God and to one another. His argument would seem to suggest that if the church is going to evangelize those in a digital culture, it will be because the church, as individuals and corporately, will understand itself to be a witness to the reign of God that is marked by the power and presence of the triune God and that in this way it will be a sign, foretaste and instrument to the kingdom. In this way, the church's being in community, especially with regard to one another and to those in need will serve as witness, more than what the church does or says. This is in fact the promise that Jesus makes to the disciples before his ascension in Acts 1:8 — But you will receive power when the Holy Spirit has come upon you; and you will be my witnesses in Jerusalem, in all Judea and Samaria, and to the ends of the earth." Simply put, churches must understand themselves as being incorporated into the mission of God (i.e., missional) which has as its emphasis the reign of God and extends beyond getting persons to "come to church (building)."

57. Ibid.

This emphasis of doing that outflows from being, rather than doing as defining being also has implications with regard to the challenge of the rapidity of change in our current cultural environment.

Rapidity and Discontinuity of Change and the Ability to Respond Effectively

One of the major results of the ^supposed shift from modernity to ^so-called postmodernity and the rapidity of technology is the impact that it has on change, especially in regard to how churches who function under a Christendom/modernity paradigm and ethos. As we discussed in the section with regard to mission, many churches, created in and for modernity, and thus influenced by both volunteer and for-profit organizations, have systems in which both clergy and members are understood as interchangeable parts that fulfill specific functions and that are kept in order by systems with the emphasis on efficiency and effectiveness. More often than not, the effectiveness and efficiency on churches, and of its leaders are based on numbers (i.e., number of members, size of budget, staff, building(s), etc.). In this way, many churches and many mainline denominations operate more as *ecclesial machines* whose sole purpose is to make the church a vendor of religious goods and services. Rather than understanding themselves as an living organisms, specifically as the body of Christ, indwelt by the Holy Spirit, whose value is not determined by its doing, many of these churches, whether they state it or not, understand themselves as organizations and institutions which determine their worth on what they are able to produce. This understanding of themselves as an organizations or institutions, albeit religious ones, undermines many of these churches evangelistic effectiveness because if the laity or clergy are simply interchangeable parts, then it is easy for the clergy/laity to decide how, and if they will participate in the activities of the body. Robert Hamm explains the difference between "interchangeable and install parts" and "transplanted and regenerated" parts well when he writes,

> A living body has identifiable "parts," certainly. Yet those parts are not static objects that are installed like a belt, a pulley, or even a computer chip. The parts of a living body grow and develop out of the very DNA of the body. If a part dies or is "removed," a new part is grown by the body of is "transplanted" from another

body. The difference is not merely semantic. An *installed* part is "bolted on" but a *regenerated* or *transplanted* part is, or becomes one with the body. This means that as the body itself grows and changes in response to the environment, the transplanted part changes along with it and actually becomes a part of the whole organism.[58]

Before Hamm wrote these words, the Apostle Paul described how all of the parts of the body of Christ were necessary and an integral part of something larger than the collective sum of the parts in 1 Corinthians 12. As Paul writes in vivid detail, each part is a vital component and has a necessary function that is not of its choosing, but rather is chosen, and assigned by God, and gifted and graced by the Holy Spirit for a specific service. Like Hamm's regenerated or transplanted body parts, for Paul each member (i.e., part) of the Body of Christ, grows, changes and becomes a part of the whole organism, while that organism grows and changes as well. More important, than their functionality, each part/member of the Body of Christ is essential in its diversity and is needed for the edification and support of the body as it pertains to individuals and corporately.

More importantly, than failing to rightly recognize itself as an organism, rather than an institution, it is very difficult for the "machinery" of institutions to respond to change, especially when it is discontinuous and rapid. For example, almost half of the Fortune 500 companies that existed ten years ago are no longer in business. Sadly, of the Fortune 500 firms that existed in 1955, 87 percent no longer exist.[59] Even more staggering is that during this period, the consulting firm CSC reported that of the 1700 top firms they surveyed, 69 percent of U.S. firms and 75 percent of European firms tried at least one reengineering project. The result—85 percent reported little to no gain in their efforts and less than 50 percent were able to report any improvements in market share. The reason for the low rates of success? The change needed was incongruent with the established culture.[60] Probably no one has understood the problem of the failure of these organizations better than the late Steve Jobs when he asked why big companies failed:

> The company does a great job, innovates and becomes a monopoly or close to it in some field, and then the quality of the

58. Hamm, *Recreating the Church*, 3.

59. CSInvesting, "Fortune 500 Extinction."

60. Elwin, "The Cost of Culture, a 50% Turnover of the Fortune 500."

product becomes less important. The company starts valuing the great salesman, because they're the ones who can move the needle on revenues. So salesmen are put in charge, and product engineers and designers feel demoted: Their efforts are no longer at the white-hot center of the company's daily life. . ..The salesmen who led the companies were smart and eloquent, but 'they didn't know anything about the product.' In the end this can doom a great company, because what consumers want is good products.[61]

Although Jobs is referring to corporate America, one can see the many parallels between these organizations and most mainline denominations and churches that were created in and for modernity. As more and more mainline denominations, and even some of the once flourishing megachurches of the latter twentieth century continue to emphasize "salesmanship" (i.e., the personality of the pastor), and utilize slick marketing campaigns and programs over the quality of the product (the Gospel), the life-giving and transforming message of the Gospel of Jesus Christ is watered down to a monotheistic deism that has no importance or impact on person within and outside of Christian communities.

An additional aspect of change under postmodernity and in the midst of profound technological paradigm shifts is that of the difference between continuous and discontinuous change. Discontinuous change is a "non-incremental, sudden change that threatens existing or traditional authority or power structures, because it drastically alters the way things are currently done or have been done."[62] Simply put, discontinuous change is change that is unpredictable, sudden and requires a complete paradigm shift in how things are done. On the other hand, continuous change is gradual, ongoing and expected change which is the next logical step in how an organization or group has continued to function, all the while keeping current power and administrative functions intact. With continuous change, change follows patterns of the old way of doing things such that there are clear links between past and future. With continuous change working harder and smarter means better results, and the same basic rules of engagement of organization work. Under continuous change, transition is easier because all the organization has to do is to repackage the old paradigm (i.e., moving from traditional to contemporary music in worship). The important element for leadership

61. Denning, "Peggy Noonan on Steve Jobs and Why Big Companies Fail."
62. *BusinessDictionary.com*, s.v. "Discontinuous Change."

and organizations to be successful is to master the technical aspects so as to gain efficiency.

On the other hand, following the same old patterns under discontinuous change prove to be disastrous because first and foremost, you do not see discontinuous change coming. Not only is not planned for, there are no clear links between the present circumstances and past circumstances such that standard operating procedures do not and will not work. Thus, many organizations that were created in and for modernity do not understand that working harder will only produce diminishing results. All of this makes the transition harder because at every level of the organization, people are facing anger, loss, confusion, frustration, failure, etc. because the basic rules of engagement are challenged. Under discontinuous change what is required is a wholesale paradigm shift, which does not and cannot rely solely on mastery of technical skills for a particular system, but rather must rely on adaptive skills that require a clear understanding of what the mission is, and the ability to exegete both the mission of the organization, the context in which they find themselves.

To lead traditional organizations in times of discontinuous change, especially those created in and for modernity, leaders have to have tremendous people skills and have to continue to remind those who follow of the larger mission and provide a way for persons to "own the change." This means that leadership has to focus on helping persons inculcate the values of the organization through mentoring and by allowing them to try to implement change on their own. A shortcut way of thinking what is required for persons to navigate discontinuous versus continuous change is to think of the difference between a chef and a cook at a fast-food restaurant. The training of the fast-food cook is to help them master technical skills over a few machines. Each new product that is introduced simply utilizes the same machines for different time periods. On the other hand, while the training of chef does include technical skills, the focus on the training is more with regard to helping the person "be" a chef, rather than do, such that a true chef can because of their experience with a wide range of flavors, equipment, etc., can reinvent or create new dishes based on what is available and because of who they are, their more detailed understanding and familiarity and their experience.

A perfect example of how discontinuous change and continuous change are at play in many denominations and congregations developed in and for modernity is to look at the lament that many aging congregations have with regard to the lack of youth in Sunday school, or the belief that young heterosexual families "will save the church" and take them back to the glory days of the church's flourishing. What many of these congregations simply do not realize is that there are other options for families on Sunday morning for either church and/or Sunday school. More importantly, as recent Barna Group studies on young adults and church attendance demonstrates not only do more young people have no interest in attending church, much less Sunday school; but that for many young adults who have been "churched" already, they have no desire to go attend church because of the issues they already have with church in general or because they believe they have "graduated" from the elementary teachings on the faith whether from Sunday School or Sunday worship. Many also have no desire to attend because of how the church presents itself to them, either as irrelevant to their concerns, too judgmental, homophobic or money-hungry.[63]

While we have noted the rapidity of change and technology, as well as the shift between modernity and postmodernity, another key issue with that affects evangelism concerns issues of multiculturalism, pluralism and diversity. We will turn to these now.

Rising North American Pluralism and Multiculturalism and the North American Church's Inability to Effectively Deal with Multiculturalism and Diversity

Rising American pluralism and multiculturalism is also affecting the church's evangelistic efforts. According to the U.S. Census Bureau, America is rapidly becoming more diverse such that by 2060, non-Hispanic whites will no longer be the majority race in America. During the period between 2010 and 2060, the Census Bureau projects that so-called minority populations will increase from 37 percent of the total population of the United States to 57 percent. In addition to the rising racial and ethnic diversity, the Census Bureau also projects other important statistics, especially as it refers to race and ethnicity. First, the Baby Boomer generation, those born between 1946 and 1964, currently comprise 76.4 million persons, or almost 25 percent of the current population; by 2060, this number is expected to drop to 2.4 million Baby Boomers or 0.6 percent.

---

63. See Kinnaman and Lyons, *Unchristian*, and also Barna Group, "Americans Divided on the Importance of Church."

In addition, the overwhelming majority of these are non-Hispanic whites (72 percent of Baby Boomers are white, compared to 63 percent of the total U.S. population). This means that younger generations of Americans are increasingly diverse. Furthermore, this diversity is not only driven by immigration, but also by increased birth rates in non-white populations.[64] In addition to these population shifts, overall global Christianity is causing the nexus of Christianity to move from North America to the global South and East.

In the midst of this growing diversity, many mainline American denominations such as the United Methodist church, are recognizing their inability to minister effectively. This is easily understandable given the fact that in many places across the Christian landscape in the United States, eleven o'clock Sunday morning still remains the most segregated hour, a fact that Martin Luther King, Jr. observed over forty years ago. Commenting on the inability of many churches to effectively manage issues of diversity, *Time* magazine religion reporter David Van Biema, in an 2010 article discussing race/ethnicity, wrote,

> Since Reconstruction, when African Americans fled or were ejected from white churches, black and white Christianity have developed striking differences of style and substance. The argument can be made that people attend the church they are used to; many minorities have scant desire to attend a white church, seeing their faith as an important vessel of cultural identity. But those many who desire a transracial faith life have found themselves discouraged—subtly, often unintentionally, but remarkably consistently. In an age of mixed-race malls, mixed-race pop-music charts and, yes, a mixed-race President, the church divide seems increasingly peculiar. It is troubling, even scandalous, that our most intimate public gatherings—and those most safely beyond the law's reach—remain color-coded . . .[65]

Further compounding the problem is that past church growth strategies such as the homogenous unit principle (HUP), prioritized numerical growth and practicality over racial righteousness. In such instances, some mega-churches lulled themselves into believing that they practiced true diversity, when in fact many persons of color within their midst were

---

64. United States Census Bureau, "U.S. Census Bureau Projections Show a Slower Growing, Older, More Diverse Nation a Half Century from Now," December 12, 2012, http://www.census.gov/newsroom/releases/archives/population/cb12–243.html.

65. Van Biema, "Can Mega Churches Bridge the Racial Divide?"

simply assimilated into already existing cultural worship and administrative styles that privilege white, middle class, heterosexual, cultural norms. Thus, while there has been education to make persons more sensitive to issues of race/ethnicities and the social aspects of inequalities such that some churches are becoming more diverse, in many cases, this level of diversity has yet to impact the leadership of some of these churches. Van Biema makes this observation when writing in 2010 of the gains of Willow Creek in the area of racial integration:

> By February 2009, Willow had hit the 20%-minority threshold that signifies an integrated congregation. Today its membership is 80% Caucasian, 6% Hispanic, 4% Asian, 2% African American and 8% "other" ethnicities.
>
> Yet in the past few years, desegregation proponents have wondered whether Willow's commitment extends to giving minorities a truly representative voice. . . Hybels never promoted a nonwhite member to a pulpit pastorship or senior staff position at the main Willow campus . . . Curtis Sallee, a black 15-year "Creeker," comments that while "what Bill has done racially has been nothing less than miraculous, there needs to be someone who speaks for the church, a teaching pastor or staff, who's a minority. That's the next step. I don't know whether they are ready to take it. But they're going to have to address it sooner or later."
>
> Willow's predicament is hardly surprising. To some white congregants, naming a person of another color to tell you what Scripture means, week in and week out, crosses an internal boundary between "diversity" (positive) and "affirmative action" (potentially unnerving). Daniel Hill, a former Willow young-adult pastor who founded his own fully multicultural River City Community Church in Chicago, says, "There's a tipping point where the dominant group feels threatened."[66]

In addition, evangelicalism seems to be a factor in hindering racial reconciliation. In their 2001 book, *Divided by Faith: Evangelical Religion and the Problem of Race in America*, Michael O. Emerson and Christian Smith found that while white evangelicals tended to believe that their faith was a powerful impetus for bringing the races together, many of them had fewer non-white friends than their non-Evangelical counterparts. They further reported that many white evangelicals believed racial inequality to be imaginary or the result of personal sin, not attributed to any societal or historical issues. This contributed to a church culture

66. Ibid.

that unofficially and unintentionally discouraged minority participation through their systems and practices. Chief of these was the failure to believe that colorblind policies and practices actually were predicated on non-minority systems which were seen as "normal" or "common sense." Thus, rather than driving races together, evangelicalism often had the unintended consequence of driving them further apart further adding to the racial fragmentation of society.[67]

Not all of these issues have been satisfied by the increase in mission and cross-cultural trips by persons from mainline denominations. While cross-cultural mission trips have expanded the vision of persons beyond American culture, albeit overwhelmingly suburban culture, as Lupton, Rieger and Cleveland write in many ways, forays across cultures, whether they be racial/ethnic or urban/suburban contexts are simply new spins on colonialistic practices of the past which dismiss the ability of those on the receiving end of being necessary and mutually equitable partners and colleagues. By equating money and numbers with success, and failing to recognize the effects of privilege, many of these "missionaries" come to the relationship failing to recognize that all present, regardless of race, ethnicity, or socio-economic status, come to the table with assets and needs. In many of these instances, while racial/ethnic stereotypes may be addressed on an individual basis little is done to address systemic injustices.[68]

The net result of these overt and covert instances of racism and classism is that while it is apparent from all of the secular research that the twenty-first century will be the century of a truly multiracial, multi-ethnic, and multigenerational in which no group will be the prevailing majority, there are less than 4 percent of US congregations that are truly diverse, meaning that diversity is reflected and influences every aspect of a church's worship, administration, and evangelistic/mission practices. This means that in every instance in society in which people have to effectively deal with diversity, the church is woefully unprepared to minister in the face of such diversity. Soong-Chan Rah offers the following as the scathing critique of why mainline denominations in the U.S., especially white evangelical churches are ill-prepared to handle and a solution to the problem when he writes, "If we were to hear of any other institution, such as a government agency or an institute of higher education, that was

67. Emerson and Smith, *Divided by Faith*.

68. See Lupton, *Toxic Charity*; Rieger, "Theology and Mission between Neocolonialism and Postcolonialism"; and Cleveland, "Urban Church Plantations."

integrated by less than four percent, there would be justifiable outrage and protest. Yet, the American evangelical church marches along in our single-ethnic ministries focused on numerical growth over the biblical value of racial reconciliation and justice."[69]

While Rah writes mostly with regard to the evangelical church and critiques the system of white privilege, my own experience bears witness to the fact that there are many racial-ethnic churches which have adopted much of the same principles as their white counterparts such that they are as racist and classist, albeit in an intra-racial way as any other. This is not to say that I do not recognize the need for there to be churches which are may be comprised primarily of one particular racial-ethnic group in order to provide support for persons who experience racism beyond the church doors. However, I submit that these churches must also be sensitive to the need for racial reconciliation and justice which understands that culture is a gift from God, not to be subsumed into some Christianized version of the American melting pot or a Christian spin on the American Dream. Rather, culture as God's gift, is designed to help manifest a multifaceted expression of the glory of God that in which all persons are recognized as integral and needed, and that recognizes that the gifts of leadership are predicated on the gifting of the Holy Spirit (Eph 3:10; 1 Cor 12). Further, while it can be argued that many of these churches are the "holders" of the history of raced-persons in America, they must see that the history they hold is a history that must be shared across race and ethnicities if various racial ethnic groups are to be "regenerated" and transplanted members of the Body of Christ that causes the whole to grow and change. In addition, they too must be challenged to be multicultural churches as well in order to meet the growing inter-race relationships among younger generations.

In addition to the diversity issues with regard to race and ethnicities, the report from the U.S. Census Bureau also evidences additional potential diversity issues with regard to age. As the Census Bureau report projects, Baby Boomers will be the largest percentage of the U.S. population with regard to age (25 percent currently). In fact, the census report projects that by the year 2056, Baby Boomers over sixty-five years old will outnumber those under 18. Whereas in the past, marketing strategies have been targeted toward young adults and youth because of their disposable income, businesses now are being advised to "seniorize" their

69. Rah, *Next Evangelicalism*, 85.

marketing strategy.[70] With an adult in the U.S. turning fifty every seven seconds, businesses, as well as other governmental and nonprofit entities are stepping up their strategies to meet the needs of these individuals. With regard to the wealth and spending habits of senior citizens and baby boomers, the following statistics are of particular interest to the church as it develops its evangelism and outreach strategies:

- The 55+ age group controls more than three-fourths of America's wealth (ICSC).

- Boomers' median household income is 55% greater than post-Boomers and 61% more than pre-Boomers. They have an average annual disposable income of $24,000 (US Government Consumer Expenditure Survey).

- One-third of the 195.3 million internet users in the U.S., adults aged 50+ represent the Web's largest constituency (Jupiter Research).

- Two-thirds of Americans 50+ buy from e-retailers online (Pew).

- In 2012, baby boomers (47–65) spend 27 hours per week online, 2 hours more per week then Millenials (16–34) at 25 hours per week (WSL/Strategic Retail).

- The current pre-retirement market is about 65% bigger than what is was 20 years ago (Bureau of Labor Statistics).

- Pre-retirees feel that enjoying retirement and making sure their spouse is taken care of is a bigger focus than leaving an inheritance (MetLife).

- In the next ten years, U.S. baby boomers will increase their annual spending on wellness-based services from approximately $200M to $1 trillion (Paul Zane Pilzer, *The Next Trillion*).

- Americans 55+ are the fastest-growing age group among gym members, up more than 266 percent since 1987 (IBISWorld).

- 43.5 million family caregivers care for someone 50+ (Alzheimer's Association).

- 37 percent of caregivers have children or grandchildren under 18 living with them (National Alliance for Caregiving in collaboration with AARP).[71]

---

70. Beesley, "Marketing to Seniors and Baby Boomers."
71. Immersion Active, "Resources 50+ Facts and Fiction."

What these statistics point to is an aging population that has larger disposable income, is more internet savvy and health conscious than previous generations of senior citizens, and who are committed to caring for someone older and/or younger. This affects significantly four primary aspects of the possibility of church growth. First, whereas the church may have been able to rely on osmosis in terms of senior attendance, giving and volunteerism at church, this new group of active seniors quite frankly has others things to do which means that churches will have to develop evangelism strategies for an aging population. This is in stark contrast to the strategy of many mainline denominations to focus their evangelism and mission strategies on young adults with families. Second, the amount of time these adults spend gleaning information on the internet means that not only will brick-and-mortar churches need to have an online presence, but that the same challenges with regard to the need for brick-and-mortar churches posed by younger generations may be expressed by boomers. The fourth and most important aspect relates to church human and financial resources. If Boomers are more committed to quality of life and leisure in retirement and/or committed to care for others, then it is safe to say that many congregations may not be able to rely on the human power and sacrificial giving of the past from older members. Simply put, if the aging Boomer population has other places for their human and financial capital, then we must question how current brick-and-mortar congregations will be maintained. Not only will churches have to deal with the issues of dealing with a technologically savvy older congregation, but as was mentioned earlier church leaders may have to be able to navigate generational diversity to the same degree as racial/ethnic diversity.

The Growing Divide between the Haves and Have-Nots

In addition to issues of race and ethnicity, it can be said that the same issues of race/ethnicity that divide churches are the same across class. In an age of the Occupy movement which brought to the forefront the economic disparities between the rich and the poor; the declining middle class, and the alarming un- and underemployment rate of young adults, in particular the high rate of underemployment among college graduates, many young adults are questioning what they refer to as an "overemphasis" by the church on economic success. In fact, the Pew Forum's recent research on the increasingly number of American adults who identify as spiritual but not religious, the "nones," reported that 70 percent of those surveyed, as compared with 51 percent of the general U.S. population believed that churches and other religious organizations were too preoccupied with money and power.[72] Simply put, many are seeing the opulence and celebrity-like status of some church leaders, as well as the emphasis of some on prosperity preaching as indicative of a deeper spiritual problem—materialism and greed.

At issue is the church's emphasis on giving/tithing when families are cash-strapped in order to keep what are perceived to be ineffective ministries (i.e., ministries that are mostly inwardly focused) afloat. At issue as well is whether or not large donors believe these churches are also capable of managing large gifts even if they did extend their ministries beyond the church walls.[73] In fact, in informal surveys by internet evangelists, many persons were loath to give their finances to brick and mortar churches when they could receive the same services online and contribute their resources to those organizations that were seeming to have a direct impact and influence on local and global communities.

The Rise of the "Nones" and the "Spiritual but Not Religious"

In October 2012, the Pew Research Center released one of the most significant reports with regard to evangelism and church growth, "'Nones' on the Rise." Their research, conducted over a five-year period, found that as of 2012 one-fifth of the U.S. adult population designated themselves as religiously unaffiliated, with one-third of adults under thirty designating themselves as religiously unaffiliated. Simply put, while many of these unaffiliated adults affirmed a belief in God, many simply wanted nothing to do with organized, and particularly Christian organized religion. The study also revealed that not only were these adults not affiliated with any particular religion, they were not looking to become a part of a particular religious group. Rather, many designated themselves as "spiritual, but not religious," citing their engagement with spiritual practices that they felt did not require church affiliation. In addition, researchers found that the

72. Pew Forum on Religion and Public Life, "'Nones' on the Rise."

73. For more on the perception of persons within and outside of the church's willingness and ability to effectively manage financial resources in order to combat societal ills, see J. Clif Christopher, *Not Your Parent's Offering Plate.*

growth of religiously unaffiliated persons was significantly concentrated in one group—Protestant whites.[74] According to researchers, the main reasons these younger adults, many of whom grew up attending church, gave for wanting little to nothing to do with the church:

- Organized religion is too concerned with politics, money and power.

- Organized religion is too judgmental, homophobic and hypocritical.[75]

Other reasons cited for the increase of the religiously unaffiliated included the postponement of marriage and parenthood among younger adults, the broad decline in social engagement in terms of civic and volunteer organizations, and the increasing secularization and pluralism of American society.

Further research from the Barna Group discovered that while a majority of these persons have been exposed to church via youth groups and vacation Bible school, that there was almost a perception that just as one graduates from school, one "graduated" out of church (i.e., been there done that, have all of the information). The same study found that also many young adults did not like many of the church's evangelism strategies that they referred to as "bait-and-switch" tactics that seemed to demonstrate the church's care and involvement with them until they became members.[76]

Both the Pew Center and the Barna Group's research demonstrates that continuing to evangelize young adults and youth utilizing strategies that may have worked with previous generations will be futile.

Nominal Christianity That Is Influencing Boomers, Gen-Xers, and Millennials

In her book *Almost Christian: What The Faith of Our Teenagers Is Telling the American Church*, Princeton professor Kenda Creasy Dean contends that the primary reason youth and young adults in mainline American churches are unable to fully claim and/or defend their Christian heritage is that the faith being promoted in many of these churches is a nominal Christianity based on Moralistic Therapeutic Deism. Moralistic

---

74. Pew Forum on Religion and Public Life, "'Nones' on the Rise," 21.

75. Ibid., 29.

76. Kinnaman and Lyons, "Get Saved," 67–89.

Therapeutic Deism is the religious belief system of many American teens and their families as defined by Christian Smith, one of the sociologists and lead researchers of the National Study of Youth and Religion. Its basic tenets are as follows:

1. A god exists who created and ordered the world and watches over human life on earth.

2. God wants people to be good, nice, and fair to each other, as taught in the Bible and by most world religions.

3. The central goal of life is to be happy and to feel good about oneself.

4. God does not need to be particularly involved in one's life except when God is needed to resolve a problem.

5. Good people go to heaven when they die.[77]

The issue with Moralistic Therapeutic Deism is that it bears little resemblance to the Christian faith of the early church in that it reduces Christian ethics to goodness, is preoccupied with the comfort and happiness of those who practice it, and provides no means of hope for those who suffer tragedy and hardship and/or when the formulaic platitudes of utilitarian Christianity (i.e., the 3, 5, 40 easy steps to achieve "X") do not yield desired results. In addition, Moralistic Therapeutic Deism provides no answers as to how Christianity is different from any other religion or secularism. Thus, Dean argues, contrary to popular belief teens and young adults are not hostile to religion, simply indifferent to it.

To combat Moralistic Therapeutic Deism, Dean suggests that churches must first recognize that Moralistic Therapeutic Deism is not only the religion of youth and young adults, but also of their parents. Relating Moralistic Therapeutic Deism to John Wesley's sermon entitled "Almost Christian," Dean contends that at issue with the faith of many in our congregation is that they are nominal Christians—good people who are Christians in name only. Dean contends that the only way to combat Moralistic Therapeutic Deism or nominal Christianity is for the church to reclaim a "missional imagination" based on the self-giving love of God as seen in the incarnation, life, death and resurrection of Jesus Christ for the church overall. Further, Dean contends that we must stop treating youth and young adults as an "alien" species but to allow them to become equally important fellow contributors to the ministry and mission of the church by helping them to claim their story within the Christian story as

77. Dean, "Moralistic Therapeutic Deism?"

contained in the Old and New Testament and by providing opportunities for them to be mentored on the way.[78]

In addition to the Moralistic Therapeutic Deism of youth, young adults and their parents, Peter Scazzero maintains that emotional immaturity is critical in cultivating mature Christian faith that provides witness to a watching world. Scazzero further suggests that nominal Christianity is fueled by a preoccupation of Christian works over the cultivation of a deep relationship with Christ and with others which causes persons to change from the inside out. Simply put, Scazzero contends that until Christians have a deep recognition of the love of God for them personally which makes them aware of patterns of relating that have been inherited from their families and communities of origins, they will never be able to move to deep, abiding relationships with others, especially those who are different from them both inside and outside the church. In this way, these Christians, as the church will always represent a fragmented body of Jesus by privileging tribal and family loyalties and by having no way to resolve conflict or to incorporate others into their faith communities beyond superficial levels.[79]

Is There No Hope?

While the current issues with regard to evangelism, the distinction between personal holiness, social holiness and social justice can seem overwhelming, the good news is that this is not the first time in the history of the church, especially those churches that are descendants of the faith tradition started by John and Charles Wesley. The early church found itself in a non-privileged position in a diverse, pluralistic and secular society in which class stratifications were extreme. As evidenced by the letters to the Corinthian church in particular, while there may have been spiritual gifts in operation, the church had to contend with the emotional immaturity of its adherents. A quick perusal of the sermons, expository notes and journal entries of John Wesley provide ample evidence that the society to which John and Charles Wesley ministered was replete with nominal Christians which privileged tribal and familial loyalties over the mandates of the gospel. Their society was also one marked by extremes in terms of racial and class inequalities. And yet, the Wesleys became

78. Dean, *Almost Christian*.

79. Scazzero, *The Emotionally Healthy Church*.

agents of renewal and revival during their time, not only affecting how Christians conducted themselves with regard to issues of personal piety, but also impacting the social ills of their day.

As will be demonstrated in the next and final chapter, it can be argued that the Wesleys' privileging of the sacraments, in particular the Eucharist, coupled with their system of catechesis and accountability—the class system provided the foundation for such renewal. While the Wesleys could not have imagined such complexities as the church currently faces and given the gains in our knowledge of such wide and varied topics as sociology and psychology, it can be argued that their understanding of how to live as sacramental people in the world can shed some light on our current predicament. In this way, it may just be possible, that a more faithful theology and practice of the sacraments, in particular the Eucharist might provide some helpful answers to the predicaments that many mainline denomination, and in particular the United Methodists, find themselves.

Questions for Consideration

1. What are the consequences when the church conflates social holiness and social justice? What distinctions are there with these two concepts?

2. How does John Wesley use the term holiness in relation to God's Grace? How does Wesley relate social and personal holiness in the practice of the Christian life? What are some of the misconceptions the church has had about Wesley's understanding of social holiness?

3. What is the danger of solitary religion to the Christian faith?

4. What distinctions are there between mission and missions and evangelism? Are these distinctions helpful?

5. What importance does the notion of the *missio Dei* have in the practice of mission in the Wesleyan tradition? In the practice of social justice and evangelism?

6. How significant is the corporate nature of the church to the ministries of evangelism and social justice?

7. What are the strengths and weaknesses of the propositions of evangelism offered in this chapter? What is helpful about the author's proposed definition of evangelism? How is such a definition at odds with other definitions of evangelism throughout the church?

8. What are the contemporary challenges to the church's identity with the collapse of Christendom in North America? What opportunities now exist to engage more imaginatively in the practice of evangelism, mission, and social justice in a post-Christendom context?

9. What challenges does the church face as it moves from a modern to a postmodern age? Are the categories of modern and postmodern useful to understanding what is happening in the wider culture? Why? Why not?

10. What obstacles to ministry are created with the rapidity of change in technology and the emphasis on organizational efficiency (e.g., the notion of the church as an "ecclesial machine")? What aspects of the church's identity are lost in this change in self-understanding (e.g., the church as a living organism, as the body of Christ)?

11. What are the effects of pluralism and multiculturalism on the church today, internally and externally? Are there limits to pluralism? To

multiculturalism? If so, what are they? What are the gifts of pluralism and multiculturalism?

12. How does information regarding the wider generational and economic s changes in North American culture help the church in its practice of evangelism and social justice?

five

Table Matters: Living as Sacramental People

> Then Elijah said to all the people, "Come closer to me"; and all the people came closer to him. First he repaired the altar of the Lord that had been thrown down; Elijah took twelve stones, according to the number of the tribes of the sons of Jacob, to whom the word of the Lord came, saying, "Israel shall be your name"; with the stones he built an altar in the name of the Lord. (1 Kgs 18:30–32 NRSV)

Introduction

That the twenty-first-century North American church is in decline is no surprise to anyone. In fact, according to the aforementioned studies by the Barna Group and the Pew Forum on Religion and Public Life, not only is the church in decline, but one could surmise that as an organization it could be on the verge of extinction—similar to those companies who once found themselves at the top of the Fortune 500 lists, who are now either not in existence or of such insignificance to really not matter except to those who refer only to past glories. While this outlook can seem dismal indeed, I suggest it is only dismal if one considers the church to be an organization—an institution, per se. However, the church is not an institution, or any other humanly created thing.

As the New Testament tells us over and over again, the church is called into being by the triune God made known in the life, death, resurrection, burial, and ascension of Christ, and sustained because of its union with God through Christ in the power of the Holy Spirit. Simply put, Scripture and Christian history, tradition and doctrine all communicate that the church is not an *organization*, it is an *organism* (i.e., body) instituted by God, whose head is Christ and whose life is the Holy Spirit. Its particular mission is to witness to the reign of God made known in the life, death, resurrection and ascension of Christ. The church understands herself not as a collective of separate, autonomous individuals who come together and who are committed to one another as long as their individual needs are met. Rather, the church understands herself as a communion—a body of persons called by Christ who, in participation with his crucifixion and resurrection, understand themselves as continuously being given for the sake of the world. As such, the church understands that as individual members of the body, no one part of the body can demand assimilation such that the uniqueness of individuals is annihilated or subsumed so that there is no distinction. Neither can any body part dismiss itself because of its perceived "unworthiness." As in a body, so is the church, the parts are uniquely crafted and empowered such that their "diversity in unity," provides a living witness to the triune God (1 Cor 12).

What all of the issues described in the previous chapter point to is not the church in North America's demise, rather they point to its malaise—not only a malaise of loss of mission (the *missio Dei*), but a loss of its identity (*witness*). As we will discuss further, the research points to a church that has exchanged its worship of the triune God as made known in the Hebrew Bible and New Testament for the lesser gods of the consumer market place that have been made with human hands. Worse still, this exchange has not been wholesale. Rather, it has come because of syncretization of the church and market, and subjugation of church to market. The language of the church in worship has been coopted so as to signify the world—albeit the world in Christian garb. Because of our desire to equate marketplace ideals such as "success" and efficiency with Christianity to appeal to the greatest number of North Americans, we have been like Esau, so hungry during the latter part of the twentieth century for evidence of our relevancy that we have sold our birthright—to be the body of Christ in the power of the Holy Spirit for the transformation of the world. And like Esau, we have paid dearly in that later generations of North Americans want nothing to do with our amalgamated religion, even though they desire "spiritual encounters," and long for authentic community where they can share their problems without fear of rejection and find hope and acceptance.

The question is, "how then can we begin to unravel the mess that we have made and reclaim our both our mission and our identity?" Let me suggest that before we begin the process of unraveling, we must clearly identify what the key issues are that led us to this state in light of our identity and mission. Second, we must be clear that the unraveling is not our work. It is the work of the triune God through the power of the Holy Spirit that is always working, not to assist us in having a clean heart, but in creating in us a clean heart (Ps 51: 10). This suggests that we must be clear that the healing and renewal of the church is not based on our efforts, but rather is the agency of the triune God through us. Thus, in this process of unraveling, we will have to remember that we are simply the branches and not the vine. The fruits of conversion and sanctification are not up to us, but are up to God (John 15 and Acts 2: 47). In this way, it is critical that we are clear about what means of grace God has extended to us so that we might be more fully open to the power and presence of God, so that it is not we who live, but Christ who lives within us. Simply put, if the North American church is to thrive as the organism (i.e., the Body of Christ), then it must be committed to understanding that what the Bible teaches is that God is not a God of resuscitation, but of renewal and re-creation. Contrary to the belief of some, the North American church will not be renewed by resuscitation—going back to the glory days of the past and re-implementing the strategies of forty or fifty years ago.[1] We can, however, review the rich storehouse of Scripture, sacraments, and the theology and practices of those revivalists who found themselves in times similar to ours to see how we regain our birthright as those called

---

1. What I have in mind here is the practice of some mainline and evangelical denominations practice of church revitalization that emphasizes obtaining a new young, and often heterosexual male pastor, in order to attract young families that can serve as "implementers" of the church's past life. I am also critiquing the "vampire theology" of some churches that swoop on young adults, in particular young marrieds with children, as having the "life blood" the church so desperately needs to survive.

to be in union with the triune God made known to us in Jesus Christ in the power of the Holy Spirit.

As a means of looking at this unraveling in this final chapter, we will attempt to summarize the problem of the church that the issues point to, then discuss how a Wesleyan—albeit United Methodist—understanding of the importance of the sacraments not only helps the church to reclaim both its mission and identity, but also serve to "rebuild the altar" as Elijah did in the quoted Scriptures above so that the people, both those within the church and those outside, can discern the triune God we worship in a pluralistic culture in which the church has become a syncretized and poor imitation of what God intended. Further, to assist us in our analysis by reviewing our initial questions around the poor practice of the sacraments, we will delve into the work of the impact of ritual on formation. Next, utilizing, the work we have already done in understanding the Wesleys' sacramental theology, we will describe what living sacramentally as Christians—albeit Wesleyan, United Methodist Christians—might look like. Finally, we will offer some suggestions as to how current United Methodist church leaders might reclaim this Wesleyan sacramentally for themselves and their congregations as more than "the next new program," but rather as the organizing principle for their self-understanding in terms of their overall identity and mission.

Summary of the Problem: The Substitution of Consumer-Market Christianity for Biblical Christianity

When we review the current issues with regard to evangelism and mission along with the biblical narratives of the early church, especially as found in the book of Acts, we can surmise that, for the most part, the modern church is off mission. In fact, when one carefully reviews the Pew study on the "nones," what one finds is that the fundamental reason for the increase in the "spiritual, but not religious" category is that many of these persons have had experience with the church and find it lacking. Specifically, the Pew researchers contend that the reason for the primary reasons for the decline are that organized religion is "judgmental, homophobic, hypocritical, and too political."[2] In addition, Sally Morgenthaler, in her research on the "seeker-service movement," found that contrary to the belief that what draws seekers is giving them what they want from a

---

2. Pew Forum on Religion and Public Life, "'Nones' on the Rise," 29.

consumeristic stand point, what seekers want is to participate in a community that helps them to meet and worship God, not to be entertained.[3] Simply put, what both the Pew researchers and Morgenthaler found was that when people came to church, they were not looking for a political activist organization, neither an entertainment venue. What the people wanted was the opportunity to experience the presence of God. Although written in the late 1990s, these words from Morgenthaler, which excerpts from William Hendricks' 1993 book *Exit Interviews: Revealing Stories of Why People Are Leaving the Church* and Chuck Lofy's 1993 taped presentation "The Voices of Change," seem to be a prophetic warning of the current place where we find ourselves:

> The most significant benefit of a worship service is connecting with God. It does not matter how chatty and interesting the celebrity interviews, how captivating the drama, how stunning the soloist, or how relevant the message. When personal interaction with God is absent, church loses much of its appeal. Hendricks warns, *"It's a serious matter, because the question, Where is God?—the doctrine of God's imminence—lies at the heart of why people come to church. They expect to find God there. And why not? If you can't find God in a church . . . then where can you find Him [sic]?* Chuck Lofy agrees. "When the church is no longer a sacrament, when the church is no longer transparent to the divine and people don't feel the presence of God, they will drift, unless all they want is the security of forms."[4]

Furthermore, Morgenthaler also found that when churches were more focused on addressing members, and potential members' needs, these churches were more likely to be an "essentially insulated, narcissistic subculture, involving very few people outside of our own churches," less likely to share the gospel with others and less likely to tolerate questions, doubts or the people who hold views radically different from theirs.[5]

Paul Metzger summarizes these findings by maintaining the church has become a "fallen power" that is unable to provide a corrective to hyperindividualistic, consumeristic North American culture that is unable to discern between the triune God's forces for good and "the powers of darkness disguised as angels of light" (2 Cor 11:13–14). Metzger

---

3. Morgenthaler, *Worship Evangelism*, 21–23.

4. Ibid., 24.

5. Ibid., 27.

describes the fallen nature of many North American evangelical churches when he writes,

> The church becomes a fallen power when it loses sight of its fundamental allegiance to the God's kingdom, when it becomes proud and autonomous and thus distorted in its use of power, seeking political advantage in the secular sphere so as to win benefits for its members, benefits that will allow them to achieve and maintain a Laodicean standard of living and leisurely life-style, as they are—in the meantime—reduced to a function of the state, market and consumer culture. How, then, are we to battle the Balrog [i.e., the sin or demon] that is within each of us? We will not be able to conquer the consumer Balrog by catering to affinity groups. We will only be able to conquer the Balrog when a profound sense of inclusive beloved community centered in the triune God consumes us.[6]

While Metzger focuses the majority of the argument on evangelical Christians, highlighting the fact that evangelical Christianity's emphasis on individual piety and otherworldliness prevent them from evaluating current social contexts and structures (and understanding how these structures and systems benefit them at the expense of others), I contend that his argument with regard to the church as a fallen power is also applicable to those churches that focus solely on the social justice aspects of the gospel, which are typically referred to as liberal. I suggest that at issue in both cases is a clear understanding of what it means to be the church that understands itself as

> a power instituted by God . . . designed with the particular mission of bearing witness to God's advancing kingdom of beloved community through participation in the crucified and risen Christ, and of being consumed by him on behalf of the world for which Christ died. As such, that beloved community [the church] should be breaking down divisions between male and female, Jew and Gentile, slave and free, and it should be confronting those demonic forces that distort and reduce people to races and classes, to rugged individuals in isolation, people whose values lie in how much they produce and consume.[7]

While it may be the case that there are churches in which the boundary between church and world is almost indistinguishable except for the

---

6. Metzger, *Consuming Jesus*, 37.

7 Ibid., 36.

language used, all churches are destined to become fallen when they forget that the reason for their being and the source of who they are lie in their love for God. What Metzger forgets in his analysis is that in Revelation, the church at Ephesus was found wanting as well in that while it was good at maintaining the works of the Lord, it had been negligent in the love of the Lord of the works. And when the Lord of the work is neglected then both churches become fallen powers in that something other than the triune God becomes the object of their worship. The problem of both the Laodicean and Ephesian churches is that they have forgotten that it is their worship of Jesus Christ as Lord and their understanding that it is in the power of his spirit that they are able to do anything that should drive their ethics (i.e., mission) and evangelism. Fundamentally, what both churches have forgotten is that it is being consumed by and assured of the love of God that allows one to love oneself and others in the manner that God does in the power of the Holy Spirit—and that should determine the ministry, evangelism, and mission of the church. Or to put it another way, *lex orandi, lex credendi, lex vivendi, lex agenda*—the law of prayer/worship orders our beliefs, our lives, and what must be done.

It can be asserted that this is the way of Jesus and the early disciples of Christ. All throughout the Gospels, we are told that Jesus retreated to spend time in prayer with God and that this was the source of the fulfillment of his mission. In fact, of all the things that the disciples could have asked—teach us to do miracles, teach us to preach like you, they only asked Jesus one thing—teach us to pray. Furthermore, while Jesus was clear with regard to his mission, he was also very clear he understood his mission as being an emissary of the One who sent him. It can also be ascertained from the gospels that the entirety of Jesus' life and ministry of which, he commissioned the church to emulate was done in the power of the Holy Spirit. As recorded by the early followers of Christ also understood themselves as being sent by the Sent One Jesus in the power of the Holy Spirit. Their ministry, which can be argued was both priestly and prophetic centered on the finished and salvific work of Christ and what this meant for them and the world in terms of ushering in the reign of God that was both present and not yet. Furthermore, a quick perusal of the New Testament, in particular, the book of Acts, provides ample evidence that the sacrificial work of the early church was based on the grace and love of Christ.

Simply put, because of the sacrifice of Christ for them, they willingly sacrificed themselves for the spread of the reign of God. Furthermore, it can also be argued that they, in particular the apostle Paul, kept central the *missio Dei* and the necessity of the communal aspects of Christianity. They did this with a particular understanding of the culture of their day, building bridges between cultural norms and Christianity so as to incorporate others into Christianity without compromising its fundamental message. As such, it can be argued that pre-modern Christianity met the very current challenges of postmodern society and the concern for liberation and freedom for all those who are oppressed without becoming so relativized as to be indistinguishable from the very fallen powers, or anti-gods of its day. In fact, Christopher Wright, building on the work of Martha Frank, contends that we must interpret the Bible from this sort of missional hermeneutic which keeps central its worship of the triune God made known in Jesus Christ, and which is also able to hold within creative tension the cultural, local, relational, and narrative aspects of the text. Rather, than rely on the abstract nature of doctrines or on programs alone, Wright maintains that what the church has to offer the postmodern world in search of an encounter with God is a "coherent story with universal claim" that affirms "humanity in all of its particular cultural variety" without losing the cohesion of the story.[8] Carl Braaten also makes this point when he writes, "This Trinitarian grounding of mission should make clear that God and not the church is the primary subject and source of mission. Advocacy is what the church is about, being God's advocate in the world. The church must therefore begin its mission with doxology, otherwise everything peters out into social activism and aimless programs."[9]

Thus, taking into account the work of Morgenthaler, Metzger, Wright, and Braaten, it would seem then that at the heart of what the church must do is to make worship that creates opportunities for those gathered to participate in encountering the God in which we worship, such that all are transformed in the encounter. Now that we understand what must be done, the question of how now comes into view. However, before we can offer suggestions into the what, or even understand how we might discern a path that is faithful to our Wesleyan, albeit United Methodist roots and which answers our initial question of whether or not a more "faithful practice" of the sacraments might assist us in developing Christ-centered, Spirit-empowered communities focused on the love of

8. Wright, *Mission of God*, 46–47.
9. Braaten, "Mission of the Gospel," 127.

God and love of neighbor, and which serve as a sign and foretaste of the reign of God to a watching world, it will be helpful if we take a small detour to understand the way in which rituals work in the formation of persons and communities.

Understanding the Impact of Ritual on the Formation of Persons and Communities

In a provocative essay entitled "The Science of the Sacraments: The Being and Becoming of Persons in Community," Brent Peterson utilizes the science of ritualization to answer the question of how rituals, specifically communal rituals transform or malform individuals and communities. To determine the effects of rituals on individuals and communities, Peterson highlights the work of Arnold Van Gennep, Victor Turner, Ron Grimes, Tom Driver, and Mary Douglas, which directly concern rituals of initiation, liminality and the rise of communitas in liminal spaces. While Peterson's work is quite extensive, we will only highlight those areas that are pertinent for our discussion.

First and foremost, Van Gennep has found that in "modern," "civilized," Western societies there is a growing absence of communal rituals that are there in cultures that are perceived to be "less civilized." The loss of communal rituals is especially so with regard to those rituals that are rites of passage. According to both Van Gennep and Grimes, although these supposedly more "civilized and modern" societies have less communal rituals, they are nonetheless highly ritualized, it is just that the rituals are "far less intentional and embodied" and are designed to produce autonomous individuals.[10] Thus, rather than developing community (*communitas*), these rituals produce collectives—loosely held groupings of persons who are gathered in the same place at the same time, who are primarily concerned with individual concerns and who deem themselves as having the freedom of movement in and out of the group at will.[11]

10. Peterson, "Science of the Sacraments," 180–81.

11. The difference between a collective and *communitas* is that in a collective the totality of the group is limited to the sum of the individuals, whereas with a *communitas*, there is an overarching bond such that the group is greater than the sum of the individuals while at the same time being affected by each individual. An example would be consumers at a Walmart. Although there is a large number of consumers and it would seem that they are at Walmart for the same purpose, these consumers are more committed to how Walmart meets each of their individual needs (or perhaps

Further, Peterson contends that the loss of communal rituals in western culture is due to two primary factors. First, he maintains that rituals have become "disembodied from the community narrative from which they were birthed." Thus, like our earlier joke regarding the newly married couple and the truncated roast, rituals become rote and the people become ritualists, meaning that we continue to do the rituals because this what we have always done, not because they have any meaning for us or because we have any commitments to them. Furthermore, once a ritual loses its ability to speak to the real life situations of the persons that are engaged in them, Driver suggests that "ritual boredom" sets in, which further separates the ritual from the person who is engaged in them. In this way, rituals/rites are reduced to ceremonies that have little to do with the communities that gave rise to them, which means that the value of the community that produced them becomes increasingly irrelevant. Thus, even though the ritual may have been important in the formation of a community, people may engage in them for reasons other than the original intention. For example, many Christian rituals such as baptisms, burials, and marriage have become such that it is perceived that anyone can conduct these or that these are simply the "products" that churches and/or other religious organizations offer to the wider community. According to Peterson, in this way what are meant to be significant rituals in the church are now reduced to mere civic duties.[12]

The second reason that rituals lose their value is that in societies that value reason and rational discourse, rituals are highly suspect in that we are not sure that they "do" anything.[13] The point here is that when everything is reduced to what can be explained, then rituals can be abolished because they are determined to be irrelevant and unimportant. Building on the work of Louie Marie Chauvet and Mary Douglas, Peterson explains the danger of this position when he writes,

---

the needs of their families) than they are to one another (a fact easily demonstrated by the number of fights that have broken out in recent years during Christmas sales at Walmart). The primary issue is one of allegiance in that in collectives people continue to attend these as long as their individual needs are met; but as soon as someone can better meet their needs or if they feel as if their needs are not being met, they leave. The relationship to the overarching entity (i.e., Walmart) is only as good as the last transaction. So, in essence, there is not a "communal" experience, but the same individualized experience happening a multiplicity of times.

12. Peterson, "Science of the Sacraments," 182–83.

13. Ibid., 182.

It seems that this issue of being a ritualist is the very excuse that many evangelical Protestants use in their derision of high liturgy and weekly celebration of the Eucharist. Douglas suggests that many Protestants denounce what they view as irrelevant rituals, oppose ritualism as a whole and prefer and "exaltation of the inner experience and denigration of its standardized expressions; preference for intuitive and instant forms of knowledge; rejection of mediating institutions . . . In its extreme forms of anti-ritualism is an attempt to abolish communication by means of complex symbolic systems.

It begs an important question as to whether Protestants in their allegiance to modernity hold "truth" captive by being skeptical of the sacramental and symbolic world. Mystery and paradox are often equated with that which is irrational or ignorant. Hence, many in the evangelical culture no longer see the need for naïve archaic rituals, but prefer knowledge and spiritual formation through instantaneous cognitive assent to propositional statements or individual emotions. This position is dangerous. Louis Marie Chauvet suggest that the denial of mediation and claim of divine immediacy is the very definition of idolatry. . .Only by doxologically acknowledging God's otherness and absence can God be truly encountered as such. *If God's transcendence is collapsed into complete immanence, that idea of "god" quickly becomes idolatrous* [emphasis mine].[14]

In addition to the idolatry that can arise in terms of this collapse between immanence and transcendence, Grimes suggests that persons will utilize the rituals in an appropriate ways such as personal growth or self-enhancement as a means to navigate various rites of initiation or when encountering life transitions. When these rituals are dislocated from the community, it still leaves persons isolated and alone, left to navigate the mysteries of life on their own. When this occurs, Grimes contends that persons attempt to cannibalize the rituals of other societies in order to "name and bring to light that which ambiguous and powerful." Thus, while persons may participate in rituals designed to foster community, once the ritual is over and because the ritual has been dislocated from its communal function in the past and in the present, then persons are still left with feelings of isolation and loneliness.[15]

14. Ibid., 183.
15. Ibid., 186.

The solution for disembodied rituals and the overreliance on reason is to first understand that authentic rituals *transform* both the person and the community because of three primary aspects of rituals: "First, [authentic] rituals embody the values of a group where the past is made present; second, rituals create liminal space in an anti-structure which enables the work of transformation and thus transitions person and groups of people into these newly remade structures and communities; and third, in liminal space, the group going through a ritual can become a *communitas*."[16]

Simply put, embodied rituals tell us who we are and whose we are by providing identity for those within the group by affirming that those present are part of a continuing tradition that is being refashioned such that they communicate to modern day participants the meanings of the past that defined the group. Rituals also create liminal space—space that is not the past, nor the future, but rather can be called the "in-between" space in which persons are invited to leave the old behind so as to be prepared for a future status. Once persons enter this liminal space, then there is opportunity for something new to arise and/or for renewal to occur. Peterson maintains that it is in the context of liminality, or this in-between time and space that communitas occur. Furthermore, because these communitas occur in liminality, they have a unique perspective by which to critique structures outside of the communitas which means that they can become loci for radical transformation in society. Peterson explains the radical nature of communitas in liminality when he writes:

> Within *communitas* there is an underlying equality and union that attempts to throw off social status and titles. It is a recoiling from a self-referential identity. It is in this facing of others where individuals really become united as persons in community. As opposed to institutional structures which offer a cognitive encounter between persons, "communitas has an existential quality; it involves the whole [person] in his[her] relations to other whole [persons]." It is an embodied and existential encounter allowing person to really be encountered as such and thus become.
>
> . . . *Communitas* in liminality is dangerous because it calls outside structures into question . . . that which is holy is dangerous and ambiguous, calling structures into question. *Communitas* often occurs among the marginalized who become groups of

16. Ibid., 187.

social transformation against the very structures that marginalized them.[17]

As demonstrated in an earlier chapter the sacraments, both baptism and Eucharist, when combined with a robust liturgical practice, are
meant to be embodied rituals that tell those present and those watching
who and whose those gathered are. In the United Methodist liturgies of
both baptism and Eucharist, those present are reminded that they have
entered liminal space where not only Christ and they are present, but
they are in the midst of a kingdom that has already begun, is present and
is yet to come. The liturgies also further remind those who participate,
that they have become *communitas*, not only with humanity, present and
past, but in the fact that they are mystically enveloped into the life of the
triune God by virtue of their baptism into the body of Christ and their
partaking of the bread and wine of Eucharist. Specifically, as both Wesley
explains in his abridgement of Brevint's *On Christian Sacrament and Sacrifice*, the practice of the sacraments, in particular, the Eucharist, are not
to be ceremonial or memorial. Rather, the *anamnesis*, the remembering
of Christ's atoning work, is to create a re-membering that has implications for how those who participate are to live in community with one
another and in response to the world.

If the sacraments are to enable participants to fully comprehend
and embody what they practice such that the liturgy does not become
dead, then we must keep in mind Mary Douglas' caution against creating
ritualists. Ritualists, as Douglas asserts, are those who perform "exter-
nal gestures which imply commitment to a particular set of values but
[they are] inwardly withdrawn, dried out and uncommitted."[18] To move
persons from being ritualists to being those whose inner commitments
equal their outer action, we must catechize those who participate in the
sacraments via liturgy, ethics and evangelism not only through our practices, but even more importantly with regard to how we embody these
at an organic level in terms of how we relate to one another within our
communities of faith and how we relate to those outside of them. Simply
put, is who we say we are as Christians in our practice of the sacraments
evidenced in how our churches are administered, how we tend to those
within and outside of our community, especially those who are the least,

17. Ibid., 192.
18. Douglas, *Natural Symbols*, 2.

the last, the lost and the lonely, and how we invite others to become parts of our faith communities.

How the Sacraments Help Us Reclaim Our Mission and Identity and Thereby Help Us Respond to the Current Issues and Challenges

As we have seen from the previous chapter, persons are choosing not to engage in traditional churches, not because they are not interested in God, but because they are not interested in the manner in which we have presented God. Simply put, what all of the research seems to suggest is that people within and outside of our congregations are sick and tired of "going through" the motions of traditional church and want an encounter with the living God that helps them deal with the pressures of life in the twenty-first century. It is tragic that in an epidemic in which approximately seventy-six million Americans report being lonely, and in which two million persons a day go to the Internet to search for questions about God, especially about how God can help them deal with the tragedies of their own life, that many report the church, especially traditional and mainline church, is the last place to find community and assistance with the questions of life. Far worse is the accusation that one cannot be vulnerable and/or authentic within the walls of most churches.

As Robert Martin reminds us, a return to the sacraments, not as disembodied rituals but as foundational to our understanding of the church as sacrament and, as such, an "actual embodiment and enactment of Christ," has the opportunity for the church to reclaim her missional focus and place our doctrinal, institutional, and practical work of the church in their proper place—as the "means to the primary objective of living the 'way' [of Christ]."[19] In this way, our worship directs the totality of what we do and who we are. Understanding the church as a sacrament in and of itself serves as a rubric that reminds us the church is not a kind of institution, albeit a religious one, but rather an organism. When the church believes that its primary function is that of institution, then we forget our sacramentality and thus collapse the symbol and what it signifies. The other problem is that when we privilege the church as institution, then we forget that the church receives her sustenance from God, not because of clever techniques or gimmicks. As sacrament, the church's primary task

19. Martin, "Toward a Wesleyan Sacramental Ecclesiology."

as signifier is to serve as sign(witness), foretaste and an instrument of the reign of God as inaugurated by Jesus' death.

But to be sacramental, the church has to regain a full appreciation of those particular sacraments in which Christ has promised to be with us—baptism and Eucharist. In addition, our practice of the sacraments cannot be to reduce them to mere disembodied memorials or ceremonies of Christ's past work, but they must also point us to Christ presence with the sacraments are practiced and help persons to understand how our union with Christ in his sacrificial offering for us is that which determines our life together, not as a collective of individuals consuming Christ, but as a individual members of one body that are called to give itself as an offering to the world.

While the work of the United Methodist Church in sacramental renewal, especially the work done in both *By Water and the Spirit*, the document on our baptism practices, and *This Holy Mystery*, the problem has been that many congregations received this information "as one more tool to help us grow," and subordinate to the preached word and the many programs of the church, rather than as foundational as preaching to the life of the church. In many ways, these studies provided most of us with information, but little was done to help many pastors understand the sacraments on a practical level. Thus, although while many appreciated the importance of the sacraments, there was little to no link on how these related to church growth. In era of seeker-services in which time was of the essence and the emphasis was on not doing anything that made unchurched persons uncomfortable, the sacraments were reduced either in their frequency or in terms of following the liturgy. In addition, for those traditions that practiced the sacraments more frequently, the way in which they were practiced either as ceremony/memorial and the elements used (individual wafers or individual wafer/cups). Added to this was the fact that some televangelists and megachurch preachers who rightfully understood that the Christ's sacrifice in the sacrament secured benefits for partakers of the sacraments began to emphasize that persons should commune daily by hawking individual wafer cup/combination or

books, which reduced the meaning of the sacrament into spiritual vitamins, guaranteeing to make one healthy, wealthy and wise.[20]

For the Wesleys the sacraments were not complements to the "main
components of church life," (i.e., the preached word, programs and
administration), they were integral and foundational. Simply put, for
Wesley salvation is not possible without baptism and Eucharist. This is
evidenced in his sermons and other works, especially his "A Treatise on
Baptism," "The Marks of New Birth" and "The Duty of Constant Communion." Wesley understood the purpose of the sacraments to be salvific in that they served as the means for justifying and sanctifying grace
which culminated in union with Christ and other believers. In this way,
the sacraments help to make manifest "a communion which is cultivated
in the Eucharist as personal and corporate (social) holiness of heart and
life, the defining characteristic which is love." In this way, the sacraments
do not serve only as ceremonial, or disembodied ritualistic symbols of
Christ's previous work; but rather as conduits for God-human encounters regardless of space and time. For Wesley, baptism makes possible the
mystical union between believers and God and other believers, while the
Eucharist continues to foster and develop that union such that persons
are growing in love of God and of neighbor—personal and social (corporate) holiness.

20. From a transcript between televangelists Paula White and Perry Stone on
the Paula White show, October 9, 2004 in which both Stone and White insinuate in
the following conversation that by buying Stone's book and taking communion, one
would receive a magnificent financial blessing:

Paula White: "I believe that as you take communion that there is protection through
that blood. Then the Bible declares that the blood not only saves us, not only protects
us, but it also provides for us. You said there's a couple that we know very dear that
had a financial need."

Perry Stone: "Yes!"

Paula White: "And their father, a great pastor, pastor Scott told them God gave him
a revelation."

Perry Stone: "Yes."

Paula White: "To take communion once a day."

Perry Stone: "He said, 'Take it everyday and as you're praying thank God for blessing you financially. Thank Him that that's part of the provision. They needed $50,000
and they got an amazing, remarkable $50,000 miracle, this couple did!'"

Paula White: "Call that toll free number! We want you to get the 'Meal That Heals!'"

Televangelist and Pastor Gregory Dickow offers a 30-day prepackaged self-contained communion kit for individuals and emphasizes that through daily communion,
one is "to take communion today over a situation where you don't feel God has turned
to your favor." (See Thorton, "Can You Say, 'Uh-Baugh-Mih-Nay-Shun?'")

The difference it would seem between the Wesleys and many main-line denominations who are focusing on people in the pew by placing their emphasis on seeker-services designed not to alienate persons or programs that appeal to their growth as self-determined, self-actualized human beings is that the mission of "making disciples of Jesus Christ for the foundation of the world"[21] was understood in the context of holiness, not as a slogan for another cultural institution. Growing in love of God and love of neighbor was the underlying rubric by which everything else was developed as evidenced by the Wesleys' sermons, hymnody, liturgy, class meetings/bands and supplemental writings. Contrary to many modern sermons which focus on how God's power can be used to help persons "create the life they want," Wesley did not provide his listeners with simplistic platitudes that turned God into a genie and Scripture into motivational material, Wesley challenged his listeners as whether or not they had an authentic relationship of heart and head with the triune God that was accompanied by Christian faith such that "not only to believe that Holy Scripture and the Articles of our Faith are true, but also to have a sure trust and confidence to be saved from everlasting damnation by Christ. It is a sure trust and confidence which [humans] hath in God, that, by the merits of Christ, his [or her] sins are forgiven, and [s]he reconciled to the favor of God; whereof doth follow a loving heart, to obey [God's] commandments."[22]

Further because of his commitment toward the maturity, the Wesleys developed an entire schema utilizing class meetings, bands and creative worship services that provided Wesley's congregants with the means by which to grow in love of God and neighbor through mutually beneficial and disciplining/discipling relationships in which persons were accountable one to another. Also, as discussed earlier, Wesley understood the discipling of children to be critically important and also created materials for families to utilize at home to help their children grow in holiness. His insistence upon constant communion and his reworking of the Sunday service to include the *Hymns on the Lord's Supper* brought together catechesis and worship in ways that made deep theological concepts accessible to everyday persons. The liturgy and hymnody consistently reminded persons of Christ's salvific work and their obligation in union with Christ in the power of the Holy Spirit to engage in that work

21. This is the official mission statement of the United Methodist Church.
22. John Wesley, Sermon 2, "The Almost Christian."

with Christ—joyfully. Wesley also challenged his listeners with regard to how their love of God and love of neighbor was made manifest beyond the church in terms of evangelism and missions. Wesley's writings display that he clearly understood that love of God and love of neighbor included not only charitable works, but also required prophetic stands against injustice.

What is apparent when one reviews the corpus of materials developed by the Wesleys, is that they are consumed with saving souls and making mature disciples. Even in the cases where John Wesley is either summarizing or directly abridging other critical theological works to make them accessible, it is obvious that in so doing he did not lose their essential meaning. Furthermore, as in the case of Brevint's *Christian Sacrament and Sacrifice*, he often either added some practical dimension that further enhanced the catechesis of his followers. In the case of mission, charity and justice are not abstract ideas for those who "feel called" to such work. Wesley also does not allow persons to become too comfortable with their cultural status such that they can easily maintain their status while engaging with the poor or disenfranchised. Rather, as they were personally to John, consistent engagement with the poor, not only in works of charity, declarations against injustice or benevolent paternalistic friendships in which benefits were only seen as coming from those who were privileged, were vital components to growth in personal and corporate holiness. This is easily seen in Wesley's correspondence with Miss J. C. March, who lamented that she could not spend time with the poor because of her "busy schedule" in pursuing personal holiness and because of her belief that associating with the poor would be detrimental to her in that "good Christian persons should not associate with the poor," wherein he writes,

> I have found some of the uneducated poor who have exquisite taste and sentiment; and many, very many, of the rich who have scarcely any at all. But I do not speak of this: I want you to converse more, abundantly more, with the poorest of the people, who, if they have not taste, have souls, which you may forward in their way to heaven. And they have (many of them) faith and the love of God in a larger measure than any persons I know. Creep in among these in spite of dirt and an hundred disgusting circumstances, and thus put off the gentlewoman. Do not confine your conversation to genteel and elegant people. I should

like this as well as you do; but I cannot discover a precedent for it in the life of our Lord or any of His Apostles.[23]

Wesley further advocates in his correspondence with Miss March who believes that she can only grow in holiness through personal piety and by associating with people of her own social class is not "random acts of kindness" or "short-term missions" activities. Rather, Wesley is encouraging, and finally strongly recommending, is that Miss March seeks mutually beneficial friendships with the poor so that she can begin to know them as persons and not as projects. In fact, further in the letter, Wesley contends that without such friendships and because she has placed a higher emphasis on her social class, she will experience "lower degrees of usefulness and holiness than she is [you are] called to."[24]

It is this unrelenting emphasis on holiness matured through works of piety, which includes a robust theology and practice of the sacraments, in particular, the Eucharist, in creative tension with works of mercy (charity) and justice that provides rich and fertile soil for evangelism and mission work that early Methodists were known for. As we have noted earlier, whereas the worship services of early Methodists were enlivened and participatory, Wesley, by advising persons to go and develop friendships amongst the poor, disenfranchised and marginalized, Wesley demonstrated that one's worship of the triune God went beyond "religious" or liturgical activities within church, or within communities of faith that did not extend beyond one's social class. In this way, the faith communities he developed and mentored served as tangible witness to the reign of God in the midst of his day. Thus, Wesley also was able to interweave worship, ethics and evangelism such that church too demonstrates its own sacramentality by being the symbol of that which signifies.

Whereas it is easy to see how the Wesleys' theology and practice develop a sacramental ecclesiology that is heavily influenced by the constant practice of the Eucharist, the question still remains, if and how United Methodists might borrow from their theological forefather this theology and practice such that we might have a credible witness in the face of the issues facing the North American church in the twenty-first century. We will now turn our attention to how this might be done in ways that are comprehensive and comprehensible to the United Methodist Church at all levels.

23. John Wesley to Miss March, February 7, 1776, in Wesley, *Letters*, 6:206–7.
24. Ibid.

Living as Sacramental People: Towards a Sacramental Practice within and beyond the Church

When one looks at the key issues facing the church as it pertains to evangelism, it can be discerned that these issues arise from within the church. What I am suggesting is that we analyze the issues that face the church not so much a commentary about persons outside of the church or of a growing secularity, but rather as a barometer of the church's witness in a rapidly changing North American culture in which Christianity has been dislodged from her privileged position. Newbigin, Guder, and others clearly point to the fact that critical to the North American church's effectiveness is the realization that Christendom is dead. And while this knowledge is commonplace amongst scholars and perhaps even a few clergy, it is a fact that is widely unknown by many in our churches. Thus, many faithful church leaders and parishioners keep up practices that grow more and more ineffective daily in that they have no relation or relevancy to many within or outside of the church. Therefore, doing more of the same or trying variations of the same practices, prove to be ultimately unfruitful, even if they seem so for a time.

The second most critical element with regard to the issues facing the church concerning evangelism is that for many both in the pew and in the pulpit, our rituals have become disembodied from our theology and our heritage. While it is true that we as United Methodists have document after document, study after study, with regard to our theological and doctrinal beliefs, and that many churches in our denomination have developed mission statements based on the mission statement of the United Methodist Church—to make disciples of Jesus Christ for the salvation of the world—the truth of the matter is that in many ways the rituals developed around these theological and doctrinal positions often are simply the ways that persons go through the motions. In this way, these actions can be described as disembodied rituals that leave persons to make meaning of their practices for themselves unattached to their theological heritage. The Wesleys rightly understood that if they were to have persons committed to holiness—the love of God and the love of neighbor—they, in the spirit of English Armenians, sought to form those within the Methodist societies according to "primitive Christianity" and was able to do so due to the *ressourcement*.[25]

---

25. Westerfield Tucker, "Wesley's Emphasis on Worship," 227–35.

The key difference in this approach of the Wesleys and some of their modern North American descendants is that it can be said that the Wesleys practiced and privileged "Gospel," whereas their descendants practiced and privileged "mediating authorities" such as the Bible, doctrine and institutional maintenance/growth strategies (i.e., "seeker service"). Edward Farley describes the difference between the two types of practice (i.e., of Gospel vs. of mediating authorities) when he posits,

In this way the Wesleys and those within the Methodist Movement did more than "practice and privilege Gospel," they embodied it and by doing so demonstrated the church's sacramentality and witness. Their methodology was simply the means (in the same way that water, bread, and wine serve as means) they used to foster the embodiment and growth of the Body of Christ. For them, every aspect of the church's life—its worship/liturgy style, its process of catechesis and spiritual formation, and its works of charity and social justice—was designed to foster holiness, understood as love of God and neighbor, at every stage of Christian development. Simply put, each aspect of their organization did not serve as collection of individual elements, but rather was synergistic in that each aspect fed into one another such that the overall effect was greater than the sum of the individual elements. Their theology was not as much "practiced" as it was lived and embodied.

I suggest that under Christendom and even with the fine research and work done by academicians, clergy and judicatories regarding the sacraments, many North Americans churches have not been "practicing Gospel" such that it become habitus—an embodiment of the Gospel. They have either been practicing administration/ bureaucracies, therapeutic/ motivational/self-help, or moralistic organizations by subordinating the message of the Gospel to whatever gets the most bodies in the pews or are in congruence with prevailing popular religion. Edward Farley explains how orienting how churches function in their worship, evangelism and ethics according to the prevailing paradigms of our day—bureaucratic, moralistic, and therapeutic—has detrimental consequences for churches:

These three prevailing paradigms of ministry or leadership mirror and foster the prevailing trends of current secular society. A subtle secularism colors the congregation that focuses totally on the welfare of its individual member, offers to them moralizing or therapeutic bromides, and directs most of its energies to its own growth and success. When Gospel [i.e., *missio Dei*] is the congregation's paramount referent and symbolic world, bureaucracy, moralism and individualism may not disappear, but they will lose paradigmatic status. *When church leaders are oriented toward the prophetic summons of authentic faith, they resist defining themselves by their institutional functions. Their task is not simply to maintain the social institution but to assist a community of redemption to transcend its own self-orientation.*[26]

The reason why persons do not come to church or either self-identify as "spiritual but not religious" is because they can find what the churches are currently offering elsewhere—either face-to-face or online, and/or because they are seeking an encounter with God which will change them so that they can become world changers—exactly who the church is when she embodies Gospel. What I am proposing here is that the church analyzes how it uses the terms "practices" and "embodies," and which would lend itself more readily to helping persons to form Christian, albeit Wesleyan and specifically, United Methodist identities. For example the word "practices" can suggest that I engage in an activity that may have nothing to do with how I identify myself (i.e., "I practice painting, but I am not an artist"). The term "embodiment" relates to the fact that it is my identity that fashions my practices (i.e., "I am an artist, therefore I paint.") I suggest that a difference in terminology would first of all help us to claim our identity, first as Christians, specifically, as those who are Wesleyan, specifically United Methodist in our orientation. A difference in orientation from "practice" to "embodiment" would help us understand who we are individually and collectively. A re-orientation from "practice" to embodiment of Gospel who also have the effect of combating the prevailing notion of individualistic piety as the sole marks of the Christian faith in that our identities as Christians begin by being baptized *into a community of faith*, not as individuals; and that it is sustained by our relationship to the Eucharist not as a panacea for individual sin and/or a memorial service. Rather, a reorientation from "practice" to embodiment" means that we know and understand that in the liturgy of the sacraments is the memory of the life, death, resurrection of Christ, as well as the liturgical practice of the post-Paschal communities, which mandates mutually accountably discipleship and care and concern for fellow Christians, especially the poor and marginalized. It is an understanding that since they coincide with the birth of the church, the sacraments are but one important

26. Farley, *Practicing Gospel*, 10.

element of the formation and understanding of this Christian identity,[27] which includes *kerygma* (preaching and teaching), *koinonia* (fellowship), and *diakonia* (service).[28] It is to heed Augustine's words to recognize beginning with baptism one is baptized into a particular catholicity which has under the authority and teaching of the church that has a rightful claim to one's life.[29] As Louis-Marie Chauvet maintains,

> Christian identity is linked to the confession of faith Christians make their own and as a consequence to the meaning which, on this basis they give to their lives. Christian identity entails a personal commitment. However, this identity does not bypass the church as institution. Christian identity is not self-administered; to obtain it, one must receive baptism, and one does not baptize oneself; one is baptized by another person acting as the minister of the church in the name of Christ . . .
>
> . . . Similarly, there is a general pattern of Christian identity; it is impossible to call oneself a Christian if one does not adopt as one's own the few marks characteristic of a Christian.[30]

From understanding who are first, then our practices in the world would be driven by our identity, not by administrative, therapeutic or moralistic factors which do not have the wherewithal to stand against the anti-gods of hyperindividualism and rampant consumerism. By making all of practices the embodiment of who we are, we have the ability

---

27. Chauvet, *Sacraments*, xii.

28. See Farley, *Beyond the Formal Principle*, in which she contends that as important the relationship is between liturgy and ethics, that how the baptized live in community with one another communicates Christian identity to individuals within and outside the Christian community. Specifically, Farley asserts, "Many Christians experience the liturgy today, the public forms of worship in the church, as deadening not enlivening, impoverishing not enriching. With notable exceptions, there is a gap between the needs of the Christian believer and the present possibilities of shared worship. The human spirit is often dulled, distracted, burdened, as it is touched and awakened, freed in faith and hope. Far from "building up" the body of Christ, common worship often paralyzes it. The parity and reciprocity between believing, praying and living is not such that each is nourished by the other. Liturgical experience, to a great extent, is not one of opening to the presence of God among us, nor does it for in us dispositions of love in relation to our neighbor." Farley, "Beyond The Formal Principle: A Reply to Ramsey and Saliers," 191–202.

29. Augustine of Hippo, *Concerning Baptism* 5.8.9, as translated in Sheerin, *The Eucharist*, 272–73, See also MacIntyre, *After Virtue*, especially chapter 15, "The Virtues, the Unity of a Human Life and the Concept of a Tradition."

30. Chauvet, *Sacraments*, 19–20.

to create authentic community. The question now is what are some first steps that we can do this. ⌣

Back to the Future . . . A Way Forward That Claims Our Wesleyan Heritage in Embodied Ways

When we consider the renewal movement of John and Charles Wesley, we must keep in mind that the emphasis of their movement was not to make disciples of those who were unbaptized. The emphasis of their movement was how adults were living out the vows made in their baptisms and had they been born again. At question was not the faithfulness of God in their baptisms, but their unfaithfulness to God as evidenced by their lives; not whether God's Grace was made available in baptism, but had they responded to it or if they had responded, had "lost" it. Unlike other revivalists of his day, John Wesley was not convinced that those who "had made a decision for Christ" were indeed born again. Rather, he believed that those who had responded to his sermons were under convicting/converting grace.[31] As such, they lived with the faith of a servant attempting to please God by obeying God's commands in their own strength, but remaining under the power of sin. These persons, whom John referred to as "awakened," were now yearning for the new birth by which they would

> have power so to believe in thy name as to become a child of God; as to know and feel he hath "redemption in thy blood, even the forgiveness of sins;" and that he "cannot commit sin, because he is born of God." Let him be now "begotten again unto a living hope," so as to "purify himself as thou art pure;" and "because he is a son," let the Spirit of love and of glory rest upon him, cleansing him "from all filthiness of flesh and spirit," and teaching him to "perfect holiness in the fear of God!"[32]

Wesley also makes clear the distinction between having a form of godliness without experience an inward change in his sermon "The Almost Christian." For Wesley, although one may outwardly perform what would normally be considered Christian acts sincerely, without the assurance of Christ's atoning work for him/her personally which enabled them to grow in love of God and neighbor, they still had not experienced the new birth and were not yet born of the Spirit. While Wesley

31. Knight, "Significance of Baptism," 133.
32. John Wesley, Sermon 18, "The Marks of the New Birth," IV.6.

acknowledges that there are many who are not even "almost Christian," he is clear that good intentions or good deeds are insufficient to make one a Christian when he writes,

> But, supposing you had, do good designs and good desires make a Christian? By no means, unless they are brought to good effect. "Hell is paved," saith one, "with good intentions." The great question of all, then, still remains. Is the love of God shed abroad in your heart? Can you cry out, "My God, and my All"? Do you desire nothing but him? Are you happy in God? Is he your glory, your delight, your crown of rejoicing? And is this commandment written in your heart, "That he who loveth God love his brother also"? Do you then love your neighbour as yourself? Do you love every man, even your enemies, even the enemies of God, as your own soul? as Christ loved you? Yea, dost thou believe that Christ loved thee, and gave himself for thee? Hast thou faith in his blood? Believest thou the Lamb of God hath taken away thy sins, and cast them as a stone into the depth of the sea? that he hath blotted out the handwriting that was against thee, taking it out of the way, nailing it to his cross? Hast thou indeed redemption through his blood, even the remission of thy sins? And doth his Spirit bear witness with thy spirit, that thou art a child of God?[33]

Thus, the entirety of the Wesleyan movement was centered on helping persons progress from convicting/converting to justifying and sanctifying grace. As evidenced by the class system whereby members were held accountable to Methodist doctrine, and the sermons and treatises on the Christian life, John Wesley believed that that sanctification worked in the heart of every believer should be properly directed by effective catechesis and spiritual formation. Furthermore, Wesley's system of class meetings created a habitus whereby persons were incorporated into a community of love and discipline in such a way that they nurtured and were nurtured by it. More importantly, they were held accountable. In this way, the Wesleyan habitus created a system of catechesis that required more than mental assent or the performance of rituals without examination of one's life in the midst of community. When one surveys the sermons of John Wesley, and the work done by both Charles and John in *The Hymns on the Lord's Supper*, it is obvious that they understand their priestly function as mediators of holiness. The genius of the Wesleyan system was the creative

---

33. John Wesley, Sermon 2, "The Almost Christian."

tension which tied the embodiment of worship, ethics and evangelism together that was understood not to be a human creation, but rather as the work of the Holy Spirit within us (i.e., sanctifying grace). I suggest that a way forward would be to develop process (i.e. means) that are along the lines of worship, ethics and evangelism and that are oriented toward helping persons and congregations to embody holiness.

Sacramental Worship as an Embodiment of Holiness

First and foremost, we will have to help persons understand and embody Wesleyan theology. This is to say we have to help persons get past theological and doctrinal statements (i.e., mental or written assents) and help them discover ways to embody these in ways that have meaning within their contexts. For example, rather than asking candidates for ministry their written understanding of prevenient, justifying and sanctifying grace or doctrinal questions regarding the sacraments, a more pertinent question may be how often do they preach on sin or the need for justification. How often does the sermon relate to communion and in what ways? How often and how do they practice communion? How often do they teach their persons regarding communion? Is their practice of the sacraments ritualistic only or is it embodied, meaning how is it tied to tradition and made meaningful for the persons present so that they might understand that Jesus is present, or even the concepts of Sacrament and Sacrifice? These questions should go beyond Bible study and should be a part of the main worship services whenever they occur. Critical here would be what is their process to help ensure that persons understand and embody their Wesleyan, United Methodist Christian identity. In particular, it should be asked how catechesis during worship provides one with the opportunity of an encounter with God and participation with the gathered community.

I offer these as a way forward because a quick perusal of Wesley's sermons demonstrates a couple of things. First, it is obvious that his sermons are catechesis on the Christian faith, not platitudes about how to utilize Christian principles for a self-directed/self-actualized life now and in the hereafter (i.e., how the Bible makes you a better employee/parent, etc.). For the most part, his sermons challenge persons, especially those persons who could easily consider themselves "good" in understanding their need for justification and sanctification. His sermon on the duty of constant communion, which flies in the face of the practices of other Christian communities, but which seems to be more reliant on early church history, along with his abridgement of the Sunday Service provides no way out for those who consider the Eucharist either irrelevant or secondary to the Christian life. The *Hymns on the Lord's Supper* create a joyful atmosphere that catechizes persons through song that sings of grace and sacrifice. For Wesley, everything leads to Christ and Christ's Presence made known in the preached word, in the liturgy and in the sacraments.

In addition, the function of the sacraments go beyond worship. For the Wesleys, the sacraments have a discipling and disciplining function. Further, as with the other means of grace, there is a congruence between the sacraments as works of piety in tension with works of mercy and social justice. The sacraments are also not ends unto themselves, but like all means of grace, they are meant to foster holiness—personal and corporate which in turn extends beyond the faith community to evangelism and social justice. Evangelism and social justice are not the function of a few persons or only the clergy, they are the natural by-products of the Wesleyan pursuit of holiness and the submission of all activities to it. Thomas B. Dozeman makes the same assertion that the sacraments are the means by which holiness is not only transferred to the clerical order of believers but to all believers as the primary means by which they are meant to transform the world:

> The priestly vocation describes the status of a select group of humans, the priests, who become holy through sacramental ritual, allowing them to work safely in the presence of God in order to mediate holiness to the whole people of God. The priestly vocation requires that we explore the nature of the priesthood, especially in sacramental worship, and its continuing influence in ordained ministry. But the priestly vocation is never limited to priests in biblical literature. All biblical writers agree that the goal of the priestly vocation is for the entire people of God to become a priestly nation in service to the world . . .[34]

As demonstrated in our extended analysis of the Wesleys' *Hymns on the Lord's Supper* and John Wesley's sermons, it is obvious that within the Wesleyan theological framework is the insistence that every aspect assist believers from moving from awakening to embodying holiness in all

---

34. Dozeman, "Priestly Vocation," 117.

aspects of the lives of those called Methodists. And while no one would suggest that we full appropriate the Wesleys' methodology, it is obvious that we do need a pattern to assist us in helping that sacraments to be more than "spiritual vitamins" or empty rituals. I offer the following as a case study on how to proceed forward.

Corinth: A Biblical Case Study in Embodying Personal Holiness, Social Holiness, and Social Justice

Utilizing the sacraments as a means of discipling and disciplining persons so that they might embody holiness was not a new concept to the Wesleys. Both the Hebrew Bible and the New Testament are replete with examples of both prophets and apostle admonishing the people of Yahweh to embody in their dealings with one another and with those who were disenfranchised and most vulnerable in society this love and mercy extended to them by the grace of God. For example, Isaiah 58 recounts the prophetic response to the Israelites who are complaining that they have accurately and adequately performed God's required liturgical rituals with no corresponding blessing from Yahweh. Through the prophet, Yahweh responds that it is because the Israelites did not embody the holiness that the rituals portend, especially when they pertain to the poor and disenfranchised, but rather mimic the societal norms of those who around them. To rectify their situation, Yahweh explains that the people of God live in such a way that demonstrates their love of God is exemplified not only through liturgy, but through concomitant acts of social justice.

While Isaiah 58 demonstrates a biblical example of the link between sacramental practice, personal holiness, social holiness and social justice, the book of 1 Corinthians, specifically chapters ten through thirteen, provide an example that closer mimics contemporary society. According to Richard Hays, the ancient city of Corinth that Paul was writing to in the latter part of the first century was a city that was commercially prosperous, religiously pluralistic and very diverse. Corinth was also well known for its commitment to athletics in that the renowned Isthmian Games, an athletic festival held every two years which was second only to the Olympic games. In addition, the city of Corinth that Paul addressed was a relatively new refounded Roman colony that had been reestablished under Julius Caesar and populated with former slaves. Unlike many other Roman city-states, Hays notes that in particular, these former slaves enjoyed the particular status of being able not only hold office, but the opportunity to be elected as *duoviri*, the chief magistrates of the city. Thus, "Paul is writing to a church in a city only a few generations removed from it founding by colonists seeking upward mobility," a point which Hays contends suggests "a strong analogy between Paul's Corinthian readers" and American readers of the letter.[35] In addition to its prosperity and religious pluralism, Corinth was also well known for its sexual promiscuity and its mores regarding wealth and the mistreatment of the poor.[36]

We can surmise from Paul's correspondence to the church at Corinth in 1 Corinthian 11, that he is concerned not only with the unity of the church at Corinth along, what can only be argued as "interchurch denominationalism," but also how the church embodies the holiness that is implied in sacramental practice. In particular, this can be seen by a close reading of 1 Corinthians 10–12.

Paul first mentions the idea that the sacraments have both a unifying and a discipling effect on the Corinthian church in 1 Cor 10:1–4 when he repeats the story of the Exodus in terms of both baptism (verse 2) and Eucharist (verses 3 and 4). He also does something else interesting. He incorporates the Israelites into the people of God separated from the status quo of Egypt through the passing of the sea and by consuming "the same spiritual food and drink;" and also incorporates this mostly Gentile church into the Israelite story by using the word "forefathers" and contending that the rock that provide water to quench the Israelite thirst is the same Christ that provides spiritual food and drink for those who partake in the Eucharist. Paul continues his rhetoric and correlation of the Eucharist to the Jewish worship when arguing against eating meat sacrificed to idols when he writes,

> Therefore, my dear friends, flee from the worship of idols. I speak as to sensible people; judge for yourselves what I say. The cup of blessing that we bless, is it not a sharing in the blood of Christ? The bread that we break, is it not a sharing in the body of Christ? Because there is one bread, we who are many are one body, for we all partake of the one bread. Consider the people of

35. Hays, *First Corinthians*, 2–3.
36. Sampley, "First Letter to the Corinthians," 10:774–75.

Israel; are not those who eat the sacrifices partners in the altar?
What do I imply then? That food sacrificed to idols is anything,
or that an idol is anything? No, I imply that what pagans sacrifice, they sacrifice to demons and not to God. I do not want you
to be partners with demons. You cannot drink the cup of the
Lord and the cup of demons. You cannot partake of the table of
the Lord and the table of demons. Or are we provoking the Lord
to jealousy? Are we stronger than he? (1 Cor 10:14–22)

In addition to utilizing the baptism as constructive liturgy to re-
inforce the theme of unity within the body of Christ despite racial,
socioeconomic and denominational differences, in chapter eleven of 1
Corinthians, Paul's argument of verses 16 and 17 is picked up and more
thoroughly fleshed out in 1 Cor 11:17–34. First, as Walls, Sampley, and
Wright contend, for Paul, behavior is always grounded in the traditional
practice and teaching of the faith community. In 1 Cor 11:23 Paul bases
his condemnation on how the Corinthians practice the Lord's supper by
explaining that what he received from the Lord, he passed on to them.
While many commentators debate about whether Paul actually received
instructions from the Lord regarding the Eucharist, one thing is clear his
case against the behavior of the Corinthian church and more specifically
against its wealthier members is grounded in his reliance upon Christian
tradition to evaluate behavior.

Paul's condemnation of the Corinthians in their practice of the Lord's
Supper, stems from the church's tradition that the Eucharist re-presents
and represents the unification of all believers into the body of Christ, an
economic sharing and breaks down all barriers, in particular class barriers. While some scholars note that what Paul is confronting is how the
Corinthian church is celebrating what would be better understood as a
love feast, Hays maintains that what we now know as the Eucharist was
a part of a common meal.[37] Thus, Paul's critique is not one of doctrine
(i.e., "a problem of sacramental theology") but social relations. For it is
only the wealthier ones who can come early, and who gather together in
cliques, and who eat and drink without abandon while the less fortunate
go away hungry. For Paul the *anamnesis* (the remembrance of Christ's
life, death, and resurrection) is to remind those gathered of the new covenant relationship that requires to remember what Christ has done and
what one has committed to in this covenantal relationship—to love God
and neighbor wholeheartedly in thought, word and deed, and to be in

37. Hays, *First Corinthians*, 193.

solidarity with one another, especially those poor and disenfranchised. For Paul, the way that the wealthier Corinthians are eating and drinking at the Lord's Supper is slanderous because it does no re-present the reign of God that Jesus proclaimed and ushered in. Rather, their practice disregards the new covenant relationship that they are to have with Christ and one another, and reemphasizes the social mores that the Corinthians are supposed to be leaving behind.[38] For Paul to "eat the bread and drink the cup of the Lord unworthily" is not only a condemnation of personal sin. The failure to discern the body and blood of Christ, is to perform the liturgy correctly without behaving in a manner which represents and re-presents the body of Christ, but rather sacralizes the existing social structures that oppress. In other words it is to enter into the covenant in word only, without the corresponding actions and surely without the intention to have the sacrament shape one's life. Simply put, the sacraments have some claim on those who partake of them in terms of personal holiness, social holiness and social justice.

This notion of the sacraments as discipling and disciplining the body is further seen in Paul's further explanation of the how the Corinthian church is to embody the holiness implied in both their baptismal and Eucharistic practices in 1 Corinthians 12 and 13. In 1 Corinthians 12, Paul makes the point that because all have been baptized all are important and necessary; and more importantly neither racial (Jew or Greek) nor socioeconomic class stratifications (slave or free) are grounds for division, isolation and under or over utilization (1 Cor 12:12–13). The triune God has gifted, empowered and placed persons in the body of Christ based on God's design and God's choice. In fact, Paul makes the assertion, not only in chapter 12, but also early on that those whom the world would look down on are the very ones God has honored in a way that turns Corinthian and our cultural mores upside down (1 Cor 1:26–29; 12:21–25). Furthermore, for those who the world would deem "less than" or undesirable, the entire body is called to suffer with and to rejoice in God's honor of them. Paul's treatise on baptism, especially as it ties the body of Christ with the church and lifts up those who are disenfranchised has many implications for how we the church is to engage in social justice. In 1 Corinthians 13, Paul is clear, that while demonstrations of the presence of the Holy Spirit through charismatic gifts might be present, the true mark of the church is love or the embodiment of holiness, and

---

38. Long, *Goodness of God*, 161.

that Christian maturity is demonstrated when love as described in 1 Corinthians 13 is manifested within the integrated, incarnational body of believers.

Throughout the entire book of 1 Corinthians, two things are evident. First, Paul is basing his catechesis of the Corinthians on the tradition of the people of God; and second, that Paul is concerned with more than rote performance of church practices, liturgical and otherwise, or the demonstration of charismatic gifts. Not denying the emphasis on love of God, Paul is as clear as the prophet is in Isaiah 58. The liturgical practices are not ends, but rather the means of God's Grace; and how one embodies the holiness implied in them is important to the triune God.

Maple Park United Methodist Church: A Modern Case Study in Embodying Personal Holiness, Social Holiness, Evangelism and Social Justice

In the spring of 2006, I was asked to go to Maple Park United Methodist Church in the East Morgan Park/Maple Park community on the south side of Chicago as the interim pastor. As a doctoral student and commissioned candidate for elder in the United Methodist Church, I saw this as an opportunity to fulfill the requirements for ordination. In addition, as a former urban pastor and community developer/activist, I had been missing working with communities in the areas of community and economic development and social justice. Whereas most of my previous experience had been working with the poor and working class persons on Chicago's west side, the Maple Park opportunity would require that I work with a solidly middle, mostly college educated African American congregation who had planted their church some forty plus years prior to my arrival and who had fought hard to gain their socio-economic status by breaking through racial barriers in corporate, governmental and academic settings. Although my academic background clearly indicated that I was a "good fit" for this congregation and the type of pastor they were used to, in terms of academic training, I was unclear with regard to how my passion for urban ministry, especially amongst the poor and working class, fit this congregation. This would become evident in a few short months after my arrival and once I had been appointed as the Senior Pastor of this congregation.

It must also be noted at this time that my academic studies were taking a turn as well. I had just completed two courses that would forever mark me. The first was a course in Marxism and theology taught by the previous leader of several base communities in Brazil in which I first came across the term "organic intellectual." Second, I took an advanced theology course comparing the theology of Jürgen Moltmann and Jon Sobrino. As a final paper for this course, and after reading the book *Preaching to the Black Middle Class*, I argued for the need for middle-class African American churches to become more involved with the often very poor communities surrounding their churches. It was also at this time that I was reviewing the United Methodist's new literature on the sacraments in preparation for ordination. A worship professor had also suggested that I read *Torture and Eucharist*, by William T. Cavanaugh, given my increasing frustration over academic discussions that the frequent practice of the sacraments were sufficient to change behavior.

After several months of being at Maple Park, I noticed several things. First, our "church" was in fact, more social club than congregation. Second, although many in the congregation had been through every type of training the United Methodist Church had to offer, persons had often adopted the ritual, without understanding the full meaning behind it. Finally, I often had to justify why we did what we did either theologically or biblically, especially as it pertained to United Methodist theology, practice and doctrine because many in the congregation were more directly influenced by the mores of their socio-economic class, sorority/fraternity, social club and/or popular televangelists. The church was also highly divided because of socio-economic and familial cliques.

When I arrived, the immediate order of business was to get the congregation stable financially. As this happened, other issues began to emerge. None was more obvious than the growing disdain of the congregation for the new and poorer neighbors who were beginning to move into the community surrounding the church due to the regentrification that was occurring in Chicago's downtown. The folks in my church and the established folks in the community were highly outraged that the neighborhood they had fought so hard to secure and that the hard work they had done to leave behind the stigmas of race and class were about to be lost because of "those" people. Admittedly, they had some legitimate concerns. These new neighbors were younger and brought more children with them, were clearly inexperienced in maintaining single family homes, and brought an increasing element of drugs and violence closer to this community than it had experienced before.

More than anything else, I was amazed by language used by the congregation to describe persons who looked like them, and who, in many cases, had the same or worsening economic conditions than they had experienced a generation before. As an African American, I was appalled in that I could not believe that my congregation utilized the same terms regarding our new neighbors that had been used by the Anglo community towards them when they first arrived to Maple Park. Also, and probably because of the African American Christian congregations which had nurtured my formation, it was shocking that Christians, especially African American Christians, who prided themselves on their grasp of Black history were unwilling to engage, at least on a large scale, in W. E. B DuBois' concept of the "talented tenth" and saw as their African American Christian duty "the uplift of the race."[39]

In addition to the behavior towards our poorer, and often younger neighbors, the behavior of the congregation internally seemed to be more determined by the norms of their workplaces or because of non-UM religious traditions rather than by biblical or doctrinal standards. While many practiced high degrees of personal piety and had been exposed to much of the United Methodist training our annual conference or the denomination offered in terms of biblical study, church management and the like, these had little impact on how we lived our lives together. When I arrived, this congregation was also suffering from financial issues and from the loss of the previous pastor due to illness, as well as that of several key members, either due to illness or transfer of membership.

To begin to bring healing to this fractured community and in the midst of my aforementioned studies, in partnership with several leaders, we decided to do a few key things. First, the congregation asked if we might, as a congregation, go through Rick Warren's *Purpose-Driven Life: What on Earth Am I Here For?* as an all-church study, which included the Sunday services and small group studies for six weeks. During this

39. *Uplift* is a term utilized within African American circles, especially between slavery and the civil rights era, to describe both the personal and corporate spiritual and social transcendence of this worldly oppression and misery. It has also been utilized to describe African American liberation and advancement within democratic society, primarily through education. In this way, Kevin Gaines describes uplift as a form of African American liberation theology in which middle-class African Americans were tied to the Black masses by utilizing their privilege to assist others in attaining socioeconomic progress. For more on "uplift," see Gaines, *Uplifting the Race.*

time, we not only included the traditional small groups, but reached out to several young adults to lead and start a small group. Because of the success of this church-wide study, it was decided that we would bring in a consultant to work with the church to begin to vision what could be possible for us together as a church. Utilizing a strategic planning approached that highlighted the strengths, weaknesses, opportunities, and trends for this congregation, as well as Warren's *Purpose-Driven Church* to set our objectives against.

At this time, I changed the structure of our sacramental practice in that not only would Holy Communion be served every first Sunday, we would also conduct baptisms every fifth Sunday and reinstitute the Baptismal Remembrance Service. In addition, the sermons on the days of our sacramental practice would focus on the sacrament itself, relating the practice to early church and our current congregation's life together. While I acknowledged the United Methodist practice of "open communion," I also explained the implications of each of the components of the service (i.e., confession, passing of the peace, *epiclesis*). We also included the reciting of the Apostles' Creed during this time. With regard to baptisms, I was adamant that they would occur after a process of catechesis and commitment. Finally, we also changed the actual practice of the Eucharist, moving from individual wafers to whole loafs of bread; and using hand sanitizer rather than plastic gloves for those serving communion.[40] We also changed the worship songs during the Eucharist to include those which highlighted unity and the corporate nature of the church, as well as those which included atonement and personal piety themes.

As we made changes with the Sunday services, especially with regard to our practices of baptism and Eucharist, the sacraments and the Sunday service in its entirety became a way to discipline and disciple our congregation, both internally and externally. Our retreat highlighted the need and the call to move beyond our borders. Our worship practice served as a way for us to discuss how we were to treat our neighbors, internally and externally. Our worship practice, also became a way for us to discuss how we were going to operate as the body of Christ. We worked hard to

---

40. Prior to my arrival, the practice of using medical plastic gloves had been instituted because the senior pastor was working quite a bit with another UM congregation that ministered to the LGBTQ community, and there were some concerns that the congregation might be open to infection or disease. Although this change had happened during the late 1980s and early 1990s, this practice had not changed in ten years, even though some attitudes had.

stop using the language of nonprofits, to the language of the church (i.e., "who wants to volunteer?" v. "who is being called?"). The combination of the changes to our worship practices, our life together, spilled over into the way we evangelized and engaged in social justice such that at the completion of my tenure, the congregation had developed a community development corporation to meet the needs of the community and was regularly evangelizing the community surrounding their church.

Back Where We Started: Moving beyond Rote Practices

As the biblical and personal ministry examples demonstrate above, in order to assist congregations in moving beyond simply rote sacramental practices, more than catechesis is required regarding the "appropriate way" to conduct the practice. Teaching needs to be done with regard to the links, biblically and theologically, between liturgy, specifically sacramental liturgy, personal holiness, social holiness, evangelism and social justice (ethics). Specifically, an emphasis must be made on how the people of God, individually and corporately are to embody what their liturgical practices portend. As the discussion on rituals demonstrate, this teaching will need to be more than a Bible study or a book study, but rather needs to be the orienting, or as I have maintained the discipling and disciplining, way that the church understands its life together and its calling in the world. This is what it means to "practice Gospel." If those of us who are inheritors of both John and Charles Wesley, are to fully live into our Methodist, specifically United Methodist, heritage, then it is critical that not only a reclamation of the practices of baptism, reaffirmation of baptism and Eucharist occur, but that these dictate how we conduct ministry, especially as it pertains to evangelism and social justice. It is the only way that the church can begin to demonstrate that it is something different than the world and offer the panacea that the world, especially those who describe themselves as "spiritual, but not religious," so desperately desires.

Questions for Consideration

1. What are the dangers of a "consumer-market driven" Christianity?

2. How does consumerism offer a challenge to biblical Christianity?

3. What importance do rituals have on the formation of persons and communities?

4. What theological resources do John and Charles Wesley offer in terms of the formation of identity in the face of contemporary cultural challenges?

5. What does it mean to live as a sacramental people in the areas of evangelism, mission, and social justice?

6. How do the sacraments of Holy Communion and baptism provide a moral and theological alternative to the kind of administrative, therapeutic, and moralistic trends presently in vogue in North America?

7. How do the theologies of Charles and John Wesley assist the church in participating in God's mission in our contemporary context, specifically in terms of *a life of holiness?

8. How may the Wesleyan "habitus" of faith formation help the church today shape the identities of persons as they move from convicting/converting grace to justifying/sanctifying grace? What kind of mutual accountability in the life of the church needs to be cultivated to achieve this end?

9. What resources does the Wesleyan theological tradition offer in terms of discipling and disciplining? How are these two aspects of the church's witness related, and how did the early Methodist societies, bands, classes, and conference practice such means to attain such holy ends?

10. How might Christians in the Wesleyan theological heritage continue to embody holiness today as they go about living the gospel in the areas of mission, evangelism, and social justice? What contemporary challenges does the church face in these areas?

Bibliography

Abraham, William J. *The Logic of Evangelism*. Grand Rapids: Eerdmans, 1989.

Anna Howard Shaw Center. *Clergywomen Salaries*, Case Study. http://www.bu.edu/shaw/publications/umc-salary-study.

Arias, Mortimer. *Announcing the Reign of God: Evangelization and the Subversive Memory of Jesus*. Philadelphia: Fortress, 1984.

———. "Contextual Evangelization in Latin America: Between Accommodation and Confrontation." In *The Study of Evangelism: Exploring a Missional Practice of the Church*, edited by Paul W. Chilcote and Laceye C. Warner, 345–51. Grand Rapids: Eerdmans, 2008.

Augustine of Hippo. *Concerning Baptism* 5.8.9. Translated by Daniel J. Sheerin. In *The Eucharist*. Wilmington, DE: M. Glazier, 1986.

Barna Group. "Americans Divided on the Importance of Church." March 24, 2014. https://www.barna.org/barna-update/culture/661-americans-divided-on-the-importance-of-church#.U8QC-o1dUoJ.

Beesley, Caron. "Marketing to Seniors and Baby Boomers: Have You Seniorized Your Marketing Strategy Lately?" The U.S. Small Business Administration. http://www.sba.gov/community/blogs/community-blogs/small-business-matters/marketing-seniors-and-baby-boomers-have-you-s.

Behr, Thomas C. "Luigi Taparelli and Social Justice: Rediscovering the Origins of a 'Hollowed' Concept." *Social Justice in Context* 1 (2005) 3–16.

Billings, J. Todd. "What Makes a Church Missional?" *Christianity Today*, March 5, 2008, 56–59.

Borgen, Ole E. *John Wesley on the Sacraments: A Definitive Study of John Wesley's Theology of Worship*. Grand Rapids: Francis Asbury, 1985.

———. "John Wesley: Sacramental Theology No Ends without the Means." In *John Wesley: Contemporary Perspectives*, edited by John Stacey, 67–82. London: Epworth, 1988.

———. "No End Without the Means: John Wesley and the Sacraments." *Asbury Theological Journal* 46 (1991) 63–86.

Braaten, Carl E. "The Mission of the Gospel to the Nations." *Dialog* 30 (1991) 124–31.

Branaugh, Matt. "Willow Creek's 'Huge Shift.'" *Christianity Today*, June 2008, 13.

Brevint, Daniel. *The Christian Sacrament and Sacrifice*. New ed. Oxford: J. Vincent, 1847.

Brewer, Brian C. "Evangelical Anglicanism: John Wesley's Dialectical Theology of Baptism." *Evangelical Quarterly* 83 (2011) 107–32.

Brewer, Chris Boyd. "Music and Learning: Integrating Music in the Classroom." *New Horizons for Learning.* http://education.jhu.edu/PD/newhorizons/strategies/topics/Arts%20in%20Education/brewer.htm.

Brock, Rita Nakashima, and Rebecca Ann Parker. *Saving Paradise: How Christianity Traded Love of This World for Crucifixion and Empire.* Boston: Beacon, 2008

Brueggemann, Walter. *Biblical Perspectives on Evangelism: Living in a Three-Tiered Universe.* Nashville: Abingdon, 1993.

Canty, Kyle. "A Black Missional Critique of the Missional Movement." *Vergenetwork. org.* http://www.vergenetwork.org/2013/07/26/a-black-missional-critique-of-the-missional-movement/.

Carter, J. Kameron. *Race: A Theological Account.* New York: Oxford University Press, 2008.

Cavanaugh, William T. *Torture and Eucharist: Theology, Politics, and the Body of Christ.* Malden, MA: Blackwell, 1998.

Chauvet, Louis-Marie. *The Sacraments: The Word of God at the Mercy of the Body.* Translated by Madeleine Beaumont. Collegeville, MN: Liturgical, 2001.

Chilcote, Paul W., and Laceye C. Warner, eds. *The Study of Evangelism: Exploring a Missional Practice of the Church.* Grand Rapids: Eerdmans, 2008.

Choi, Hee An, and Jacqueline Beatrice Blue. "The Clergy Women's Retention Study II, Summary," 2013, 2. http://image.s4.exct.net/lib/fe891570706c0d7a7d/m/1/CW+Retention+Study+2.pdf.

Christopher, J. Clif. *Not Your Parent's Offering Plate: A New Vision for Financial Stewardship.* Nashville: Abingdon, 2008.

Cleveland, Christena. "Urban Church Planting Plantations." *Christena Cleveland* (blog), March 18, 2014. http://www.christenacleveland.com/blogarchive/2014/03/urban-church-plantations.

Coakley, Sarah. "Resurrection and the 'Spiritual Senses': On Wittgenstein, Epistemology and the Risen Christ." In *Powers and Submissions: Spirituality, Philosophy, and Gender*, 130–52. Oxford: Blackwell, 2002.

Cobb, John B., Jr. *Grace & Responsibility: A Wesleyan Theology for Today.* Nashville: Abingdon, 1995.

CSInvesting. "Fortune 500 Extinction." *csinvesting.org*, January 6, 2012. http://csinvesting.org/2012/01/06/fortune-500-extinction/.

Dean, Kenda Creasy. *Almost Christian: What the Faith of Our Teenagers Is Telling the American Church.* Oxford: Oxford University Press, 2010.

———. "Moralistic Therapeutic Deism?" Kenda Creasy Dean website. http://kendadean.com/moralistic-therapeutic-deism/.

Denning, Steve. "Peggy Noonan on Steve Jobs and Why Big Companies Fail." *Forbes*, November 19, 2011. http://www.forbes.com/sites/stevedenning/2011/11/19/peggy-noonan-on-steve-jobs-and-why-big-companies-die/.

Douglas, Kelly Brown. *What's Faith Got to Do with It? Black Bodies/Christian Souls.* Maryknoll, NY: Orbis, 2005.

Douglas, Mary. *Natural Symbols: Explorations in Cosmology.* New York: Routledge, 2002.

Downey, Michael. *Clothed in Christ: The Sacraments and Christian Living.* New York: Crossroad, 1987.

Dozeman, Thomas B. "The Priestly Vocation." *Interpretation* 59 (2005) 117–28.

Drane, John. *The McDonaldization of the Church: Consumer Culture and the Church's Future*. Macon, GA: Smyth & Helwys, 2012. Kindle edition.

Edmiston, John. "The Ubiquitous Gospel." Presentation given at Biola Digital Ministry Conference 2013. http://open.biola.edu/resources/the-ubiquitous-gospel?collection=biola-digital-ministry-conference-2013.

———. "The Ubiquitous Gospel: PowerPoint Presentation." *Cybermissions.org*. http://www.cybermissions.org/articles/The%20Ubiquitous%20Gospel.pdf.

Elwin, Toby. "The Cost of Culture, a 50% Turnover of the Fortune 500." *Toby Elwin* (blog), February 4, 2010. http://www.tobyelwin.com/the-cost-of-culture-a-50-turnover-of-the-fortune-500/.

Emerson, Michael O., and Christian Smith. *Divided by Faith: Evangelical Religion and the Problem of Race in America*. New York: Oxford University Press, 2000.

Farley, Edward. *Practicing Gospel: Unconventional Thoughts on the Church's Ministry*. Louisville: Westminster John Knox, 2003.

Farley, Margaret A. "Beyond the Formal Principle: A Reply to Ramsey and Saliers." *Journal of Religious Ethics* 7 (1979) 191–202.

Felton, Gayle Carlton. *By Water and the Spirit: Making Connections for Identity and Ministry*. Nashville: Discipleship Resources, 2013.

———. *This Holy Mystery: A United Methodist Understanding of Holy Communion*. Nashville: Discipleship Resources, 2005.

Ferrel, Lowell O. "John Wesley and the Enthusiasts." *Wesleyan Theological Journal* 23 (1988) 180–87.

Finke, Roger, and Rodney Stark. *The Churching of America, 1776–1990: Winners and Losers in Our Religious Economy*. New Brunswick: Rutgers University Press, 1992.

Gaines, Kevin K. *Uplifting the Race: Black Leadership, Politics, and Culture in the Twentieth Century*. Chapel Hill: University of North Carolina Press, 1996.

Global Media Outreach. "How Can I Reach the World for Christ?" Global Media Outreach. http://www.globalmediaoutreach.com/.

Guder, Darrell L., ed. *Missional Church: A Vision for the Sending of the Church in North America*. Grand Rapids: Eerdmans, 1998.

Hamm, Robert L. *Recreating the Church: Leadership for the Postmodern Age*. St. Louis: Chalice, 2007.

Harrell, Pat E. "Jewish Proselyte Baptism." *Restoration Quarterly* 1 (1957) 159–65.

Hawn, C. Michael. "Hymnody and Christian Education: The Hymnal as a Teaching Resource for Children." *Review & Expositor* 87 (1990) 43–58.

Hays, Richard. *First Corinthians*. Interpretation: A Bible Commentary for Teaching and Preaching. Louisville: John Knox, 1997.

Hultgren, Arland J. "Baptism in the New Testament: Origins, Formulas and Metaphors." *Word & World* 14 (1994) 6–11.

Hunter, Justus H. "Toward a Methodist Communion Ecclesiology." *Ecclesiology* 9 (2013) 9–18.

Idleman, Kyle. *Not a Fan: Becoming a Completely Committed Follower of Jesus*. Grand Rapids: Zondervan, 2011.

Immersion Active. "Resources 50+ Facts and Fiction." Immersion Active. http://www.immersionactive.com/resources/50-plus-facts-and-fiction/.

Jennings, Theodore W., Jr. *Good News to the Poor: John Wesley's Evangelical Economics*. Nashville: Abingdon, 1990.

Jones, Scott J. *The Evangelistic Love of God and Neighbor: A Theology of Witness & Discipleship*. Nashville: Abingdon, 2003.

Kallenberg, Brad. *Live to Tell: Evangelism in a Postmodern World*. Grand Rapids: Brazos, 2002.

Keefer, Luke L. "John Wesley, the Methodists and Social Reform in England." *Wesleyan Theological Journal* 25 (1990) 7–20.

Kinnaman, David, and Gabe Lyons. *Unchristian: What a New Generation Really Thinks about Christianity and Why It Matters*. Grand Rapids: Baker, 2012.

Klaiber, Walter, and Manfred Marquardt. *Living Grace: An Outline of United Methodist Theology*. Nashville: Abingdon, 2001.

Knight, Henry H. "The Significance of Baptism for the Christian Life: Wesley's Pattern of Christian Initiation." *Worship* 63 (1989) 133–42.

LaBoy, Felicia Howell. "Women by the Numbers: U.S. Women, Racial-Ethnic Clergy Increase; Still in Smaller Pulpits, More Likely to Leave Pastoral Ministry." *The Flyer*, December 2012. http://www.gcsrw.org/Portals/4/WomenByTheNumbers/2012/2012_12_WBTN.pdf.

Law, William. *A Demonstration of the Gross and Fundamental Errors of a late Book*. 2nd ed., corr. London, W. Innys and R. Manby, 1738.

Lohfink, Gerhard. Does *God Need the Church? Toward a Theology of the People of God*. Translated by Linda M. Maloney. Collegeville, MN: Liturgical, 1999.

Long, D. Stephen. *The Goodness of God: Theology, the Church and Social Order*. Grand Rapids: Brazos, 2001.

Lupton, Robert D. *Toxic Charity: How Churches and Charities Hurt Those They Help, and How To Reverse It*. New York: HarperOne, 2011.

MacIntyre, Alasdair. *After Virtue: A Study in Moral Theory*. 2nd ed. Notre Dame: University of Notre Dame Press, 1984.

Maddox, Randy L. *Responsible Grace: John Wesley's Practical Theology*. Nashville: Kingswood, 1994.

Martin, Robert K. "Toward a Wesleyan Sacramental Ecclesiology." *Ecclesiology* 9 (2013) 19–38.

McCraken, Brett. "The Church in a 'Missional' Age." *Biola Magazine*, Spring 2009. http://magazine.biola.edu/article/09-spring/the-church-in-a-missional-age/.

McMickle, Marvin Andrew. *Preaching to the Black Middle Class: Words of Challenge, Words of Hope*. Valley Forge, PA: Judson, 2000.

Metzger, Paul Louis. *Consuming Jesus: Beyond Race and Class Divisions in a Consumer Church*. Grand Rapids: Eerdmans, 2007.

Miles, Rebekah L. "Happiness, Holiness, and the Moral Life In John Wesley." In *The Cambridge Companion to John Wesley*, edited by Randy L. Maddox and Jason E. Vickers, 211–18. New York: Cambridge University Press, 2010.

Moltmann, Jürgen. *The Church in the Power of the Spirit: A Contribution to Messianic Ecclesiology*. Translated by Margaret Kohl. New York: Harper, 1977.

Moore, R. Laurence. *Touchdown Jesus: The Mixing of Sacred and Secular in American History*. Louisville: Westminster John Knox, 2003.

Morgenthaler, Sally. *Worship Evangelism: Inviting Unbelievers into the Presence of God*. Grand Rapids: Zondervan, 1999.

Newbigin, Lesslie. "Foolishness to the Greeks." In *The Study of Evangelism: Exploring a Missional Practice of the Church*, edited by Paul W. Chilcote and Laceye C. Warner, 345–51. Grand Rapids: Eerdmans, 2008.

Peterson, Brent. "The Science of the Sacraments: The Being and Becoming of Persons in Community." *Wesleyan Theological Journal* 44 (2009) 180–99.

Pew Forum on Religion and Public Life. "Nones on the Rise." October 9, 2012. http://www.pewforum.org/2012/10/09/nones-on-the-rise.

Platt, David. *Radical*. Mardel Christian and Education, May 3, 2010. https://www.youtube.com/watch?v=a0icm4wnQ4c.

———. *Radical: Taking Back Your Faith from the American Dream*. Colorado Springs: Multonomah, 2010.

Rah, Soong-Chan. *The Next Evangelicalism: Freeing the Church from Western Cultural Captivity*. Downers Grove: IVP, 2009.

Rattenbury, J. Ernest. *The Eucharistic Hymns of John and Charles Wesley*. 3rd American ed. Akron: OSL Publications, 2006.

Rieger, Joerg. "Theology and Mission between Neocolonialism and Postcolonialism." *Mission Studies* 21 (2004) 201–27.

Russell, Letty M. "God, Gold and Gender: A Postcolonial View of Mission." *International Review of Mission* 93 (J 2004) 39–49.

Ruth, John Lester. "Lex Agendi, Lex Orandi: Toward an Understanding of Seeker Services as a New Kind of Liturgy." *Worship* 70 (1996) 386–405.

Saliers, Don. "Liturgy and Ethics: Some New Beginnings." In *Liturgy and the Moral Self: Humanity at Full Stretch before God; Essays in Honor of Don E. Saliers*, edited by E. Byron Anderson and Bruce T. Morrill, 15–35. Collegeville, MN: Liturgical, 1998.

Sampley, J. Paul. "The First Letter to the Corinthians." In vol. 10 of *The New Interpreter's Bible: Acts–First Corinthians*. Edited by Leander Keck. Nashville: Abingdon, 2002.

Scazzero, Peter L., with Warren Bird. *The Emotionally Healthy Church: A Strategy for Discipleship That Actually Changes Lives*. Upadted and expanded ed. Grand Rapids: Zondervan, 2010.

Segundo, Juan Luis. *The Sacraments Today*. Translated by John Drury. A Theology for Artisans of a New Humanity 4. Marknoll, NY: Orbis, 1974.

Sider, Ronald J. *The Scandal of the Evangelical Conscience: Why Are Christians Living Just Like the Rest of the World?* Grand Rapids: Baker, 2005.

Smith, James K. A. *Who's Afraid of Postmodernism? Taking Derrida, Lyotard and Foucault to Church*. Grand Rapids: Baker Academic, 2006.

Stamm, Mark W. *Sacraments & Discipleship: Understanding Baptism and the Lord's Supper in a United Methodist Context*. Ashland City, TN: OSL Publications, 2013.

Stevick, Daniel B. *The Altar's Fire: Charles Wesley's "Hymns on the Lord's Supper, 1745"; Introduction and Exposition*. Peterborough, UK: Epworth, 2004.

Stookey, Laurence Hull. *Baptism: Christ's Act in the Church*. Nashville: Abingdon, 1982.

Tennent, Timothy C. *Invitation to World Missions: A Trinitarian Missiology for the Twenty-First Century*. Grand Rapids: Kregel, 2010.

Thompson, Andrew C. "From Societies to Society: The Shift from Holiness to Justice in the Wesleyan Tradition." *Methodist Review* 3 (2011) 141–72.

Thorton, Brian. "See Can You Say, 'Uh-Baugh-Mih-Nay-Shun'? I Knew You Could Do It." http://voiceofthesheep.wordpress.com/2007/01/11/can-you-say-uh-baugh-mih-nay-shun-i-knew-you-could-do-it/).

Thumma, Scott, and Dave Travis. *Megachurch Myths: What We Can Learn from America's Largest Churches*. San Francisco: Jossey-Bass, 2007.

Towns, Elmer L. *An Inside Look at Ten of Today's Most Innovative Churches*. Ventura, CA: Regal, 1990.

Tuttle, Robert G. Review of *Social Justice through the Eyes of Wesley: John Wesley's Theological Challenge to Slavery*, by Irv A. Brendlinger. *Wesleyan Theological Journal* 43 (2008) 220–21.

The United Methodist Church. *The Book of Worship*. Nashville: United Methodist, 1992.

Van Biema, David. "Can Mega Churches Bridge the Racial Divide?" *Time*, January 11, 2010. http://content.time.com/time/subscriber/article/0,33009,1950943–1,00.html.

Vicedom, George. *The Mission of God: An Introduction to the Theology of Mission*. Translated by Gilbert A. Theile and Dennis Hilgendorf. St. Louis: Concordia, 1965.

Vickers, Jason E. "Wesley's Theological Emphases." In *The Cambridge Companion to John Wesley*, edited by Randy L. Maddox and Jason E. Vickers, 190–206. New York: Cambridge University Press, 2010.

Wagner, C. Peter. Preface to *Understanding Church Growth*, by Donald A. McGavran, vii–xi. 3rd ed. Grand Rapids: Eerdmanns, 1990.

Walls, Andrew. "Converts or Proselytes? The Crisis over Conversion in the Early Church." *International Bulletin of Missionary Research* 28 (2004) 2–6.

Warner, Laceye. "Mega Churches: A New Ecclesiology or an Ecclesial Evangelism?" *Review and Expositor* 107 (2010) 21–31.

Warren, Rick. *The Purpose-Driven Life: What on Earth Am I Here For?* Grand Rapids: Zondervan, 2002.

Wesley, John. "The Almost Christian (Sermon 2)." http://www.umcmission.org/Find-Resources/John-Wesley-Sermons/Sermon-2-The-Almost-Christian.

———. "The Almost Christian: Sermon 2—1741." In *John Wesley's Sermons: An Anthology*, edited by Albert C. Outler and Richard P. Heitzenrater, 62–67. Nashville: Abingdon, 1991.

———. "Christian Perfection (Sermon 40)." Wesley Center Online. http://wesley.nnu.edu/john-wesley/the-sermons-of-john-wesley-1872-edition/sermon-40-christian-perfection/.

———. "The Duty of Constant Communion." In *This Holy Mystery: A United Methodist Understanding of Holy Communion*, by Gayle Carlton Felton, 65–69. Nashville: Discipleship Resources, 2005.

———. "The Great Privilege of Those That Are Born of God (Sermon 19)." In *John Wesley's Sermons: An Anthology*, edited by Albert C. Outler and Richard P. Heitzenrater, 184–85. Nashville: Abingdon, 1991.

———. *The Letters of John Wesley*. Quoted in J. Ernest Rattenbury, *The Eucharistic Hymns of John and Charles Wesley*, 31. Akron: OSL Publication, 2006.

———. *The Letters of the Rev. John Wesley*. Edited by John Telford. Standard ed. London: Epworth, 1931.

———. "The Marks of the New Birth (Sermon 18)." In *John Wesley's Sermons: An Anthology*, edited by Albert C. Outler and Richard P. Heitzenrater, 173–82. Nashville: Abingdon, 1991.

———. "The Means of Grace (Sermon 16)." Wesley Center Online. http://wesley.nnu.edu/john-wesley/the-sermons-of-john-wesley-1872-edition/sermon-16-the-means-of-grace/.

———. "The New Birth (Sermon 45)." Wesley Center Online. http://wesley.nnu.edu/john-wesley/the-sermons-of-john-wesley-1872-edition/sermon-45-the-new-birth/.

————. "The New Birth (Sermon 45)." In *John Wesley's Sermons: An Anthology*, edited by Albert C. Outler and Richard P. Heitzenrater, 340–44. Nashville: Abingdon, 1991.

————. *A Plain Account of Christian Perfection.* In *The Works of John Wesley*, edited by Thomas Jackson, 11:366–446. London: Wesleyan Methodist Book Room, 1872.

————. "Salvation By Faith (Sermon 1)." Wesley Center Online. http://wesley.nnu. edu/john-wesley/the-sermons-of-john-wesley-1872-edition/sermon-1-salvation-by-faith/.

————. *Thoughts Upon Slavery.* London: R. Hawes, 1774.

Wesley, John, and Charles Wesley. *Hymns on the Lord's Supper.* https://archive.org/stream/hymnsonlordssupp00wesl#page/52/mode/2up.

Westerfield Tucker, Karen B. "Wesley's Emphasis on Worship and the Means of Grace." In *The Cambridge Companion to John Wesley*, edited by Randy L. Maddox and Jason E. Vickers, 225–42. New York: Cambridge University Press, 2010.

White, James F. *Sacraments as God's Self Giving.* Nashville: Abingdon, 2001.

————. *The Sacraments in Protestant Practice and Faith.* Nashville: Abingdon, 1999.

Willow Creek Community Church. "GSCRW/GCORR, Case Study." *What Willow Believes.* http://www.willowcreek.org/aboutwillow/what-willow-believes.

Woodward, J. R. *Creating a Missional Culture: Equipping the Church for the Sake of the World.* Downers Grove: InterVarsity, 2012.

Wright, Christopher J. H. *The Mission of God: Unlocking the Bible's Grand Narrative.* Downers Grove: IVP Academic, 2006.

Ziegler, J. J. "What Is Social Justice? From Taparelli to John Paul XXIII." *The Catholic World Report*, April 10, 2013. http://www.catholicworldreport.com/Item/2173/what_is_social_justice.aspx.

Index

Made in the USA
Middletown, DE
26 January 2021